# The
# Prairie
# Homestead
# Cookbook

# The
# Prairie
# Homestead
# Cookbook

*simple recipes for
heritage cooking
in any kitchen*

## JILL WINGER

FLATIRON
BOOKS
NEW YORK

THE PRAIRIE HOMESTEAD COOKBOOK.
Copyright © 2019 by Jill Winger.
Foreword copyright © 2019 by Joel Salatin.
All rights reserved. Printed in China.
For information, address Flatiron Books,
175 Fifth Avenue, New York, N.Y. 10010.

www.flatironbooks.com

Photography by Lindsay Linton Buk of
Linton Productions

Styling by Greta Eagan

Book design by Jan Derevjanik

The Library of Congress Cataloging-in-Publication Data
is available upon request.

ISBN 978-1-250-19019-2 (paper over board)
ISBN 978-1-250-30594-7 (ebook)

Our books may be purchased in bulk for promotional,
educational, or business use. Please contact your local
bookseller or the Macmillan Corporate and Premium Sales
Department at 1-800-221-7945, extension 5442, or by
email at MacmillanSpecialMarkets@macmillan.com.

First Edition: April 2019

10 9 8 7 6 5 4

To the special souls
who possess the grit
to transform from a
reader into a doer

# contents

# foreword

We naturally fear what we don't know. The American love affair with pseudo-food and convenience, promising to extricate us from the visceral monotony of domestic culinary duties and farm chores, has now morphed into remorse. We bought a promise of ease and leisure only to find nutrient deficiency, unpronounceable ingredients, and dubious additives.

More and more people question this trade of domestic duty for corporate and industrial care. More and more of us are skeptical about the type of food and farm care this century-long trade created. As we opted out of historical participation in food and farming, the skills and knowledge went to the grave as our elders passed away. Common knowledge is no longer common.

I don't know much about computers or video games. I don't even know much about fashion or Hollywood celebrities. But I know what a heifer is. I know you don't need a rooster for hens to lay eggs. I know how to plant tomatoes and how to make applesauce. I know the difference between a raccoon attack on chickens and an opossum attack. I enjoy leftovers, and carrots with some telltale dirt still clinging to their little hairy roots. I know how to keep pigs in an electric fence, how to dig a pond, and what good hay smells like. These rural arts and skills too often get shoved to the margins of our sophisticated society.

In this unsettled time, in limbo between what was lost and a return to personal involvement with food and farming, fear of the unknown now rules the day. Questions like "How do you make a hamburger?" and "Why are you short of eggs in November?" require coaching. The compounded and profound food and farm ignorance most Americans now face leads to food fears. What to eat, how to cook, where to buy create tension and turmoil in families and workplace potlucks.

When the distrust of the food conglomerate orthodoxy and frustration of not knowing anything reach the stomach-turning point, literally, here comes Jill Winger, hand-holder and cheerleader for personal responsibility and home-centricity. I have preached forever that the foundation of an integrity food system must be laid in domestic culinary arts. All of us simply need to know more about food and its production in order to stem the trajectory toward nutrient deficiency, foodborne pathogens, and techno-fragility.

But it's such a tall order, this desire and imperative to rediscover lost arts. *The Prairie Homestead Cookbook* might be the best friend and coach for a

fearful pilgrim into the lost arts of home and hearth. The pictures bring tears of appreciation that mingle with salivating eagerness. Written in a welcoming and nonjudgmental style, this is far more than a cookbook; it's a callback to do-it-yourself food. Don't let the word "homestead" in the title put you off. If you're locked in an urban condominium for now, you have plenty of practical ways to quit supporting food's dark side. Jill's winsome and inspirational demeanor will have you diving into sauces and pickles before you have time to realize you don't know how to do this. That's a good thing.

With calm reassurance and "I've been there and done that" encouragement, Jill brings you to success regardless of your starting point. This wonderful book hands the gift of can-do to anyone ready to embrace the kitchen and the corral. Lots of cooking insights, great recipes, and a good smattering of homestead gardening and livestock advice drew me affectionately through the pages. I know you'll be eager to see what this tried-and-true homesteader has to say because the best antidote to fear is knowledge. Thank you, Jill, for helping thousands of aspiring participators overcome their trepidation and become doers. Fire up the stove, don the apron, pull on the boots, and bring the bucket. It's a world of healing and discovery; let the journey begin.

—JOEL SALATIN

*Going back to a simpler life
is not a step backwards.*
—YVON CHOUINARD

# returning to our roots

## Two City Kids and a Compost Pile

Splashing in the creek, chasing fireflies at dusk, and living life at the end of a dirt road. Nope, that wasn't my childhood. I wasn't raised a homesteader. In fact, I didn't even grow up out in the country. Like many folks, I have homesteaders and farmers on branches of both sides of my family tree, but my childhood was spent in a regular little neighborhood on a small lot in rural northern Idaho—no acreage, no chickens, and no big red barns.

My upbringing may have been suburban, but I had a fascination with all things country right from the start. While all my friends were playing dress-up, I pushed a wheelbarrow around our tiny yard and pretended I was living on a farm and mucking stalls. (Yes, really.) The other girls giggled about their latest crush while I doodled sketches of my future barns and corrals. In high school, the thought of Saturdays spent roaming the mall bored me to tears. I much preferred using my weekends to help local ranching friends build fences and clean pens. I never really fit in with the crowd, but I never really wanted to either.

I've been obsessed with horses since I was two years old, so after graduating from high school, it only made sense to pursue a career in the equine industry. Instead of staying close to home, I packed up my F-150 truck and drove to Wyoming to begin a grand adventure 1,100 miles away from everything and everyone I had ever known. I was scared to death, but promptly fell in love with the ruggedness and wide-open spaces of the Cowboy State and swore to never leave. A few years into that adventure, I met my future husband, Christian. It was a totally romantic first encounter—I was shoveling liquid cow manure in the college arena the first time he laid eyes on me. Now that I think about it, it had to be some sort of a foreshadowing of our future lifestyle. He wasn't raised on a farm or ranch either, but our early dates were filled with talk of our shared dreams of owning land and cattle someday. He proposed on horseback and we were married soon after.

The concept of homesteading couldn't have been further from our minds as newlyweds, but we had a couple of horses and knew for certain we didn't want to live in town. We saved up a down payment and began to shop for our first home. Instead of playing it safe and, like rational people, buying one of those cute little starter homes three minutes away from the grocery store, we fell head over heels for a neglected property 40 miles from town. The tiny hundred-year-old home boasted 900 square feet of shoebox-sized rooms with an awkward layout. The accompanying cinder-block barn and shop (circa 1940) were filled waist-deep with junk and rusty car parts. The fence posts were rotted, leaning, and laced with ancient strands of broken barbed wire. And my personal favorite—there was a dead washing machine in the front yard full of moldy clothes. The place radiated charm.

Our friends thought we had completely lost our minds, and when I look back at those early photos, I suppose I can see their point. But tumbledown fences and trashy buildings aside, the sad little property gave two city kids with a small budget a chance to become the proud owners of 67 acres of prairie land. And it was glorious.

Blinded by potential, we feverishly dove into setting new fence posts, reconstructing crumbling outbuildings, and hauling away over 20 tons of trash (and that lovely washing machine). Since then, the entire place has undergone a complete transformation, and it looks nothing like it did back then. Thankfully, Christian and I are both home-improvement junkies, so we've enjoyed (almost) every second of building, fencing, digging, painting, remodeling, and planting.

I wish I could say there was a profound or poetic moment that sparked our first official homestead endeavor, but the truth is, the catalyst was horse manure. There was a growing pile in the back pasture, and it would be years before our budget could handle the purchase of a tractor. And so the pile grew larger by the day and drove me crazy every time I looked at it. I was desperate for a solution, so when a library book introduced me to the idea of turning animal manure into rich plant food, I was wildly inspired.

Christian built two compost bins out of salvaged scrap lumber on the edge of the yard. I remember surveying the completed bins and feeling an awakening I'd never quite experienced before. Our new little property felt so ripe with possibility, I was beside myself. I schemed about how our land could become profitable (or at least earn its keep), and I was hit with a powerful desire to start

growing food. I checked out every library book I could find about vegetables, dairy goats, and chickens, and found myself lying in bed at night, unable to sleep as my heart pounded with excitement at the potential of what we could create here on our little piece of land.

We had created something from almost nothing, we were opting out of cultural norms, we were preparing to grow food, and we were one step closer to sustainable self-sufficiency. It was intoxicating. I became addicted right then and there and immediately began to plan the next project. Shortly thereafter, I impulse-bought a flock of Rhode Island Red chickens, followed by a pair of pregnant dairy goats (when I was nine months pregnant myself). There was no turning back.

After several naysayers told me gardening in our corner of Wyoming wasn't worth bothering with, I set my sights on mastering vegetables. Despite more than a few mistakes and plenty of weeds, I eventually harvested pumpkins, potatoes, onions, corn, carrots, and beans by the basketful. The milk cow came a little while later, and so did the hogs, cheese making, and chickens. We don't grow every single bit of our food ourselves and likely never will, but our efforts have paid off handsomely and we enjoy many, many meals made with ingredients grown right here on our prairie homestead.

As our homesteading adventure progressed and we added children into the mix, our life felt so unusual and exciting, I wanted to talk about it. A lot. The problem? I didn't have any homesteading friends at that point, and my family members were getting tired of goat talk. So like a true child of the Internet age, I took my passions to the World Wide Web, and in 2010, I began rambling away on my blog, *The Prairie Homestead* (theprairiehomestead.com). Little did I know that this little blog would eventually become a thriving community of online homesteaders with many millions of visitors each year. There were other people out there who loved composting. And chickens. And baking bread. What a thrill! My favorite emails are the ones where people tell me how reading the blog inspired them to take action and dive into their own homesteading adventure. Connecting with so many people all over the globe with a shared love for this modern twist on an old-fashioned lifestyle has been one of the greatest privileges of my life.

For us, homesteading has been the gateway to building a life we love. Christian and I have never wanted to live our lives just going through the motions—homesteading is how we have chosen to live with intention and purpose. It helps us stay grounded and in sync with the cycles of nature. To put it simply, homesteading makes us feel more alive.

But that was only the beginning. Once I broke out of the box in one area of life, I couldn't help but keep busting down my other self-imposed walls too. This notion of purposefully creating what we wanted rather than allowing ourselves to be pulled along by the cultural current of passivity began to creep into all other areas of our lives.

What began as a simple passion for rural living and good food has resulted in opting out of the nine-to-five lifestyle, becoming entrepreneurs, schooling our children at home, and exploring natural medicines, among many other things. Homesteading invited Christian and me to design the life we had dreamed of and has taken us further than we ever could have imagined. Sometimes I look at where our life is now and I have to pinch myself. The little girl who pushed her wheelbarrow to the country finally has stalls to muck, plus a whole lot more. And it all started with one humble compost pile.

## Homesteading Redefined

There's no shortage of debate these days over what the term *homesteader* should mean. Some folks even assume the strictest definition of the word and email me wanting to know how we got our land for free. (Spoiler alert—we had to buy our property just like everyone else!)

I call our lifestyle *homesteading* because that particular label seems to fit our unique routine better than others. Considering we don't sell food to the public or make an income from our animals and crops, calling ourselves farmers or ranchers feels awkward to me. The "homesteading" label feels most natural when someone asks why we do what we do, and it's easier than reciting a lengthy sermon on my philosophies of self-sufficiency and quality of life. The good news? You can call yourself anything you like—there are no real rules here, just preferences.

Back in the day, a homesteader was someone who claimed a piece of federal land and made it his or her own. As author and western historian Candy Moulton explains:

> The 1862 Homestead Act allowed men and women to claim up to 160 acres of land. Anyone who was twenty-one years old or the head of a family, who was a United States citizen or in the process of becoming one, and who had never fought in a war against the United States could claim a homestead. In order to prove up or gain title, an individual had to live on the claim for at least six months each year during a five-year development period and make improvements. After a five-year development period, the land became the homesteader's property.

The original homesteaders possessed a sizable dose of determination, courage, and grit to be willing to head into unknown territory to chase the promise of a better life and more opportunities. Many failed, but many others succeeded and ended up shaping history forever. Both sides of my family homesteaded in southeastern Idaho, and my great-grandmother Genevieve even homesteaded solo after her husband decided he didn't care for the rugged lifestyle. She kept chickens, cattle, horses, sheep, gooseberry bushes, and a vegetable garden, and was well-known for her skills with a horse and a gun. (She also challenged societal norms at the time and scandalized the community by being one of the few women who wore pants.) To me, she embodied the tenacity and fortitude of the original and the modern homesteaders alike.

In 1976, the Homestead Act was repealed, and with it, that particular definition of homesteading has been laid to rest. The enticement of free land is a thing of the past. But the spirit of homesteading is just as alive and well as it has ever been. The traits that made the original homesteaders so legendary continue

to live on in a new group of pioneers for whom self-sufficiency and freedom are as alluring as ever.

There are plenty of potential titles for this crazy existence that bucks modern-day norms. Some call it homesteading. Some call it backyard farming. Some call it urban farming. And some people don't have a name for it; it's just life. But regardless of the title, the ideology is spreading like wildfire because even in the midst of a modern culture full of ease and convenience, folks are fed up.

They're fed up with eating processed foods laced with chemicals. They're fed up with passionless desk jobs and sitting in endless traffic. They're fed up with witnessing poor stewardship of land and resources. They're fed up with their kids thinking food somehow just magically appears on the shelves at the grocery store. And they're fed up with being dependent on someone else.

This notion of modern homesteading doesn't get hung up on specific definitions because it speaks to a mind-set rather than to a specific location or list of possessions. It's a mentality of celebrating a simpler way of life, of savoring the sheer enjoyment of working with your hands, and of appreciating time-honored skills and wholesome food.

Homesteading has taught me how to appreciate the simpler, slower parts of life. In a world where life seems to move faster and faster, it's easy to become disconnected from what matters. Homesteading breaks this cycle by encouraging us to get our hands dirty and return to an intimate relationship with the cycles of nature and food production. I'm convinced this is a need every human carries and that returning to it satisfies something deep inside us.

I'm also convinced humans need an element of challenge to feel fully alive. I know I personally feel the most content when I'm knee-deep in a project and trying my best to figure it all out. Obstacles and challenges shape us, teach us life lessons, and, when we overcome them, provide a heady feeling of accomplishment that inspires us to keep going. I have a hunch that many of us are just plain bored with all of the conveniences available. Homesteading captures our imagination because it's not easy—yet we know in our gut it's going to be a thrilling ride. Why else would a perfectly rational adult spend dozens of hours coaxing tiny seeds to grow when they could zip to the grocery store and buy as many vegetables as they want in mere minutes? It's because we anticipate the rewards of labor and desire the satisfaction and gratification that come from time well spent. It's a part of our human fiber.

Modern homesteaders are people who are choosing to opt out of the rat race. They savor good food and crave playing an active role in producing what they eat. Dirt under their fingernails and manure on their boots doesn't bother them a bit, and they don't bat an eye at spending a late night putting food in jars to preserve the harvest. They appreciate the value of hard work and consider sore muscles at the end of a day spent outside something of which they can be proud.

Land ownership isn't a requirement, because homesteading is a state of mind. Sure, some homesteaders live on hundreds of acres, but you'll find many others in the most urban of settings, sprinkled across suburbia, or tending vegetables on the balconies of their high-rise apartments.

Regardless of where a homesteader lives, our objectives remain the same. We long to return to our roots. We crave self-sufficiency. And we yearn for the freedom to write our own story—just like our pioneer ancestors. If these concepts resonate with you, then you're already a homesteader, my friend.

## Cooking the Homesteader Way

*"I want to homestead SO BAD, but I don't have any land, and I won't be getting chickens for a long time. . . . Help!"*

Emails like this find their way into my inbox in a never-ending trickle, and they make me excited. Because yes, there is so much you *can* do! Modern homesteading has many different moving parts, but when you step back and look at the bigger picture, these pieces all revolve around one thing: FOOD. That is the answer. Start shifting your food habits and not only will your health improve, but you'll be well on your way to adopting the homesteading philosophy into other parts of your life too. If you're wondering exactly how to start that shift, well, you're holding the answer in your hands. This cookbook will provide you with the exact tools you need to cook like a homesteader—no matter where you live.

Try your hand at kneading bread, creating ricotta clouds in a pot of milk, or roasting a vegetable you've never tried before from the local farm stand. Ditch the boxes, cans, and frozen dinners and fall in love with colorful, fresh, whole ingredients. If you can't grow your own ingredients at the moment, begin a new habit of visiting local producers or farmers' markets. Turn off the TV and embrace the time-honored ritual of taking a moment to gather the family around the table to pause and break bread.

Food has a supernatural way of bringing humans together. It's meant to be appreciated, celebrated, and savored. Even the tiniest apartment kitchen can create farmhouse-worthy food and bring a taste of the homestead to the city. It's very possible, and extremely delicious.

## Good, Better, Best

When my out-of-state friends talk about grocery shopping, I listen to every detail with complete fascination. They'll talk about making the rounds to multiple natural food stores in their town, grabbing their favorite brand of yogurt at one store and the best coconut oil at another. All manner of raw dairy, local organic produce, and grass-fed meats are at their disposal, whether through their favorite organic chain or through one of many farmers in their area. And they can shop around to find their favorite producers and the best prices. It sounds like a blast!

In Wyoming, we have wide-open spaces, a rugged population, and not a single Whole Foods Market or Trader Joe's in the whole state. While there are farmers' markets scattered around the region, they only operate during a handful of months and even then much of the produce is shipped in from neighboring areas. I've been pleased to see more and more small local producers pop up recently, but when I first started, finding organic *anything* around here was like finding a needle in a haystack.

As frustrating as it can be to hunt down quality, whole-food ingredients in a place like Wyoming, I'm living proof it can be done. There's a precious window of time each year when I grocery shop from my garden several times per day, and nearly every meal features onions, potatoes, beets, squash, or green beans picked just hours prior. As beautiful as that time of year is, it doesn't last very long, so we rely on other options during the rest of the year, including frozen or canned produce or things picked up in town. I have zero reservations about buying nonorganic produce from trusted producers who don't use pesticides or herbicides, as the organic certification process is often too costly for the little guys, and I'm always delighted to support them anyway.

Growing ingredients ourselves (more on that in Part Two), combined with ordering food online and bulk buying with friends when necessary, has provided us with all the ingredients we have needed for the almost ten years we've been on our whole-food journey. I feel like a treasure hunter sometimes, but if I can cook with whole foods out here on the Wyoming prairie, then anyone can. (And these same principles apply to anyone who might live in an urban or suburban area with limited options as well!)

I use a "Good, Better, Best" scale when I'm shopping for ingredients (you can find more specifics on some of my favorite ingredients on page 330), because sometimes I have to make do with certain things, no matter how much I'd prefer better options. If you can relate to the idea of having to treasure hunt to find quality food in your area, then you'll find this helpful.

## GOOD, BETTER, BEST SHOPPING

GOOD – Upgrade the ingredients you currently use by choosing less processed or homemade versions. Swap out white sugar for dehydrated whole cane sugar, maple syrup, or honey. Buy whole chickens instead of just breasts and wings so you can make homemade stock (page 236) with the leftover bones. Even if a conventional grocery store is the only option you have available, there's so much you can do with the food there.

*Example:* Choose butter instead of margarine.

BETTER – Opt for organic at the regular grocery store or seek out whole-food cooperatives or buying clubs such as Bountiful Baskets. Even though not every single item might be USDA Certified Organic, some may still have been grown without pesticides or chemicals by growers who couldn't afford the organic certification process.

*Example:* Choose organic butter from the natural food store.

BEST – Start growing your own ingredients. If that's not a possibility, seek out local farmers from whom you can purchase directly, participate in a community garden, or join a local Community Supported Agriculture (CSA) program. Another option is to partner with friends who have a garden plot or who are able to keep chickens or larger animals, and split the labor and expenses with them.

*Example:* Choose butter from local, grass-fed cows or milk your own dairy animals.

The recipes in this cookbook are designed to fit any of these three scenarios and can be easily adapted to what is currently available to you, no matter if you're using regular grocery store ingredients or the finest, locally sourced or homegrown produce, dairy, and meats. Don't expect your cupboards to change overnight—it's a process, and trying to make all the swaps all at once will have you pulling your hair out. Focus on swapping out one ingredient at a time and enjoy the ride.

## In Defense of Balance

As passionate as I am about whole, homegrown foods, I refuse to be dogmatic about them, so allow me clarify a few things before we dive into the recipes.

I've watched various diet fads come and go over the years and have been alarmed by recent trends demanding absolute perfection. As much as I adore whole foods and do my very best to source high-quality ingredients, I'm not a purist. For the sake of my sanity, I do compromise sometimes.

I see a lot of people running themselves ragged in an attempt to make their diets perfect. I fell into this common trap at the beginning of my own

journey, and thought my efforts were a failure if every bit of every meal was not perfectly sourced and homemade. I'll never forget the time I spent an *entire* day attempting to prepare a sack lunch for a family outing. I was determined to make every single bit of it by hand (the bread, the lunchmeat, the cheese, the snacks) and I nearly drove myself to tears in the process. It was the final straw, but an important turning point. From that day forward, I stopped beating myself up for not being perfect and worked on celebrating what I did create, instead of worrying about what I didn't.

My mission is for our food to give us joy and nourished bellies, but for it also to leave us time to do other things we love. Now, I know some of you may be reading these words with one eyebrow raised saying, "You're joking, right? You milk a cow, grow a garden, and raise your own beef, for heaven's sake!" Yes, it's a funny balance we have, but a balance nonetheless. I love the process of growing and cooking food, so I intentionally choose to spend a considerable amount of time doing those things since they contribute to our overall quality of life. Not to mention, recipes calling for a "box of this" and a "can of that" always leave me feeling rather uninspired. If I'm going to cook something, I'd rather it be from scratch.

However, as much as I *love* food, my life simply cannot revolve around it all the time. In our home, whole-food and from-scratch cooking requires a sort of fluidity and a willingness to be flexible and, yes, even to compromise sometimes. What does this look like? It means some days we have roasted homegrown chicken for supper with seasoned fried potatoes from the garden and a side salad of fresh lettuce picked from right outside the door. But it also means on the busier days you might find us chowing down on nachos made with the ground beef I hastily defrosted and fried up and store-bought tortilla chips. Therefore, right here and now I'm declaring my stance as a whole-food-loving homesteader who believes it's entirely okay to cheat sometimes.

Here is where you come in, dear reader—good food shouldn't be an all-or-nothing thing. Perfection is overrated, and the process of learning something worthwhile never happens overnight. Consider *The Prairie Homestead Cookbook* your guilt-free road map to this beautiful, crazy life we call homesteading. My hope is that it inspires you to get in the kitchen, create some tasty food, and maybe even experience a spark of excitement from learning a new skill.

# Fitting Homesteading into a Modern Schedule

Homestead food is slow food. In a day and age where waiting on the microwave feels like an eternity, it seems counterintuitive to make homemade pizza dough that requires 24 hours to reach its full potential. However, the blessing of slow food is that the time required by the techniques is rarely hands-on.

It sounds impressive (and complicated!) to brag that the soup on the table contains homemade stock, homegrown sausage, and cream from the cow, but it's easier than you think. The secret? Most homegrown and homemade meals I put on the table have been created in stages. I made and canned the stock two months ago, ground and seasoned the sausage last year, and skimmed the cream this week. Putting the ingredients together in the pot and tossing in a bit of seasoning is hardly any more difficult than making a boxed dinner from the grocery store.

With a bit of forethought and the recipes in this book, you can stock your pantry and make your homemade meals a snap. Here are a few other tips for balancing homestead-style cooking with a modern schedule.

PLAN AHEAD—If I'm planning on making a recipe that includes longer wait times, it helps to pencil it into my calendar just like I would a trip to town or an appointment. It also ensures I remember to have the various ingredients on hand or defrosted before I start. If you work during the week, you may find the weekend is the best time to have homemade dairy products culturing (such as buttermilk, page 244, or cream cheese, page 245) or stock (page 236) bubbling away on the stove.

BUILD A REPERTOIRE—There's a time for complex kitchen experiments and a time for good old standbys. Create a list of five to ten from-scratch meals you know inside and out and keep the ingredients always available. Make slightly more complicated or adventurous recipes two or three times a week and fill in the other days with easier options (three cheers for scrambled eggs!). Keeping basics like Simple Roast Chicken (page 54) or Stovetop Mac 'n' Cheese (page 83) on frequent rotation also helps to eliminate decision fatigue in your menu planning (the struggle is real).

BATCH COOK—I'm famous for making gallons of chicken stock (page 236) or multiple batches of mozzarella at the same time so I only have to dirty pots and pans once. Double or triple recipes whenever possible so you can freeze them or eat them the following day.

PRESERVE LIKE CRAZY—Having jars of home-canned beans in the pantry or containers of homemade ricotta cheese (page 249) tucked away in the freezer means I can include more homegrown or organically sourced ingredients in my recipes without having to make every single part of the recipe on the same day. Food preservation is a worthwhile skill to add to your repertoire—it will save you time and money in the long run.

LET GO OF PERFECTION—There's one thing I know for certain—there are days your meals just won't come together. (Or you explode your picture-perfect, homegrown pumpkin pie just moments before sitting down at the table.) You know what? It's okay. Pop a batch of popcorn, drizzle some butter on top, and try again tomorrow.

## Time Management on the Homestead

For me, modern homesteading is about mixing the best of two worlds. We take a generous helping of our ancestors' grit and know-how and mix it with a few spoonfuls of the conveniences available to us (I *really* love running water).

Because most of us still have at least one foot firmly planted in the twenty-first century, we have the unique experience of figuring out how to juggle our modern responsibilities with tasks our ancestors would have spent the majority of their day accomplishing. It's a delicate balance, but I'm here to tell you that it can be done. While I most definitely *do not* have it all figured out, here are a few principles I've adopted over the years that keep my schedule flowing as much as possible.

RESPECT THE SEASONS—Nature does an excellent job of leading the way. To everything there is a season, and I try my best to mimic that with my schedule. Winter is for cleaning cabinets, reflection, and rest. Spring is for planting and preparation. Summer is for growth and all the outdoor projects I can possibly handle. And fall is for harvest, filling the larder, and overall regrouping. Getting the bright idea to deep-clean my cabinets in the midst of fall preservation ends with one stressed-out mama. Every single time.

There are seasons I put all my energies into gardening, seasons I focus on organizing my home, and seasons where I push hard in my businesses. I'm not convinced everything should be in perfect balance at all times—sometimes it's appropriate to put more focus on one area and let the others coast for a while.

WRITE IT ALL DOWN—Planners, calendars, notebooks, binders—it doesn't matter what you use, but make a habit of getting it out of your head and onto paper. Nothing is more stressful than a million to-dos swirling around in your brain. My planner tracks our homeschool schedule, when we bred the cows, when I planted what seeds, what I'm making for supper, and so much more. Plus, it's gratifying to be able to look back at old planners and see how far you've come.

GET UP EARLIER—This one isn't my favorite, but it works. Our days always run more smoothly when I get up even 30 minutes earlier than normal. It's enough time to do chores, put a roast in the slow cooker (page 73), or get a head start on a kitchen project before the chaos of the day is in full swing. When mornings are smooth, the mood for the rest of the day tends to follow.

LET IT GO—I gave up being a purist years ago, and I no longer beat myself up for cutting corners here and there. Sometimes I buy store-bought tortillas. Sometimes I forget to defrost the meat for supper and we just eat sandwiches. Some years I have tons of vegetables, some years I have only a few, and some years I just have dead vegetable plants. I've stopped trying to live up to some imaginary depiction of what a perfect homesteader should look like and I just do the things that make sense for us. And you know what? I like this lifestyle a whole lot better this way.

## Embracing Failure

Maybe you've already given this homesteading thing a try and it didn't work out quite like you thought. You're considering calling it quits, and wondering if you jumped in too fast. Or perhaps you're afraid you're just not cut out for this lifestyle.

I get it. I've been there. There are times this journey is so intoxicating, you have to pinch yourself to make sure it's real. And there are other times it brings you to your knees and breaks your heart.

I've wept over hail-shredded vegetables. I've been devastated over dead chickens. I've cried when I've found baby goats standing next to their dead mother. I've thrown tantrums and yelled, "*I quit!*" to anyone who would listen.

If you're wondering if it's time to throw in the towel, let me say this: If you can't get homesteading out of your mind; if the thought of chickens pecking in the front yard and vibrant jars of home-canned food in the pantry makes your

*If you want to succeed faster,*
*double your rate of failure.*

—BRIAN TRACY, bestselling
self-development author

heart beat a little faster; if the thought of eating a meal you grew with your own two hands still makes your eyes light up, stick with it. Fight the urge to play small to avoid failure—it's a surefire recipe for regret.

I invite you to not only let go of your fear of failure, but to actually embrace failure. Get all cozy with it. Own your mistakes because mistakes are proof that you're trying. You're doing the hard things. You've upgraded from spectator status, you're officially in the arena, and *you're making it happen.* In fact, if you're not experiencing some sort of failure in an area you're passionate about, perhaps you're not chasing that particular dream hard enough. Radical thought, huh?

That's the key, my friends. If homesteading is something you truly love, don't let the sting of failure stop you from pursuing it. Not for one second. Don't be one of the many whose fear of failure has paralyzed them for a lifetime. Sometimes your biggest successes can only appear after you experience your biggest failures. Burn the pie, make chewy pork chops, and bake rock-hard loaves of bread. It doesn't matter. Sometimes it has to get ugly before it can get pretty. And if you quit in the midst of the striving, you will miss out on the greatest reward of all.

It's not about talent, or genetics, or finances, or your background. It's about sheer determination and resilience. Just don't quit.

# my hopes for you and this cookbook

As I've ventured into the world of modern homesteading in all its glory and frustrations, I've discovered one trait that has served me better than all the others: action. If you can hone the ability to learn a new skill and swiftly implement it, you'll go far in this homesteading gig. The magic shows up as you dive in and make mistakes. The mastery materializes through steady, consistent attempts that don't feel very remarkable at first, but eventually add up to greatness. It's the action that yields the results.

My prayer is that you'll transform the information in this book into tangible activity. The photos might be beautiful, but this book is not meant to sit on the coffee table. It's meant to be your companion in the kitchen as you roll out flaky pie crust, brown chunks of grass-fed beef, chop crisp lettuce, and knead yeasty bread dough with the heels of your hands.

I hope the pages end up being dog-eared, wrinkled, and splattered with bacon grease and bits of flour. I hope you bond with your family and friends as you make Simple Roast Chicken (page 54), Rustic Sausage Potato Soup (page 102), and Apple Molasses Pie with Cheddar Crust (page 190). I hope you devour the meals with the TV turned off and the conversation flowing.

I hope you swell with pride as you tackle the time-honored skills from these pages and master the art of homemade butter, and ricotta, and stock. I hope you feel inspired to grow something. Anything. Even just a pot of basil in the window. I hope you'll laugh when you mess something up or when the smoke alarm goes off. And then I hope you'll try again.

If you've been homesteading for years, I hope this book brings a sense of community and validation to the lifestyle you already embrace and love.

And if you're new to this beautifully old-fashioned lifestyle, I hope you feel the rush of adrenaline as you taste the possibilities for the very first time. I hope the notion of self-sufficiency begins to shift from a dream to a concrete reality for you.

No matter what your homesteading journey looks like, I hope you are filled with deep satisfaction as you return to your roots and craft delicious foods to nourish the bellies and souls of those you love.

Now, let's get cooking!

*part one*

# RECIPES

## FARM & FAMILY FAVORITES

*Get in your kitchens, buy
unprocessed foods, turn off the TV,
and prepare your own foods.
This is liberating.*

—JOEL SALATIN

# country breakfasts

*Thick layers of nostalgia surround the notion of* mornings on a farm. Blazing orange sunrises with streaks of pink, crowing roosters, steaming cups of black coffee, and plates loaded with bacon, homemade biscuits, and sunny-side-up eggs are usually the first images that drift through our imaginations.

However, our mornings on the homestead are more similar to the average household than you may think. Like most folks', our days kick off with plenty of hustle and bustle and even a measure of regular ol' chaos at times. While I love the idea of serving a full country breakfast with all the fixings to my family each and every morning, in reality that rarely happens. We aren't necessarily rushing out the door to make the morning commute or running the kids to the bus stop, but our farm mornings aren't as leisurely as I once imagined they'd be in my pre-homesteading days.

Sure, sometimes there are indeed those picture-perfect mornings where I pull on my boots before the rest of the house awakens and steal down to the barn to do chores by myself. The rooster crows with impeccable timing as I pass the coop and I hear the hens clucking as they sit in nesting boxes leaving their eggs for the kids to find later. The mingled perfume of animals, hay, and leather (the very best smell in the entire world, by the way) surrounds me as I enter the cinder-block barn and grab a halter from the hook on the wall. Our milk cow, Oakley, stands right inside the door slowly blinking her big brown eyes as she waits patiently to be milked. The swish of milk streams hitting the bucket lulls me into deep thought as I strategize how I'll tackle the day's tasks. By the time I stroll back to the house lugging my pail filled with frothy milk, I feel centered, energized, and ready to take on the day.

But there are also the mornings that aren't exactly Instagram or Facebook worthy, the ones that make you laugh, otherwise you'd cry. They go something like this: Upon waking to do chores, I discover the kids are already awake. Not one, not two, but all three, of course. "Mommy! We want to do chores with you!" they scream as I begin the process of hauling them outside, complete with blankies and pajama-clad feet jammed into cowboy boots.

Somehow I make it to the barn without losing a child, a sippy cup, or the milk bucket, only to discover someone left the middle gate open last night. This means that instead of standing patiently in the barn, Oakley is now standing in the corner of the south pasture, as far away as she can possibly be. Back to the house I go to grab the four-wheeler. I load the kids up and drive (very slowly) down to the corner to halter her and lead her back.

We arrive at the barn. Finally. I tie Oakley in her milking spot and throw her a pile of hay in hopes that it will appease her so I can milk quickly. Her udder is a mess from lying in the mud last night, so I jog back to the house to grab an extra washing towel—the first one I brought with me is caked with mud after the first wipe.

The kids harass the barn cats as I finally sit down to milk. This annoys the dog, who starts to bark, which in turn seriously offends Oakley. And so I alternate between dodging her swinging tail and her stomping hind foot as I squeeze the milk into the bucket. I deem the bucket full enough (the calf will drink the rest today) and we start our trek back. Upon the insistence of my brood of children, we make a brief stop at the chicken coop to collect three eggs, two of which meet an untimely demise on the concrete sidewalk on the way back to the house.

By the time we finally make it inside, I stop to catch my breath as I pick flecks of dried manure out of my hair. Is it time for coffee yet? Nope. Now it's time to make breakfast. And therein lies the true, though probably surprising, romance of a morning on the homestead. I enjoy the chaos in a weird way, although I most certainly appreciate the slightly quieter mornings too. Even by itself, homesteading can be overwhelming, but when you throw kids into the mix, well, it borders on sheer insanity. And yet, I love it. This is also why our breakfasts must be hearty and nourishing but not too fussy. By the time I make it back inside, the last thing I want is to be in the kitchen for two hours.

In this chapter, you'll find a mixture of classic farm breakfast fare as well as make-aheads and quick morning meals to help you start your day, regardless of whether your morning chaos is navigating traffic and the drop-off line at school or dealing with a persnickety cow and broken eggs.

# Foraged Frittata with Potato Crust

*serves four*

The dandelions and I have officially called a truce. I used to give them death glares each spring when they'd arrogantly pop up all over the homestead, but now we have an agreement: you grow wherever you want and I'll turn you into this delicious frittata. I think it's working out well.

3 tablespoons lard (page 251) or unsalted butter

1 small onion, diced

2 heaping cups foraged greens (dandelion greens, purslane, lamb's-quarter, or chickweed all work well)

3 cloves garlic, minced

3 medium potatoes, sliced ⅛ inch thick

½ teaspoon fine sea salt

½ teaspoon freshly ground black pepper

8 large eggs

⅓ cup whole milk

¼ cup freshly grated Parmesan cheese

Heat 1 tablespoon of the lard in a 10-inch oven-safe skillet (I use my cast-iron, of course).

Sauté the onion until soft, about 8 minutes, then add the greens and garlic and sauté for 2 to 3 minutes more, or until the greens begin to wilt. Remove the greens from the skillet and set aside.

Preheat the oven to 400°F.

Sprinkle the potatoes with ¼ teaspoon of the salt and ¼ teaspoon of the pepper. Add the remaining 2 tablespoons lard to the skillet and fry the potatoes until they are softened and lightly browned, about 10 minutes. Arrange the potatoes in a layer on the bottom of the skillet.

In a large bowl, whisk together the eggs, milk, cheese, and remaining ¼ teaspoon each salt and pepper, then add the egg mixture to the greens, mixing until just combined.

Pour the mixture over the potatoes in the skillet, transfer to the oven, and bake for 20 to 25 minutes, or until the eggs are set.

*kitchen notes · If you don't live in an area where you feel comfortable foraging for wild greens, trimmed spinach, kale, chard, or collards will also work beautifully in this frittata.*

# Baked Eggs with Cream & Chives

*serves four*

Chives and eggs have to be among the most perfect ingredient combos we grow here on the homestead. Eggs fresh from the coop and chives plucked from the herb garden outside the front door elevate this homey dish to a farm-fresh masterpiece. It's one of our early-summer staples when the hens have resumed their heavy laying and the wire basket on my countertop is overflowing with speckled brown eggs.

3 tablespoons heavy cream

1 tablespoon unsalted butter

8 large eggs

3 cloves garlic, minced

2 tablespoons minced fresh parsley

2 tablespoons minced fresh chives

¼ teaspoon fine sea salt

⅛ teaspoon freshly ground black pepper

Preheat the oven to 425°F.

Place the cream and butter in a 9 x 13–inch baking dish and heat in the oven for 5 minutes to melt the butter.

Crack the eggs directly into the hot pan. (Be careful not to break the yolks!)

Combine the garlic, parsley, chives, salt, and pepper and sprinkle evenly over the eggs.

Bake for 5 minutes, then switch the oven to broil and broil for 2 minutes, or until the whites are set but the yolks are still slightly runny.

Serve with a bit of crusty bread (such as leftover Crusty Dutch Oven Bread, page 160) or toast to sop up the yolk.

## WHEN LIFE GIVES YOU WEEDS, EAT 'EM

Scouring your yard for edibles, formerly known as weeds, is extremely satisfying, not to mention strangely addictive. But before you serve up any foraged goodies, do your homework thoroughly to make sure you aren't accidentally eating something poisonous. County Extension Offices are fantastic local resources and will be glad to help you identify any plant you are unsure about. Also, only forage in areas you know have not been sprayed with herbicides or pesticides.

# Farmer's Breakfast Hash

If I put this simple hash on the menu at just the right time in late summer, I can make it completely from ingredients grown right outside my back door: home-cured bacon from the pigs; potatoes, an onion, and a pepper provided by the garden; eggs laid by our multicolored hens; and chives grown in the herb patch. It also works beautifully with your favorite variety of sausage, just in case you don't have any bacon on hand. (And if you don't have bacon on hand, we really should have a talk about priorities.)

½ pound bacon, chopped

4 or 5 medium potatoes, cubed

1 small onion, diced

1 medium bell pepper, seeded and diced

½ teaspoon fine sea salt, plus more as needed

¼ teaspoon freshly ground black pepper

6 large eggs

Fresh chives, minced

In a 10-inch oven-safe skillet, cook the bacon over medium-low heat until crispy. Remove the bacon, setting it aside on a paper towel to drain and leaving about 2 tablespoons of fat in the skillet.

Add the potatoes to the skillet and fry them over medium heat for 8 minutes, or until they begin to soften. Add the onion, bell pepper, salt, and black pepper. Cook until the potatoes are golden brown, about 10 minutes more.

Stir in the bacon, taste, and add more salt if needed. Make shallow wells in the top of the hash and carefully break the eggs into the wells. Cook over medium heat for 3 to 4 minutes, until the egg whites are beginning to set, then transfer the skillet to the oven. Broil on high for 3 to 4 minutes, or until the egg yolks are set to your liking (I personally like mine a bit runny). Sprinkle with fresh chives and serve immediately.

*kitchen notes · This recipe is incredibly forgiving, so play around with it as you see fit. You can bump up the amount of veggies, crack more eggs on top, or double the potatoes in a larger skillet. I usually make this in a 10-inch cast-iron skillet, but if you have smaller skillets, you can make personal-sized hashes in each one.*

# Crispy Hash Browns

Crispy homemade hash browns that don't turn into a gummy mess in the pan? It's a lofty request, but after making a million pans of soggy, sticky potatoes, I finally figured out how to fry up hash browns that will make your hometown diner jealous. Just a few tiny adjustments to the technique make all the difference. Get out the ketchup—you're gonna love this one.

3 or 4 large russet potatoes

1 teaspoon fine sea salt

¼ teaspoon freshly ground black pepper

¼ cup (½ stick) unsalted butter or lard (page 251)

Wash the potatoes and shred them using a box grater or a food processor fitted with a grating disc. I don't peel mine first, but you can if you like. Place the shredded potatoes in a colander and rinse them under cool water until the water runs clear.

Drain the potatoes completely; sometimes I even squeeze them with a clean dishtowel to remove as much water as possible. Season the shredded potatoes with the salt and pepper.

In a 10-inch skillet over medium heat, melt the butter until it sizzles when you place a potato shred in the pan. Add the potatoes, give them a quick stir, then pat them into an even layer. Now, this is the hard part—*leave them alone* to cook over medium-low heat. Yes, resist the urge to fuss over them. It's hard, I know. But it makes all the difference.

When the bottom of the potatoes has developed a crisp, brown crust, after around 8 to 10 minutes, flip them. I'm not quite talented enough to flip the entire bunch at once, so I do it in quarters. Cook for another 8 to 10 minutes, or until they are browned to your liking. Serve immediately with a side of ketchup.

*kitchen notes · Every stove top is different, so watch the pan closely the first time you make these. The goal is for the heat to be high enough to crisp up the potatoes, but not so hot that it burns the bottom before the middle has time to cook.*

*It's tempting to crowd the pan with more potatoes (because who doesn't want more potatoes?), but fight the temptation. In order to get that perfectly crispy finish, the hash browns need room to breathe.*

*For a complete country breakfast, serve your crispy hash browns alongside a pile of Eggs 'n' Greens (opposite) or Maple Sage Breakfast Sausage (page 34).*

# Eggs 'n' Greens

serves four

(pictured on page 35)

When it comes to buying farm animals or planting vegetables, my eyes are always bigger than my stomach. This means I'm usually dealing with a constant glut of eggs and greens in the spring and early summer. It's my own fault, but I can't seem to stop. Therefore, it's only natural to throw the abundance together with a bit of cheese, don't you think?

2 tablespoons unsalted butter

1 medium onion or leek, diced

3 cups packed roughly chopped stemmed chard, kale, spinach, or collard leaves

1½ cups sliced mushrooms

6 large eggs

½ teaspoon fine sea salt

¼ teaspoon freshly ground black pepper

¼ cup ricotta cheese (page 249)

In a 10-inch skillet over medium heat, melt the butter. Sauté the onion until softened, about 6 minutes. Add the greens and mushrooms and cook until the greens are wilted, about 3 minutes.

In a medium bowl, beat the eggs with the salt and pepper, then add them to the greens in the hot skillet. Cook until the eggs are set but not dry, about 4 minutes.

Remove the skillet from the heat, crumble the ricotta over the top, and serve immediately.

# Maple Sage Breakfast Sausage

*makes three pounds*

Savory sage and tangy mustard dance with a splash of sweet maple syrup to make this a recipe I turn to time and time again. Brown the sausage in bulk to add to Old-Fashioned Sausage Gravy (page 41) or sandwich a patty between halved Sky-High Buttermilk Biscuits (page 168). Leftovers are never an issue when this sausage is on the menu. Make a double or triple batch and freeze the patties so they can easily be thrown in the frying pan on busy mornings.

3 pounds ground pork

1 small onion, finely minced

¼ cup maple syrup

1 tablespoon fine sea salt

2 teaspoons dried sage leaves

2 teaspoons ground mustard

2 teaspoons garlic powder

¾ teaspoon freshly ground black pepper

In a medium bowl, combine all the ingredients. I use my hands to mix everything together—it's messy, but effective. For maximum impact, refrigerate the mixture for 1 to 2 hours so the flavors have a chance to mingle. But if you're in a hurry, there's nothing wrong with cooking it up right away.

To make patties, place a piece of parchment or waxed paper on the counter. Place the sausage mixture on top and pat it to ½ inch thick. Using a 3-inch biscuit cutter or the rim of a drinking glass, cut the sausage into rounds. Or if you're in a hurry, you can make free-form patties in the palm of your hand.

In a skillet over medium heat, fry the patties until they are no longer pink in the middle, about 3–5 minutes per side.

*kitchen notes · To freeze, place squares of waxed paper between uncooked patties, stack them in an airtight container, and freeze for up to 4 months.*

*Combine 1 pound cooked sausage with Eggs 'n' Greens (page 33) and wrap 1 cup of the combo in a warm tortilla (page 171) for a tasty breakfast burrito.*

# Homemade Bacon

*makes three pounds*

The hardest part of making bacon is finding the raw ingredients, but once you're the proud owner of a beautiful pork belly, it's smooth sailing from there. If you don't raise your own hogs, call your local butcher and ask if they will sell you a belly or two. There's an untold number of ways to make bacon at home, but this simple method is the one I return to repeatedly when I'm craving the perfect combination of savory spices with a hint of sweetness. It doesn't require the addition of nitrates and it can easily be made by any home cook, even if you don't own a smoker. I keep my paper-wrapped bundles of bacon hidden in the bottom of the freezer, and each slice is savored when it makes an appearance at the table.

3 pounds whole pork belly with skin removed

4 cloves garlic, crushed

3 tablespoons coarse sea salt

2 tablespoons packed brown sugar, preferably organic whole cane sugar, or maple syrup

1 tablespoon dried rosemary leaves

1 tablespoon whole black peppercorns

Rinse the pork belly under cool water and pat it dry with a paper towel.

Combine the remaining ingredients in a small bowl and rub the seasoning over both sides of the pork belly, making sure the entire pork belly is thoroughly coated.

Seal the pork belly in a gallon-size freezer bag or airtight container and refrigerate for 5 to 7 days to cure. I like to check mine daily to flip the bag over and discard any liquid that might have accumulated as the salt draws the moisture from the meat.

After the curing period, remove the bacon from the bag and rinse it under cool running water. This removes the excess salt.

Place the bacon on a rack and refrigerate uncovered for 12 hours to air-dry.

After the drying period, preheat the oven to 200°F.

Set the bacon, still on the rack, on a rimmed baking sheet and bake for 1½ to 2 hours, or until the internal temperature reaches 150°F.

Cool the bacon in the fridge for 6 hours before slicing it to your desired thickness. Divide the slices into 1-pound packages and freeze up to 3 months or store in the refrigerator for up to 7 days.

To cook the bacon: Lay the slices in a cold skillet and heat the skillet over medium heat. Fry until both sides are crispy, flipping occasionally. Be sure to pour the leftover fat into a jar and save it for use in other recipes, such as the Barn Raising Beans (page 96), Saturday Night Roast Beef (page 73), or Restaurant-Style Refried Beans (page 129).

# Homemade Chorizo

I needed a chorizo without the questionable ingredients contained in the premade options at the grocery store, but I didn't feel like hunting down a bunch of hard-to-find spices to make my own. And that's how my take on Mexican-style chorizo was born. Ancho chile powder is as specialized as I get in this recipe. I had to order mine online, but there's a good chance you have access to better grocery stores and will be able to find it locally. I don't recommend substituting regular chili powder for the slightly sweet, smoky ancho if you can avoid it. Ancho chile powder is 100 percent dried, ground poblano peppers whereas regular chili powders are usually a blend of peppers and other spices, so the taste difference is substantial. If you must, you may use chipotle chile powder as a substitute, though keep in mind that chipotle is spicier, so use a teaspoon or two less if you prefer a milder sausage.

1 pound ground pork

1½ tablespoons apple cider vinegar

1½ tablespoons ancho chile powder

1 tablespoon garlic powder

1 tablespoon paprika

1 teaspoon ground cumin

1 teaspoon dried oregano

¾ teaspoon fine sea salt

¼ teaspoon freshly ground black pepper

In a medium bowl, combine all the ingredients. I use my hands to mix everything together—it's messy, but effective. For maximum impact, refrigerate the mixture for 4 to 8 hours so the flavors have a chance to mingle. But if you're in a hurry, there's nothing wrong with cooking it up right away.

Brown the chorizo in bulk or, to make patties, place a piece of parchment or waxed paper on the counter. Place the sausage mixture on top and pat it to ½ inch thick. Using a 3-inch biscuit cutter or the rim of a drinking glass, cut the sausage into rounds. Or if you're in a hurry, you can make free-form patties in the palm of your hand.

In a skillet over medium heat, fry the patties until they are no longer pink in the middle, about 3–5 minutes per side.

*kitchen notes · To freeze, place squares of waxed paper between uncooked patties and stack them in an airtight container (or simply wrap them tightly, if freezing in bulk) and freeze for up to 4 months.*

*Add chorizo to frittatas or breakfast burritos, or substitute it for the bacon in Farmer's Breakfast Hash (page 31).*

## no-stick scrambled eggs in a cast-iron skillet

If you were to dig through my kitchen cupboards, you wouldn't find a single piece of cookware with the special nonstick coating that seems to be on everything these days.

I fell out of love with the stuff years ago. I hate how easily the coating scratches, not to mention that the fumes many of the coatings emit when heated to higher temperatures aren't especially healthy. I'll stick (pun intended) with my stainless steel and cast iron, thank you very much.

Thankfully, with these few considerations, it's entirely possible to cook eggs in a good old-fashioned cast-iron skillet.

*Start with a well-seasoned pan.* This makes all the difference—a naked pan will result in glued-on eggs every time. If you aren't confident in your skillet, see page 154 for instructions on re-seasoning cast iron.

*Don't skip the fat.* This isn't the time to try to be fat-free. I add at least 1 tablespoon of fat to my 10-inch skillet when I'm cooking scrambled eggs. Butter, coconut oil, lard, and bacon grease will all work—just don't skimp. Eggs taste better with fat, anyway. It's a win-win.

*Warm it up.* Starting with a cold pan is a surefire way to end up with a sticky mess. Heat the pan and fat well over medium heat before adding the eggs.

*Wait, then stir.* After pouring the beaten eggs into the pan, wait for 20 to 30 seconds before you start stirring with a wooden spoon or spatula.

# Baked Oatmeal with Peaches

This oatmeal breakfast cake is as flexible as they come. Swap in quick-cooking oats for the rolled ones if that's all you have, or use colorful, in-season berries for the peaches if you'd rather. I like to throw it together the night before and store it in the fridge, but it's just as tasty if you make it and serve it immediately.

3 cups rolled oats

2 teaspoons baking powder

½ teaspoon fine sea salt

½ teaspoon ground cinnamon

1 cup whole milk

½ cup packed brown sugar, preferably organic whole cane sugar

¼ cup (½ stick) unsalted butter, melted

3 large eggs

1 teaspoon vanilla extract (page 261)

4 peaches, peeled and diced (about 2 cups)

Preheat the oven to 350°F and grease a 9-inch round baking dish.

In a large bowl, combine the oats, baking powder, salt, and cinnamon.

In a separate bowl, whisk together the milk, sugar, melted butter, eggs, and vanilla, then add to the dry ingredients and stir to combine.

Mix in the peaches and pour the mixture into the prepared baking dish.

Bake for 30 minutes, or until golden brown, or cover and refrigerate to bake and serve the following morning. Serve with a drizzle of milk or cream.

*kitchen notes* · *If you use canned peaches instead of fresh, be sure to drain them very well. You may also need to increase the baking time by 5 to 10 minutes to account for the additional moisture.*

*If refrigerating overnight for baking the following morning, allow an extra 5 to 10 minutes of baking time.*

# Creamy Wheat Porridge

Oatmeal is a popular breakfast at our house, but this oatmeal alternative receives special cheers from my kids whenever they see it on the stove. Use whatever variety of wheat berries you have available, but we find we especially prefer soft wheat. We also like to make this recipe with millet. Swirl some Simple Berry Sauce (page 50) into your bowl to make it even snazzier.

1½ cups soft wheat berries or millet

2½ cups whole milk

3 tablespoons unsalted butter

½ teaspoon fine sea salt

Place the wheat berries in a bowl, cover them with several inches of water, and soak overnight.

The next morning, drain and rinse the wheat berries and place in a blender. Pulse for about 1 minute, or until the wheat berries resemble steel-cut oats. (Add 1 cup water if the blender gets stuck.)

In a large saucepan over medium heat, bring the milk, butter, salt, and 2 cups water to a gentle boil.

Add the wheat berries and cook for 12 to 15 minutes, or until softened. Serve with maple syrup, a drizzle of cream, or fresh fruit and nuts.

# Mason Jar Yogurt

*makes two quarts*

"Wait a second . . . You can actually make yogurt?!" The revelation hit me like a lightning bolt as I was reading a home dairy book one day. It was early in my homesteading journey and my mind was blown by the idea of making so many foods I previously thought could only be purchased at the store. Yogurt was one of my first from-scratch victories, and it's an ideal place to start if you're new to the world of home dairy. Even if you don't have access to raw milk and fancy cultures, you can still make thick yogurt rivaling those from the fanciest creameries with basic ingredients and a stockpot. It only takes a few minutes of hands-on time to create as much as your heart desires, and this recipe can easily be doubled if you have a family of yogurt lovers. I almost always make at least a gallon at a time and it disappears in a flash.

8 cups whole milk

4 tablespoons plain yogurt with live, active cultures

SPECIAL EQUIPMENT

2 quart-sized glass canning jars with lids

Large stockpot

Food thermometer

Small cooler (see "Incubation Tips")

Clean the jars thoroughly or sterilize them in the dishwasher. Fill the jars with the milk, leaving 2 inches of space at the top of each jar. Place the filled jars into the stockpot.

Fill the pot with water, stopping when the water level is three-quarters of the way up the sides of the jars.

Bring the water to a boil and gently simmer until the milk inside the jars reaches 180°F.

Carefully remove the hot jars from the water (don't pour out the water in the stockpot yet—you'll need it later). Loosely cover the jars with their lids and periodically check the temperature of the milk until it cools to 110°F. (You can speed up this process by placing the jars in the fridge, but it's really easy to forget about them in there!)

Add 2 tablespoons of the yogurt to each jar, stir gently, and cap the jars.

Put the jars into the cooler and fill the cooler with the leftover warm water from the stockpot before closing the lid. (If the water has cooled too much, turn the burner back on and heat it to 120°F or so before pouring it into the cooler.) Allow the yogurt to incubate for 8 to 10 hours, or until it sets up. The longer it incubates, the tangier it will be.

Chill the finished yogurt for 24 hours before enjoying. It will keep in the refrigerator for at least 2 weeks, although I've had it last much longer. (If you see mold in the jars or the yogurt develops an unpleasant aroma, toss it.)

Top your homemade yogurt with maple syrup, honey, nuts, chopped fruit, jam, or Simple Berry Sauce (page 50) and dig in!

*kitchen notes* · *Make sure the jars are very clean before you start. Sterilize them in your dishwasher if possible.*

*The step of heating the milk to 180°F changes the proteins in the milk and creates a thicker yogurt. There are methods to make unheated, raw yogurt, but they generally require specialty cultures that won't be available at your local grocery store.*

*Most high-quality brands of yogurt will contain live, active cultures, but check the back of the carton to be sure. You can use your homemade yogurt to start future batches, although the cultures seem to get "tired" after a while, so plan on buying fresh yogurt after three or four batches.*

## INCUBATION TIPS

If you don't have a cooler that fits your jars, don't worry—here are a few other incubation options:

- Briefly preheat the oven, then shut it off before placing the jars inside to incubate for 8 hours. Leave the oven light on—this should generate just enough heat to keep the yogurt happy.

- Place the jars on a heating pad and cover them with a towel.

- Use a food dehydrator (the kind with removable racks) set to 110°F.

The goal is to keep the jars at roughly 110°F during the incubation period, so there's plenty of room to get creative as long as the temperature stays constant. (I've even heard of people incubating yogurt in their hot cars during the summer!)

# Simple Berry Sauce

(pictured on page 46)

*makes about two cups*

I know, I know. "Pancake *sauce*" doesn't roll off the tongue quite as nicely as "pancake *syrup*" does, but hear me out. Maple syrup is lovely, but sometimes you just need to mix it up on the pancake front. This homemade fruit sauce does exactly that. You can use this same technique to make fruit syrup—the difference is that for syrup the solids are strained out before serving. I prefer to leave the solids in this sauce for a thicker finished result, but if you do strain them out, add them to smoothies or spoon them over biscuits or toast.

2 cups fresh or frozen berries of your choice

⅓ cup sugar, preferably organic whole cane sugar

1 teaspoon vanilla extract (page 261)

In a medium saucepan, combine the berries, sugar, and 1 cup water. Bring to a boil over medium heat and simmer for 10 to 15 minutes, stirring occasionally, until thickened.

Remove the saucepan from the heat, stir in the vanilla, and puree the berries with an immersion blender or in a regular blender with the lid slightly ajar to allow steam to escape.

Serve the warm sauce over pancakes or waffles, mix it into plain yogurt (page 48), or stir it into Creamy Wheat Porridge (page 47), or cool and store it in an airtight container in the refrigerator for up to 1 week or in the freezer for up to 3 months.

*kitchen notes · This sauce would be heavenly over ice cream. Just throwing that out there.*

*I'm partial to blueberries here, but raspberries, strawberries, or a combination of the three would be pretty tasty too.*

# hearty mains

*No matter whether you're cultivating vegetables* outside a sod house in 1889 or tending a handful of tomato plants in a suburban backyard in 2019, the heartbeat of a homestead remains the same. And that heartbeat is food.

Food is the vein that runs through all homesteads, past and present. Even in our age of industrialized food production, for those of us who choose to take a step back to a simpler way of life, food brings a structure and rhythm to our days in a way nothing else can. The cadences manifest themselves in different forms, but they are persistent and always remain at the forefront of the day.

The rhythms of production and growth determine which projects are priorities and when we might dare leave the homestead for a short vacation. When will the new baby chicks arrive? When will the garden require planting? When we will need to stay close and watch heat cycles and breed the cows again?

The rhythm of harvest determines our menu. There are times we gorge ourselves on every egg dish you can imagine, and times when squash appears in at least one dish per day. And then the seasons change and we take a forced fast from eggs or squash or whatever else we've been indulging in.

And the rhythm of mealtime determines the arrangement of our day. The anchor of our schedule is suppertime. Our goal is to have food on the table at 5:30 p.m. so we have time to do dishes and head back outside to wrap up projects before bedtime. We all feel more grounded and rooted when we take a purposeful break to sit at the table and bond over food.

Sometimes a friend or neighbor joins us (there's always a project happening outside, so it's common to have help over during mealtimes), but usually it's just our little family. We talk over Maple-Glazed Pork Chops about what we accomplished that day, discuss tomorrow's tasks over noodles smothered in Butternut Pasta Sauce, or chat over steaming bowls of Farmhouse Beef Stew about the blizzard that's blowing in. It's not a fancy affair and we don't eat on fine china (or even matching plates), but the time to draw close and reconnect is one of the best parts of the day. You don't have to live on a farm to embrace this ritual—just turn off the TV and let the flavors of the home-cooked food in this chapter bring you together with the people you love.

# Simple Roast Chicken

Everyone needs a tried-and-true lazy supper option, and this is mine. It's a hands-free meal on the day we eat it and comes with a built-in meal plan for the rest of the week too. After I serve the bird for supper, every leftover scrap of meat is pulled from the bones to make Creamy Chicken Noodle Soup (page 107) or Chicken Poblano Chowder (page 105) the following day, and the bones and drippings go right back into the pot with onions and garlic to make jars of rich, nourishing stock (page 236) for soups or stews later in the week. A whole chicken gives you a lot of bang for your buck.

6 cloves garlic, minced

1 tablespoon dried parsley

1 tablespoon dried thyme

1 tablespoon dried sage

1 teaspoon dried tarragon

1 tablespoon coarse sea salt

1 whole chicken (4 to 5 pounds)

2 tablespoons extra-virgin olive oil

6 medium potatoes, quartered

1 large onion, cut into chunks

Preheat the oven to 350°F.

Combine the garlic, herbs, and salt in a small bowl.

Rinse the chicken under cool water and pat it dry with a paper towel. Coat the chicken thoroughly with the olive oil, then rub the herb mixture over the whole chicken, inside and out.

Place the potatoes and onion in the bottom of a Dutch oven and lay the chicken on top, breast-side down. Cover and roast for 45 minutes, then increase the temperature to 400°F, remove the lid, and roast for 20 minutes more. Flip the chicken breast-side up and roast until the thickest part of the thigh reaches 165°F, about 30 minutes more.

*kitchen notes · If you're heading out for the day, use your slow cooker to cook the chicken instead of roasting it. Follow the instructions above, placing the onion and potatoes in a slow cooker instead of in a Dutch oven. Lay the seasoned chicken on top, cover, and cook on low for 7 to 9 hours. To crisp the skin, place the cooked chicken on a broiler pan and broil about 12 inches from the heat for 4 to 5 minutes, or until the skin is brown and crisp.*

# cooking an old hen (or rooster)

If you keep chickens for any period of time, you'll inevitably be faced with the task of culling the flock. There will be hens that no longer lay, mean roosters that cause you to fear for your life every time you open the coop, and those extra roosters that you were hoping were hens when you purchased them from the feed store. Whatever the reason, eventually you'll end up with nonproductive or counterproductive chickens that continue to eat food and cost you money. And they've gotta go.

I've heard of folks sending older chickens to chicken sanctuaries, but I prefer to take care of extra birds the old-fashioned way—the stockpot.

The stewing hen is a bit of culinary resourcefulness that has been pushed aside over the years. Most folks are accustomed to the broilers you buy at the store—they're young, tender, and perfect for roasting or frying. Stewing hens aren't exactly young or tender, but they have a tastiness all their own. In fact, older hens tend to be even more flavorful than younger birds—the trick is aging and cooking them properly.

After butchering an older hen or rooster, avoid cooking it right away. Instead, place it in the refrigerator, loosely covered with waxed paper, for 4 to 6 days. Similar to the process of aging beef, this allows the muscle fibers to relax and produces a much more tender result.

With older chickens, roasting is out and long, slow cooking is in. Place the whole chicken in a stockpot and cover it with water. Season it with salt, pepper, an onion, several cloves of garlic, bay leaves, and your choice of herbs. (Exact amounts aren't super important, but if you'd like more specific measurements, use the homemade stock on page 236 as a guide.) Simmer for at least 6 hours or up to 12 hours, or until the meat is tender. Remove the bird from the pot and strain the stock for use in other recipes. Once the chicken is cool enough to handle, pull the meat from the bones and use it in soups and stews. The leftover bones can be simmered again with fresh water and herbs for another batch of nutrient-rich stock. And that is how the stewing hen just keeps giving and giving.

# Chicken Stroganoff

*serves four*

A plate full of hearty stroganoff is a reliable way to fill hungry bellies after a day of working outside in the cold. I've made many variations on beef stroganoff, but I keep coming back to this chicken version with its rich sauce and hint of tarragon. We prefer our stroganoff sauce ladled over pasta, but there's nothing wrong with using rice or mashed potatoes instead. Use this recipe to transform leftover chicken into a fresh new main dish. If you plan on using cooked chicken, add it after the sauce has finished simmering to keep the meat from disintegrating into shreds.

16 ounces dry egg noodles or pasta

3 tablespoons unsalted butter

1 medium onion, diced

1 cup sliced fresh mushrooms

2 cloves garlic, minced

¼ cup all-purpose flour

1 teaspoon paprika

½ teaspoon dried tarragon

¼ teaspoon fine sea salt

¼ teaspoon freshly ground black pepper

2¼ cups chicken stock (page 236)

2 boneless, skinless chicken breasts, cut into ½-inch cubes (about 3 cups)

1 tablespoon Worcestershire sauce

¾ cup sour cream

Fresh parsley, for garnish

Cook the noodles in salted water to al dente (tender but firm) according to the package directions. Drain and set aside.

In a medium saucepan over medium heat, melt the butter. Add the onion and mushrooms and sauté until the onion is softened, about 6 minutes.

Add the garlic, flour, paprika, tarragon, salt, and pepper to the pan and cook for an additional 2 to 3 minutes, until the flour is slightly brown.

Add the stock, chicken, and Worcestershire sauce. Reduce the heat to low and simmer, uncovered, for 15 to 20 minutes, or until the chicken is cooked through and the sauce has thickened.

Stir in the sour cream and pour the sauce over the noodles. Garnish with fresh parsley.

# Sticky Honey Chicken

*serves four to six*

You just can't beat a drumstick dripping with a sticky honey-garlic glaze, especially when the entire dish only calls for a handful of ingredients. Since we raise our own birds, we usually only have whole chickens in the freezer. My favorite trick is to cut up a whole chicken (check out the instructions on page 60); use the wings, thighs, and drumsticks for this recipe; save the breasts for the Chicken Poblano Chowder (page 105) or Creamy Chicken Noodle Soup (page 107); and finally simmer the backbone with onions and herbs for stock (page 236).

⅓ cup honey

¼ cup tomato sauce (page 264)

2 tablespoons soy sauce or alternative of your choice

2 tablespoons apple cider vinegar

1 teaspoon garlic powder

1 teaspoon onion powder

½ teaspoon ground ginger

6 bone-in, skin-on chicken pieces (thighs, drumsticks, wings) or boneless breasts

Whisk the honey, tomato sauce, soy sauce, vinegar, garlic powder, onion powder, and ginger together in a small bowl. Put the chicken pieces in a large bowl or baking dish and pour the mixture over the chicken. Cover and marinate for at least 2 hours in the refrigerator, or up to overnight.

Preheat the oven to 400°F. Arrange the chicken pieces in a 9 x 13–inch baking dish skin-side up and pour the marinade over the top. (If I use breasts, I like to cut them in half to help them soak up more flavor.)

Bake for 40 to 50 minutes, or until the internal temperature of the chicken reaches 165°F, basting the chicken pieces with the liquid several times during the cooking process for maximum flavor.

For crispier chicken, broil the finished pieces on high for 3 to 4 minutes, or until the skin is brown and crisp.

I usually prefer to cook whole chickens, but sometimes recipes like Sticky Honey Chicken (page 59) make it worthwhile to piece them out. It takes practice to become proficient at this skill, but with a little work, you'll soon be slicing through that chicken like a pro. A sharp chef's knife is a must, although most of the cuts are through a joint and should be fairly easy if your knife placement is correct. Whole chickens are often cheaper than buying pieces at the store, so spend a little time mastering this skill and you'll be saving cash and getting bonus stock in the process.

**1.** Place the chicken breast-side up on a cutting board. Pull the drumstick away from the body and slice through the skin. Be careful not to slice into the breast meat.

**2.** Roll the chicken onto its side and firmly grasp the thigh. Bend it back until the thigh joint pops out. Cut through the joint and skin. Repeat on the other side.

**3.** To separate the drumstick from the thigh, place the leg skin-side down on the cutting board. There is a white fat line that runs between the thigh and the drum—it's the perfect guide for your knife. Slice through the line, wiggling the joint as you go. If you have proper placement (it will take a little practice), the knife should glide through the joint—no brute force required.

**4.** To remove the wings, use your thumb to feel for the end of the wing (press into the chicken a little ways to find this joint—think armpit) and cut through that joint.

**5.** Position the chicken breast-side up with the neck end facing you. Place the blade of your knife on top of the breast on one side of the breastbone. Glide the knife down close to the bone to separate the breast completely from the body

cavity. Stay as close to the body cavity as possible to avoid wasting any meat.

**6.** As you continue to slice down, your knife will come in contact with the wishbone in front. To break it, position the top third of the knife over the middle of the bone and use your free hand to hit the top of the knife and split the wishbone in half.

**7.** Repeat the process to remove the breast from the other side. You can slice the breasts in half or leave them whole—that's up to you. Use the backbone to make stock (page 236) and then celebrate! You've just broken down a whole chicken with zero waste.

# The Wyoming Burger

We may not be able to boast about vast vineyards or tropical fruits, but if there's one ingredient Wyoming knows well, it's beef. These juicy burgers have a dash of crushed sage to represent our ever-present sagebrush, smoky paprika to give a nod to our legendary wind, and chili powder to put a bit of fire in the belly during our frigid winters. This burger is rugged and hardy, just like the fine folks who live in the Cowboy State.

2 pounds ground beef

2 tablespoons dried sage

2 tablespoons molasses

2 tablespoons Worcestershire sauce

1 tablespoon chili powder

1 tablespoon smoked paprika

½ teaspoon garlic powder

½ teaspoon crushed red pepper flakes

½ teaspoon freshly ground black pepper

1 tablespoon extra-virgin olive oil, butter, or preferred cooking oil

Coarse sea salt or kosher salt

8 slices pepper Jack cheese or cheese of your choice

8 buns

Burger fixings of your choice, such as tomato, lettuce, onion, and pickles

Combine the ground beef, sage, molasses, Worcestershire sauce, chili powder, paprika, garlic powder, red pepper flakes, and black pepper in a large bowl and shape the mixture into eight patties.

Heat the olive oil in a 12-inch skillet over medium-high heat. Sprinkle both sides of each patty with a generous pinch of salt (about ¼ teaspoon per patty), and immediately place four patties in the hot skillet.

Fry for 3 to 5 minutes on each side, or until the patties are cooked to your liking (to an internal temperature of 145°F for medium-rare or 160°F for medium). When the burgers are just about done, top each with a slice of cheese and give it a chance to melt. Repeat with the remaining patties.

Serve on a toasted bun with your favorite burger fixings and a generous pile of Zesty Oven Fries (page 118) on the side.

# Cheddar & Herb Meatloaf

*serves six to eight*

The humble meatloaf. It may not win awards for Most Glamorous Dish, but you can't beat it when comfort food is in order. I prefer the savory herbs and cheese in this recipe to the sweeter, ketchup-laden loaves. Christian has been known to choose this recipe over a steak dinner, so I think it's safe to say it's a hit at our house. Mixing beef and pork makes this the juiciest, most flavorful meatloaf I've ever tried. I'll never go back to using only beef again.

½ cup minced onion

2 tablespoons extra-virgin olive oil

2 cloves garlic, minced

1 pound ground beef

1 pound ground pork

1 large egg, beaten

¼ cup dry breadcrumbs (page 262)

¼ cup freshly grated Parmesan cheese

1 tablespoon Worcestershire sauce

1 tablespoon dried parsley

1 teaspoon dried oregano

1 teaspoon fine sea salt

½ teaspoon freshly ground black pepper

1¼ cups shredded cheddar cheese

Preheat the oven to 400°F. In a skillet over medium heat, sauté the onion in the olive oil until softened, about 6 minutes, then add the garlic and cook for 2 minutes more.

In a large bowl, combine the meat, onion and garlic, egg, breadcrumbs, Parmesan, Worcestershire sauce, and seasonings. Mix together until completely incorporated (hands make the best mixers here), then add 1 cup of the cheddar.

Place a metal rack on top of a rimmed baking sheet. Shape the meat mixture into a loaf and place it on the rack. This allows the excess fat from the pork to drip off and keeps the meatloaf from becoming soggy as it cooks.

Bake for 45 to 55 minutes, or until the internal temperature in the center of the loaf reaches 160°F, sprinkling the top with the remaining ¼ cup cheddar during the last 15 minutes of baking.

# Saucy Spiced Beef & Onions

An economical cut of beef is transformed into tender bites of curried deliciousness in this unpretentious yet tasty recipe. If you don't have round steak handy, chuck steak or even stew meat can stand in. I usually serve this over rice, but it's also amazing poured over hot mashed potatoes.

3 tablespoons lard (page 251)

1 to 1½ pounds round steak, trimmed of fat and cut into ½-inch pieces

¾ teaspoon fine sea salt

½ teaspoon freshly ground black pepper

1 large onion, sliced

3 cloves garlic, minced

2 teaspoons ground cumin

2 teaspoons ground coriander

2 teaspoons curry powder

3½ cups beef stock (page 236)

½ cup sour cream

4 cups cooked white or brown rice

In a Dutch oven over medium heat, melt the lard. Season the steak with the salt and pepper and cook until the chunks are browned on all sides.

Add the onion, garlic, and spices and cook for an additional 3 to 4 minutes, until the onions have started to soften. Pour in the stock, reduce the heat to low, and simmer, covered, for 2 hours, or until the sauce has reduced by half and the meat is tender. Remove from the heat, stir in the sour cream, and serve over hot rice.

# Steak Bites with Mushrooms

Raising our own beef has spoiled me forever. I have access to any cut my heart desires, including the pricier cuts I never would have dreamed of buying at the grocery store in the past. And yet, there are times I find myself standing in front of the open freezer, staring at all the neatly wrapped white packages of beef and feeling completely at a loss for ideas. If you've bought beef in bulk, I bet you can relate. We eat a lot of simple grilled steaks, but sometimes I mix it up with these brightly flavored steak bites. You can even insert toothpicks into the cubes and serve them as an appetizer or party food.

1½ to 2 pounds sirloin steak, trimmed of fat and cut into 1-inch cubes

½ teaspoon fine sea salt

¼ teaspoon freshly ground black pepper

2 tablespoons unsalted butter

2 cups baby bella (cremini) mushrooms, cleaned and quartered

½ cup beef stock (page 236)

1 tablespoon balsamic vinegar

1 tablespoon dried parsley

Toss the steak with ¼ teaspoon of the salt and the pepper. Heat the butter in a large skillet over high heat until it's blazing hot, then add the steak in small batches to avoid overcrowding.

Sear the steak, turning as soon as a dark brown crust has developed, which, as long as the skillet is hot enough, should only take about 30 seconds per side. (We want the steak bites to remain pink and tender on the inside.) Continue to turn the steak until all sides are seared. Remove from the skillet and set aside. Repeat this process until all of the steak has been cooked and set aside.

Add the mushrooms to the skillet, reduce the heat to medium, and sauté for 5 minutes, until the mushrooms release their juices.

Add the stock, vinegar, parsley, and remaining ¼ teaspoon salt to the skillet. Cook for 5 minutes, or until the stock has reduced by half and slightly thickened. Pour the mushrooms and sauce over the steak and serve immediately.

# Pan-Fried Steaks
# with Roasted Garlic Butter

*serves four*

I used to make pan-fried steaks only when the grill was buried under five feet of snow and I didn't feel like digging. These days, I make them year-round, whether the grill is accessible or not. We've found we much prefer the flavor of a pan-seared steak—plus, I like the extra bit of control I have over their cooking.

The roasted garlic butter is optional, but transforms these from simple steaks into a gourmet experience, so I think you'll be glad you took the little bit of extra time to throw it together. The only downside is a slightly smoky kitchen, so turn on the fan and pop open a window before you begin. Serve your pan-fried steaks with Crispy Potato Stacks (page 114) or Beet & Potato Mash (page 113).

4 steaks (such as New York strip, sirloin, rib eye, or T-bone), around 1½ inches thick

Coarse sea salt and freshly ground black pepper

2 tablespoons unsalted butter

2 cloves garlic, smashed

Roasted Garlic Butter (page 71)

Let the steaks sit out at room temperature for 30 minutes before you plan to cook them.

Heat two skillets over high heat for at least 10 minutes. (This is the time to be breaking out your cast-iron pans, by the way.) If they start to smoke a bit, you're on the right track. Pat the steaks dry with a paper towel, then sprinkle them with salt and pepper and immediately place them in the hot, dry pans. Sear for 1 minute, then flip and sear on the opposite side for 1 minute.

Add 1 tablespoon of the butter and 1 clove of garlic to each pan. Continue to flip the steaks every minute or so, basting them with butter until they are cooked to your liking. (See the chart on page 71 for cooking times—remember, there is no shame in using a thermometer to get perfectly cooked steaks!)

Rest the finished steaks for 10 minutes and top with a pat of roasted garlic butter before serving.

# Roasted Garlic Butter

*makes half cup*

½ cup (1 stick) unsalted butter, softened

1 bulb roasted garlic (page 132)

1 tablespoon dried parsley

½ teaspoon fine sea salt

Combine all the ingredients in a small bowl until well blended. Spoon the butter onto a piece of plastic wrap and roll it into a log. Chill until firm, about 2 hours.

## STEAK COOKING CHART

| Doneness | Internal Temperature | Approximate Total Cooking Time |
| --- | --- | --- |
| Rare | 125°F | 6 minutes |
| Medium-Rare | 135°F | 8 minutes |
| Medium | 145°F | 10 minutes |
| Medium-Well | 155°F | 12 minutes |
| Well | 165°F | 15 minutes |

# Saturday Night Roast Beef

Some of my earliest food memories involve the roast beef dinners my grandmother used to make. The tender beef, smothered in rich gravy and served alongside sweet baby carrots, is forever embedded into my taste buds. As a newlywed I attempted to re-create her legendary roast beef countless times with disappointing results. Many years and failed attempts later, I finally learned the magic lies in the sear. Add a few savory seasonings, and this roast tastes just like a Saturday night at Grandma Rising's table.

2 tablespoons lard (page 251) or bacon grease

1 (3- to 5-pound) beef roast (I usually use chuck, rump, or sirloin tip roasts)

1 teaspoon fine sea salt

½ teaspoon freshly ground black pepper

1 medium onion, minced

4 cloves garlic, minced

1 cup beef stock (page 236)

2 tablespoons Worcestershire sauce

2 tablespoons soy sauce or alternative of your choice

6 fresh sage leaves, or 1 tablespoon dried sage

In a large skillet over medium-high heat, heat the lard until melted. Season the roast well with the salt and pepper. Sear it in the lard until all sides develop a deep brown crust.

Remove the roast, then add the onion and garlic to the skillet. Sauté for 3 to 4 minutes, or until softened, then add the stock, using a wooden spoon to scrape any cooked bits from the bottom of the skillet.

Place the roast in a slow cooker, along with the stock mixture, Worcestershire sauce, soy sauce, and sage. Cover and cook on low for 8 hours. Use the drippings to make brown gravy (page 258).

*kitchen notes · To make a roast in the oven instead of in a slow cooker, sear the beef and sauté the onion and garlic in a Dutch oven instead of a skillet. Return the meat to the pot, add the Worcestershire sauce, soy sauce, and sage, then cover and roast in a preheated 350°F oven for about 3 hours, or until the meat is tender and the internal temperature reads 160°F.*

# Maple-Glazed Pork Chops

*serves four*

*Dry, chewy,* and *flavorless.* Those were the words I once used to describe any pork chop that came out of my kitchen. It was downright embarrassing, especially after we started raising our own pork. After many failed attempts, I landed on this foolproof technique. The maple glaze yields tender chops bursting with layers of tangy seasoning, and I'm finally confident enough to feed homegrown pork chops to guests. Whew. Boneless or bone-in chops will work for this recipe, but I prefer bone-in since they carry more flavor.

1 teaspoon fine sea salt

½ teaspoon smoked paprika

½ teaspoon garlic powder

¼ teaspoon freshly ground black pepper

4 pork chops, 1 inch thick

2 tablespoons lard (page 251) or unsalted butter

Maple Glaze (recipe follows)

Preheat the oven to 350°F. Combine the salt, paprika, garlic powder, and pepper in a small bowl. Season both sides of the pork chops generously with the mixture and pat it into the meat.

In an oven-safe skillet over medium-high heat, heat the lard until it's melted and hot. Carefully add the pork chops to the skillet and fry for 2 to 3 minutes on each side, or until the meat begins to develop a deep brown crust.

Pour the glaze over the chops in the skillet. Cook for 1 minute more on each side. Transfer the skillet to the oven and bake for 7 to 8 minutes, or until the internal temperature of the pork is 160°F in the center. Remove from the oven and let rest for 10 minutes before serving.

## Maple Glaze

½ cup maple syrup

3 tablespoons Dijon mustard

2 tablespoons apple cider vinegar

2 cloves garlic, finely minced

Whisk all the ingredients together in a small bowl. This glaze will keep for up to 3 days in the refrigerator if you'd like to make it ahead of time.

# Slow Cooker Pulled Pork

serves five to eight

I've tried every way possible to mess up this recipe, and I'm pretty sure it can't be done. Need to cook it longer than the recipe specifies? No problem. Want to cook it a day early? You got it. How about starting with a frozen pork shoulder in the slow cooker? It'll still turn out perfectly (just add an extra 3 to 4 hours of cook time on low and you'll be set). This is my go-to crowd-pleaser when I'm working or entertaining and don't have time to fuss in the kitchen before mealtime. Homegrown or locally sourced pork makes it even better.

1 teaspoon paprika

1 teaspoon garlic powder

1 teaspoon fine sea salt, plus more if needed

½ teaspoon freshly ground black pepper, plus more if needed

1 (3- to 5-pound) pork shoulder

1 medium onion, chopped

1 cup beef or chicken stock (page 236)

In a small bowl, combine the paprika, garlic powder, salt, and pepper and rub the mixture liberally over the entire pork shoulder. Place the shoulder and onion in a slow cooker and pour the stock over the top. Cover and cook on low for 8 to 12 hours.

Remove the pork from the slow cooker and set it aside to cool until you can comfortably handle it, then separate the meat from the fat and bones. Shred the meat and season with additional salt and pepper if needed. The cooking liquid can be strained and set aside as well.

Serve with or without a bun. Also, this pulled pork is best friends with Sweet and Tangy BBQ Sauce (page 263)—you'll definitely want to serve them together.

*kitchen notes · I generally use bone-in pork shoulders, but boneless will work as well, as will other varieties of pork roast.*

*When serving a crowd, I like to cook and shred the pork the day before company arrives. On the day we plan to eat it, I pop the shredded meat and 1 cup of the cooking liquid or stock back into the slow cooker to keep it warm until mealtime.*

*To make shredding the meat easier, place several cups of meat chunks into the bowl of a stand mixer fitted with the paddle attachment. Beat on low speed for 30 to 60 seconds until it's shredded. This method is approximately 581 times easier than using two forks to do the job.*

# Butternut Pasta Sauce

*serves four*

I have squash hoarding tendencies. I like to arrange the winter squash along our basement shelves and then I stand there and admire them . . . Wait, that's not normal? Anyway, roasted squash with a pat of butter and splash of maple syrup is our standby, but when I'm in the mood to change things up, I turn to this Alfredo-inspired sauce. The butternut adds a hint of sweetness, which has turned many a squash-hater into a raving fan. Pumpkin also makes a great substitute.

1 pound bacon (page 37)

1 cup diced onion

3 cups peeled and cubed butternut squash (approximately ½ medium-sized squash)

2 cloves garlic, minced

2 tablespoons minced fresh sage leaves

½ teaspoon fine sea salt, plus more if needed

¼ teaspoon freshly ground black pepper, plus more if needed

1½ cups chicken or beef stock (page 236)

16 ounces dry pasta or 1 batch homemade pasta (see page 81)

1 cup whole milk

In a Dutch oven over medium-high heat, cook the bacon until crispy, about 15 minutes. Remove the bacon, setting it aside on a paper towel to drain and leaving about 2 tablespoons of fat in the pot.

Sauté the onion in the bacon fat until softened, about 6 minutes. Add the squash, garlic, sage, salt, and pepper and sauté for 2 to 3 minutes more to brown the cubes lightly and draw out more flavor.

Add the stock, reduce the heat to low, cover, and simmer for 10 to 15 minutes, until the squash is tender.

Meanwhile, cook the pasta, drain, and set aside.

Remove the squash mixture from the heat and pour in the milk. Using an immersion blender, puree the sauce. (Alternatively, you may transfer the mixture to a regular blender and puree.) Taste and add more salt and pepper if needed.

Add the pasta to the sauce and toss to coat. Chop the cooled bacon into bits. Serve the pasta with the bacon bits sprinkled on top.

# Fresh Pasta with Pesto Cream Sauce

I love serving homemade pasta to people who've only ever had dried store-bought noodles—the difference in flavor and texture is worth every bit of extra effort involved. Making pasta at home doesn't have to be fussy or complicated, and while pasta machines are handy, you can just as easily use a rolling pin and a knife. If pesto isn't your thing, toss homemade noodles with Rustic Fresh Tomato Sauce (page 264) or even just olive oil, Parmesan cheese, and a bit of sautéed garlic.

| | |
|---|---|
| 2 cups all-purpose flour | 3 large eggs |
| ½ teaspoon fine sea salt | Pesto Cream Sauce (page 82) |

In a large bowl, combine the flour and salt. Make a well in the center of the flour and add the eggs to the well. With a fork, gently mix the eggs with the flour, drawing in flour with each stroke of your fork until a stiff dough forms, then knead with your hands for 8 to 10 minutes. If the dough seems dry and crumbly, add water ½ teaspoon at a time until it comes together. Pasta dough is much stiffer than bread dough, so don't be alarmed if it still feels rough after a few minutes of kneading. Just keep going and soon you'll have smooth dough with a satiny finish.

Cover the dough with plastic wrap and allow it to rest at room temperature for 45 minutes. This will make the rolling process much easier.

Divide the dough into four portions. If using a rolling pin, roll each portion into the thinnest rectangle you possibly can and cut it into thin strips with a sharp knife or pizza cutter. If using a pasta machine, pass the dough through the machine several times, gradually decreasing the thickness as you go, then cut it into fettuccine or spaghetti noodles.

Cook the pasta in salted boiling water for 2 to 3 minutes, or until al dente (tender, but firm). Drain and toss with the sauce.

*kitchen notes · To freeze fresh pasta, make small nests of noodles on a baking sheet and freeze for at least 1 hour or for up to 2 hours. Transfer each portion to a plastic freezer bag and store in the freezer for up to 3 months. When ready to use, add frozen pasta to boiling water and cook for 3 to 5 minutes, or until al dente.*

## Pesto Cream Sauce

1 tablespoon unsalted butter

1 clove garlic, minced

¾ cup heavy cream

¼ cup whole milk

1½ cups Homestead Greens Pesto (page 254)

Fine sea salt

In a medium saucepan over medium-low heat, melt the butter. Add the garlic and sauté for 2 minutes, or until the garlic is fragrant.

Whisk in the cream, milk, and pesto, reduce the heat to low, and simmer for 3 to 4 minutes, until thickened. Taste and add salt if needed, then toss with hot pasta.

# Stovetop Mac 'n' Cheese

*serves four*

The average day on our homestead finds us knee-deep in projects and reluctant to take long, leisurely lunches. When we're working in the garden or fixing fence, the goal is to get in, get fed, and get back outside as quickly as possible. A person can only eat so many leftovers, which is why this stovetop mac 'n' cheese has become a favorite at our house. It's the perfect real-food alternative to those instant versions with their neon-orange powdered cheese, and it gets five-star ratings from homestead kids (and husbands). Make it heartier by tossing in a cup or two of cooked ham or chicken or steamed vegetables.

**16 ounces dry pasta (mini shells or farfalle [bow-ties] are our go-to choices)**

**¼ cup (½ stick) unsalted butter**

**¾ cup sour cream**

**1 teaspoon Dijon mustard**

**1¼ teaspoons fine sea salt**

**1 teaspoon paprika**

**½ teaspoon chili powder**

**¼ teaspoon freshly ground black pepper**

**2 cups shredded cheddar cheese**

Cook the pasta in salted boiling water to al dente (tender but firm) according to the package directions. Drain.

Place the pot back on the stove over low heat and melt the butter in it. Put the pasta back into the pot along with the sour cream, mustard, salt, paprika, chili powder, and pepper.

Add the cheddar cheese a handful at a time, mixing after each addition until the cheese is melted and smooth.

# Brick Oven Pizza

*makes four 10-inch pizzas*

Delivery isn't an option when you live more than 40 miles from the nearest pizza parlor, but once I learned how to make this easy no-knead dough, we lost our craving for those pizzas anyway. The magic of this crust lies not in the ingredients, but rather in the technique. I've thrown away all my other crust recipes and this is the only one I've used for several years now. If you have fresh basil in your herb garden, try arranging a handful of leaves on top of the mozzarella. It's perfection.

1 tablespoon active dry yeast

3½ cups warm water (95–100°F)

7¼ cups all-purpose flour, plus more for dusting

1 tablespoon fine sea salt

Pizza toppings (see notes, page 86)

RECOMMENDED TOOLS

Large plastic bucket or bowl with lid

Baking stone

Pizza peel (parchment paper can work in a pinch)

Mix the yeast and water together in a large bucket or bowl, then stir in the flour and salt. No kneading is required; just use a wooden spoon to incorporate the ingredients. It will look like a sloppy, chunky mess, and that's perfectly fine.

Loosely cover the container with the lid (don't make the seal airtight) and leave it at room temperature to rise for 2 to 3 hours or until bubbly.

Once the dough has risen, you can use it immediately or refrigerate it for up to 7 days. I recommend letting the dough age in the refrigerator for at least 1 day, as it drastically improves the flavor of the finished crust. I usually mix up my dough 1 to 2 days before I need it. Chilled dough is also less gooey to handle.

Prepare the sauce, shred the cheese, and chop and cook other toppings ahead of time as necessary so they're ready and waiting. It's easiest to work in an assembly-line process.

When you're ready to assemble and bake the pizzas, place the stone on the center rack of your oven and preheat the oven and the stone to the highest temperature setting it will allow (usually 550 to 600°F) for at least 30 minutes before you start cooking the pizzas. It's tempting to skip this part, but don't. It makes all the difference.

Remove the dough from the refrigerator and sprinkle a bit of flour over the top of the risen dough to make it easier to handle. Divide the dough into four evenly sized balls. The pizzas will be slightly smaller than average (roughly 10 inches in diameter), but this makes them easier to handle.

Place the first ball of dough on a well-floured surface and gently punch it down. Use your fists and knuckles to stretch the dough. The goal is to preserve the air pockets in the dough, so avoid smashing as much as possible.

Transfer the dough onto a well-floured pizza peel or piece of parchment and continue to gently stretch and shape it into a circle. If the dough tears as you work it, no worries. Just patch it back together and keep going. Top the dough circle with the sauce, cheese, and toppings. Reduce the oven temperature to 550°F and carefully slide the assembled pizza onto the stone if using a peel. If using parchment, set it directly on the stone.

Bake for 5 minutes, then switch the oven to broil and broil for 1 to 2 minutes, until the crust is golden brown and the cheese is completely melted and showing a few dark spots. Remove the pizza from the oven and allow it to cool for 3 to 4 minutes before slicing and serving. Repeat with the remaining dough.

*kitchen notes · I like to keep the toppings basic to allow the beauty of this crust to shine through. I usually choose Rustic Fresh Tomato Sauce (page 264), sliced mozzarella, and a handful of pepperoni. That's it!*

# Old Homestead Pie

The inspiration for this recipe came from *The Cookbook of Left-Overs: A Collection of 400 Reliable Recipes for the Practical Housekeeper,* published in 1911. I discovered the tiny volume in a dusty pile of books I inherited from my grandmother. The original recipe calls for "cold boiled mutton," which, admittedly, I don't often have, so I decided to improvise just a bit. Instead of mutton, you can use whatever leftover meat you may have hanging around—beef roast, pork roast, or bits of chicken or turkey you've collected after cooking a bird. I've written out my basic ground beef version below, but also included instructions for building your own pie depending on what's in your fridge (see page 88). Nothing says "homesteader" more than using every bit of what you have, and even though we've strayed considerably from the original mutton recipe, I couldn't resist allowing the name to live on.

1 pound ground beef

1 small onion, diced

1 green bell pepper, diced

2 cloves garlic, minced

½ teaspoon fine sea salt

¼ teaspoon freshly ground black pepper

1 cup tomato sauce (page 264)

1 teaspoon dried oregano

½ teaspoon dried basil

½ teaspoon garlic powder

½ teaspoon onion powder

2 cups shredded mozzarella cheese

BISCUITS

1¾ cups all-purpose flour

2 teaspoons baking powder

1 tablespoon sugar, preferably organic whole cane sugar

½ teaspoon fine sea salt

¼ cup (½ stick) unsalted butter

¾ cup buttermilk (page 244)

Preheat the oven to 375°F.

In a 10-inch cast-iron or other oven-safe skillet, brown the ground beef. Add the onion, bell pepper, garlic, salt, and black pepper and cook until the onion is softened, about 6 minutes. Add the tomato sauce and remaining seasonings and simmer for 15 minutes.

Make the biscuits: In a medium bowl, combine the flour, baking powder, sugar, and salt. Cut in the butter using a pastry blender or two knives (you can also use a food processor) until the mixture resembles coarse crumbs, then mix in the buttermilk. Pat the dough out to ½ inch thick on a floured countertop. Cut into rounds with a 2-inch biscuit cutter.

Sprinkle the cheese on top of the beef, then arrange the biscuits on top. Bake for 20 to 25 minutes, or until the biscuits are golden brown.

# the "build your own homestead pie" formula

When you're on day three of working through a giant ham or roast, leftovers quickly lose their charm. Use the following formula to turn tired bits of meat and veggies into a snazzy new meal. (Because really—who can resist anything topped with a homemade biscuit?)

Potpies are the perfect time to experiment with tweaking and substituting, so this formula chart is meant to be followed loosely. The amounts in the seasonings column are suggested amounts—exact quantities will depend on the meat, veggies, and other ingredients you use. Just taste test as you go and you'll be just fine.

## BASIC METHOD

1. In an oven-safe skillet, sauté the onion in 2 tablespoons of oil.
   Add 3 tablespoons of all-purpose flour and stir until lightly browned. (Omit the flour if you are using tomato or barbecue sauce as the liquid.)
   Add the cooked meat, remaining vegetables, the stock or sauce, and the seasonings to the skillet.

2. Simmer and stir until the vegetables are softened, about 5 to 10 minutes.

3. Taste and adjust the salt and other seasonings if needed.

4. Make the biscuits, sprinkle the cheese on top of the meat in the skillet if called for, and arrange the biscuits on top.

5. Bake at 375°F for 20 to 25 minutes, or until the biscuits are golden brown.

6. Watch your leftovers disappear!

| MEAT | VEGETABLES | LIQUID | SEASONINGS |
| --- | --- | --- | --- |
| 3 cups leftover chicken (see page 54) or turkey | 1 cup diced onion<br><br>1 cup diced carrots<br><br>1 cup peas | 1 cup chicken stock (page 236) | 1 teaspoon dried rosemary<br><br>1 teaspoon dried thyme<br><br>1 teaspoon fine sea salt<br><br>½ teaspoon each garlic powder, onion powder, and freshly ground black pepper |
| 3 cups leftover beef roast (see page 73) | 1 cup diced onion<br><br>1 cup sliced mushrooms<br><br>1 cup diced carrots | 1 cup beef stock (page 236) | 1 teaspoon dried rosemary<br><br>1 teaspoon dried marjoram<br><br>1 teaspoon fine sea salt<br><br>½ teaspoon each garlic powder, onion powder, and freshly ground black pepper |
| 3 cups leftover pork roast or shredded pork (see page 77) | 1 cup diced red onion<br><br>2 cups cooked pinto beans | 1 cup BBQ sauce (see page 263) | ½ teaspoon fine sea salt<br><br>½ teaspoon each paprika, dried oregano, garlic powder, onion powder, and freshly ground black pepper |
| 3 cups sliced sausage links | 1 cup diced onion<br><br>2 cups diced potato | 1¼ cups beef or chicken stock (page 236) | ½ teaspoon fine sea salt<br><br>½ teaspoon each garlic powder, onion powder, and freshly ground black pepper<br><br>(Start with a lesser amount of salt and increase as needed, depending on the saltiness of the sausage.) |
| 3 cups cooked ham | 1 cup diced onion<br><br>1 cup peas<br><br>1 cup corn | 1 cup chicken, beef, or pork stock (page 236)<br><br>1 cup shredded cheddar cheese | ½ teaspoon fine sea salt<br><br>½ teaspoon each garlic powder, onion powder, and freshly ground black pepper<br><br>(Start with a lesser amount of salt and increase as needed, depending on the saltiness of the ham.) |

# Stuffed Peppers with Kale & Sausage

*serves six*

Bell peppers seem to take *forever* to mature, but they're worth waiting for. When they're finally ready, I pluck a few from the garden, along with an onion, a handful of tomatoes, and a few bunches of kale, to make these stuffed peppers. This filling is wonderfully flexible; don't hesitate to substitute other greens or veggies.

1 pound Italian Sausage (recipe follows)

½ cup diced onion

4 plum tomatoes, chopped

2 cups chopped stemmed kale leaves

1 cup cooked white or brown rice

½ teaspoon fine sea salt, plus more if needed

¼ teaspoon freshly ground black pepper, plus more if needed

1½ cups shredded mozzarella cheese

6 large bell peppers

Preheat the oven to 375°F.

In a medium skillet over medium heat, brown the sausage with the onion, about 6 minutes. Add the tomatoes, kale, rice, salt, and black pepper and cook 5 to 6 minutes more, until the kale is wilted. Taste and add more salt and pepper if needed. Mix in 1 cup of the cheese.

Cut the tops off the bell peppers and discard the seeds and membranes. Stand the peppers upright in a 9 x 13–inch baking dish and stuff them with the sausage mixture. Top with the remaining ½ cup cheese and cover with foil.

Bake for 30 minutes, remove the foil, and bake for an additional 10 to 15 minutes, or until the cheese is melted and bubbly.

## Italian Sausage

*makes one pound*

1 pound ground pork

1 tablespoon dried parsley

1 teaspoon garlic powder

1 teaspoon onion powder

1 teaspoon dried basil

1 teaspoon dried oregano

½ teaspoon freshly ground black pepper

½ teaspoon fine sea salt

½ teaspoon fennel seeds

½ teaspoon crushed red pepper flakes

1 tablespoon red wine vinegar

Combine all the ingredients in a mixing bowl. Freeze for later or fry up to use in recipes.

# Tomato Basil Galette

The funny thing about galettes is that they are easier to make than a traditional pie, but feel substantially more elegant. These rustic free-form pies can be filled with any filling your heart desires, but this one in particular puts summer's heirloom tomato bounty to delicious use. If you're serving it as a main dish, you'll probably want to make at least two. (Thankfully, making multiple galettes isn't much more effort than making just one.) Purple, yellow, or bicolored heirloom tomatoes make for the most jaw-dropping presentation here, and be sure to select firm, ripe fruit to avoid a soggy crust.

DOUGH

1¼ cups all-purpose flour

1 teaspoon sugar, preferably organic whole cane sugar

¼ teaspoon fine sea salt

6 tablespoons cold unsalted butter, cubed

4 to 6 tablespoons cold water

FILLING

2 to 3 ripe but firm medium tomatoes, thinly sliced

½ teaspoon fine sea salt

2 teaspoons extra-virgin olive oil

⅓ cup diced onion

2 cloves garlic, minced

½ cup ricotta cheese (page 249)

½ cup freshly grated Parmesan cheese

¼ cup chopped fresh basil leaves, plus more for topping

Balsamic vinegar

1 large egg, beaten (for wash)

Make the dough: In a large bowl, mix the flour, sugar, and salt together, then cut in the butter using a pastry blender or two knives (you can also use a food processor; see notes, page 94) until the mixture resembles coarse crumbs. Add the lesser amount of water and mix, adding the remaining water a teaspoon or two at a time if necessary, until the dough comes together and forms a ball. Press it into a disc, wrap the disc in plastic wrap, and chill in the refrigerator for at least 1 hour.

Make the filling: Place the tomato slices in a single layer on a large plate or baking sheet. Sprinkle with the salt and let sit for 30 minutes to draw as much water from the tomatoes as possible.

In a small skillet over medium heat, heat the oil and sauté the onion and garlic for about 6 minutes, until softened. Cool slightly in the skillet, then mix in the cheeses and basil.

Preheat the oven to 400°F.

Unwrap the dough and roll it into a 12-inch circle on a piece of parchment. Spread the cheese mixture in the center of the circle, leaving 2 inches of dough around the outer

edge. Arrange the tomato slices over the cheese mixture. A bit of overlap is okay, but don't pile the tomatoes more than two layers high—the filling of a galette shouldn't be heaped. Drizzle a few splashes of vinegar on top of the tomatoes.

Fold the edges up over the outside edge of the tomato layer one section at a time, overlapping as you go. Brush the edges of the crust with the egg and transfer the parchment with the galette onto a baking sheet or stone. Bake for 30 to 40 minutes, or until the crust is golden brown and the filling is bubbly. Cool for 30 minutes and serve at room temperature.

*kitchen notes · It's not an absolute necessity, but using a food processor makes mixing pastry dough a snap. Give the dry ingredients a quick pulse, then add the butter and pulse until you see crumbs. Add the lesser amount of the water, pulse several times, then open the lid to see if the dough will stick together when you pinch it. If it does, remove it from the bowl of the processor and use your hands to gently press it together. If not, add the remaining water, a teaspoon or two at a time, and process for a few seconds after each addition until it comes together.*

# planting a piece of history

Thumb through an heirloom seed catalog, and you'll be struck by the incredible diversity. There are purple carrots, black tomatoes, spotted beans, white beets, chocolate peppers, brick-red lettuce, and everything in between. I'm not sure when we started thinking that tomatoes are only red and beans are only green, but that couldn't be further from the truth.

Heirloom seeds captured my imagination years ago and I haven't looked back since. I grow them almost exclusively and I've had spectacular results — even here in dry, rugged Wyoming.

The exact definition of what constitutes an heirloom seed can vary a bit, but the term usually refers to varieties of plants at least fifty years old that are open-pollinated, which means that, unlike hybrid varieties, pollination occurs without human intervention.

Many of the vegetables we find in the supermarket have been selectively bred for high yields and their ability to handle transportation. Flavor often gets pushed aside in an effort to produce a tomato that doesn't turn to mush sitting on a truck as it's driven across the country. Heirlooms haven't been subjected to this same sort of breeding, so not only have they kept their original, full flavors, but they often pack a heftier dose of nutrition too.

And then there are the stories. . . . It's easy to get lost in a seed catalog as you pore over the captions for each plant. The seeds come from all over the globe — many have been passed down through generations or are old-time market varieties that have since fallen out of favor in modern supermarkets.

Adding heirlooms to the garden is something anyone can do, regardless of where you live or how much you like to garden. The seeds aren't any more expensive than conventional ones, and unlike with hybrids, you can save seeds from heirloom plants to grow next year. Plant a bit of history next growing season and help carry on the work of the many gardeners who have come before us.

# Barn Raising Beans

One of my very favorite things about our rural community is how the word *neighbor* is a verb. Just as they've been doing for decades, the local ranchers actively practice *neighboring*, where they take turns helping each other work cattle and ship calves. Mornings of work are always followed by a big noon meal, where everyone kicks off his or her boots and fellowships over a hot meal. While barn raisings and threshing parties used to be commonplace, our culture seems to have slipped away from the idea of coming together to accomplish a shared community goal and, sadly, sometimes we don't even know the person who lives next door.

These rustic, savory beans don't require much hands-on time, so they are a perfect make-ahead meal to share with a crowd, whether you're raising a barn, working cows, coming together to clean up the neighborhood, or just inviting over some new friends. Be sure to serve them with a hunk of Green Chile Cornbread (page 175).

1 pound dried pinto or black beans

1 tablespoon bacon grease or unsalted butter

1 medium onion, diced

1 bell pepper, diced

2 poblano peppers or other mild chile peppers, diced

4 cloves garlic, minced

2 cups beef stock (page 236)

2 teaspoons dried oregano

1½ teaspoons fine sea salt, plus more if needed

½ teaspoon freshly ground black pepper

1 bay leaf

In a stockpot, cover the beans with water. Bring to a boil over high heat, then remove from the heat, cover the pot, and let the beans sit for 1 hour. Drain them and set aside.

In a second stockpot or a Dutch oven over medium heat, heat the bacon grease. Add the onion, peppers, and garlic and sauté until the onion is softened, about 6 minutes. Stir in the stock, oregano, salt, black pepper, bay leaf, and drained beans.

Cover the beans with 1 to 2 inches of water and place the lid on the pot. Simmer over low heat for 1½ to 2 hours, or until the beans are soft. (Sometimes I remove the lid for the last 30 minutes or so if there seems to be too much water in the pot.) Taste the beans as they cook and add more salt or additional water if needed.

*kitchen notes* · This recipe breaks all the rules when it comes to cooking beans. I used to religiously soak all beans overnight before I cooked them, but have since discovered it doesn't make much of a difference. (No, not even in the digestive realm, ahem.) Unsoaked beans take a teeny bit longer to cook, but not enough to make the overnight soak worthwhile for me. I use a quick soak method in this recipe, but technically you could skip the soaking altogether. If you are still set on an overnight soak, you can certainly do that. Just skip the quick boil at the beginning and proceed with the rest of the recipe.

For years I was petrified to add salt to beans while they cooked, as "they" said it would prevent them from ever softening. Imagine my delight when I discovered this wasn't true. And hey—beans taste a whole lot better if they can bask in salt as they simmer. Be a rebel. Salt those beans.

The fresher the beans, the quicker they will cook. Very old beans (over a year old) sometimes dry out to the point that they will never really soften, even after many hours of cooking.

Serving a BIG crowd? This recipe doubles like a champ.

# French Onion Soup

There's no better way to savor a bountiful crop of onions than a steaming bowl of French onion soup bubbling over with toasted cheese. I make this recipe every fall after harvesting the onions before tucking them into the basement for the winter. Well, except for the year our evil turkey systematically demolished the entire onion crop and I had to buy store onions, but I'm trying to forgive and forget. Anyway, this recipe has forever ruined me for many restaurant renditions of French onion soup. It takes a little bit of extra time to put together, but very little of that time is hands-on. Rich, from-scratch stock is absolutely nonnegotiable, and try to use several different varieties of onions for maximum flavor. (I like a combination of sweet and red onions.)

½ cup (1 stick) unsalted butter

4 medium to large red, white, or yellow onions, or a combination, halved and thinly sliced

1 teaspoon dried thyme

2 bay leaves

4 cloves garlic, minced

¾ cup red wine or stock

4 cups chicken stock (page 236)

2 cups beef stock (page 236)

2 tablespoons balsamic vinegar

1 teaspoon fine sea salt

½ teaspoon freshly ground black pepper

Slices of crusty bread or Homemade French Bread (page 159—optional)

Finely shredded Gruyère or Swiss cheese

In a Dutch oven over medium heat, melt the butter. Add the onions, thyme, bay leaves, and garlic and cook, stirring occasionally, until the onions turn a rich shade of golden brown, reducing the heat if they begin to burn. The caramelization process usually takes 45 to 50 minutes, but the depth of flavor you'll end up with is worth the wait.

Add the red wine all at once to pull the flavor from the bottom of the pan and cook, stirring, until the onions are mostly dry again, 5 to 10 minutes. Add the stock, vinegar, salt, and pepper to the pot and simmer for 20 to 30 minutes, or until slightly thickened. Taste and add more salt if needed.

Preheat the broiler to high.

Ladle the soup into oven-safe bowls or ramekins, top each serving with a slice of crusty bread and a handful of cheese, if desired, making sure the cheese completely covers the bread and the top of the soup, and broil for 2 to 3 minutes, or until the cheese is bubbly and browned.

*kitchen notes · If you have a food processor, use the slicing blade to speed the process of slicing the onions and to avoid tears.*

# Creamy Tomato Garlic Soup

*serves four*

Standing in a stifling-hot kitchen covered in tomato splatters in mid-August makes it easy to forget why I ever thought canning was fun. Thankfully, pulling a jar of bright red, homegrown tomatoes from the pantry on a cold prairie evening to create this creamy, comforting soup makes it all worth it. If you don't have home-canned tomatoes, you can substitute two 14.5-ounce cans of diced tomatoes instead. This soup also makes the perfect quick hot lunch on a chilly day.

¼ cup (½ stick) unsalted butter

½ cup chopped onion

4 cloves garlic, minced

3 tablespoons all-purpose flour

1 tablespoon sugar, preferably organic whole cane sugar

2 tablespoons dried basil

1 teaspoon fine sea salt

¼ teaspoon freshly ground black pepper

2 cups chicken stock (page 236)

4 cups crushed or diced tomatoes, undrained

1 cup heavy cream

Freshly grated Parmesan cheese, for garnish

In a Dutch oven over medium heat, melt the butter. Add the onion and sauté until softened, about 6 minutes. Add the garlic and sauté for 2 minutes more.

Sprinkle the onion with the flour, sugar, basil, salt, and pepper and stir until the flour just starts to brown, 2 to 3 minutes. Stir in the stock, then add the tomatoes with their liquid.

Using an immersion blender, puree the soup to create a creamy consistency. (If you do not have an immersion blender, simply puree the tomatoes in a regular blender or food processor before adding them.)

Reduce the heat to low and simmer for 20 minutes, or until the soup thickens slightly. Add the cream and stir. Cook for 5 to 10 minutes to allow the flavors to meld. Taste and adjust the seasonings as needed.

Ladle the soup into bowls and garnish with a sprinkling of cheese and a thick slice of crusty bread or garlic toast made from French bread (see page 159).

# Rustic Sausage Potato Soup

*serves four to six*

Heavy cream adds a smooth touch to this rustic soup. If you come for supper on a chilly night, don't be surprised to see a steaming pot sitting on the table next to a loaf of Crusty Dutch Oven Bread (page 160). This humble soup allows autumn ingredients to shine in the very best of ways. If you like spice, bump up the crushed red pepper flakes to ¾ teaspoon (or more).

½ pound bacon (page 37)

1 pound Italian sausage (page 91)

1 small onion, diced

2 cloves garlic, minced

3 cups chicken stock (page 236)

6 medium russet potatoes, halved and sliced

¼ teaspoon fine sea salt

¼ teaspoon freshly ground black pepper

¼ teaspoon crushed red pepper flakes

2 cups chopped stemmed kale leaves

½ cup heavy cream

Freshly grated Parmesan cheese, for garnish

In a Dutch oven over medium-high heat, cook the bacon until crispy, about 15 minutes. Remove the bacon, setting it aside on a paper towel to drain and leaving about 2 tablespoons of fat in the pot.

Add the sausage and onion to the pot and brown, about 6 minutes. Add the garlic and cook for 2 to 3 minutes more, until fragrant, then add the stock, potatoes, salt, black pepper, and red pepper flakes. Cover and simmer for 15 minutes, or until the potatoes are tender.

Add the kale and simmer for 3 to 4 minutes, until it is slightly wilted. Taste and adjust the seasonings if needed. Remove from the heat and stir in the heavy cream. Chop the cooled bacon into bits. Ladle the soup into bowls and garnish with cheese and the bacon.

*kitchen notes* · *If you're starting out with plain ground pork, you can easily turn it into Italian sausage with the seasoning mix on page 91.*

# Broccoli Cheddar Soup

serves four

My kids mow through broccoli like nobody's business. I've even caught myself saying things like, "Make sure you eat everything on your plate and then you can have seconds of broccoli" and "Yes, you can have more broccoli after dessert." I've tried various proportions of milk, cream, and stock with my broccoli soups over the years, but I think using primarily chicken stock with just a cup of cream gives this soup the perfect creaminess without being too heavy.

¼ cup (½ stick) unsalted butter

1 medium onion, diced

2 cloves garlic, minced

¼ cup all-purpose flour

1 teaspoon paprika

¾ teaspoon fine sea salt

½ teaspoon ground mustard

½ teaspoon freshly ground black pepper

4 cups chicken stock (page 236)

1 cup heavy cream

5 cups broccoli florets and chopped stems

2 carrots, diced

2 cups shredded sharp cheddar cheese

In a Dutch oven over medium heat, melt the butter. Add the onion and sauté until softened, about 6 minutes. Add the garlic and cook for 2 to 3 minutes more, until fragrant, then add the flour, paprika, salt, mustard, and pepper and stir to combine.

Add the stock, cream, broccoli, and carrots and simmer until tender, about 20 minutes.

If you like a smoother soup, you can puree it with an immersion blender or in batches in a regular blender with the lid slightly ajar to allow steam to escape. I puree about half of mine, since I like some chunkiness and texture.

Once the soup is the consistency you like, stir in the cheese until it's completely melted. Taste and adjust the seasonings if needed.

Serve with extra cheese and Pumpkin Pan Rolls (page 166) or Chive & Cheddar Mounds (page 167) on the side.

104    The Prairie Homestead Cookbook

# Chicken Poblano Chowder

Juicy chunks of chicken mingle with lightly spicy peppers in a creamy broth to create a simple soup that warms the belly. Poblanos grow easily in our rugged Wyoming climate, which makes me quite partial to this recipe. They tend to vary when it comes to spiciness (ranging from extremely mild to medium heat), so it can be hard to tell exactly how zesty they'll be before the soup comes together. Keep this in mind if you plan to serve this soup to anyone who's especially sensitive to spicy things. I love to serve this chowder with plenty of fresh cilantro and a bowl of tortilla chips for scooping and dipping.

2 tablespoons extra-virgin olive oil

1 cup diced onion

3 tablespoons all-purpose flour

5 roasted poblano or other mild chile peppers (see page 175), finely diced

2 cloves garlic, minced

1 teaspoon ground cumin

1 teaspoon fine sea salt, plus more if needed

¼ teaspoon freshly ground black pepper

4 cups chicken stock (page 236)

2 chicken breasts, cut into ½-inch pieces (4 cups)

2 cups shredded cheddar cheese, plus more for garnish

¾ cup heavy cream

Fresh cilantro, for garnish (optional)

In a Dutch oven over medium heat, heat the olive oil and sauté the onion until tender, about 6 minutes.

Add the flour, poblano peppers, garlic, cumin, salt, and black pepper and cook for 5 minutes, stirring frequently.

Add the stock and chicken. Bring to a boil and simmer for 15 minutes, or until the chicken is completely cooked.

Reduce the heat to low and stir in the cheese and cream. Cook until heated through. Taste and adjust the salt if needed.

Garnish with fresh cilantro, shredded cheese, and a side of tortilla chips if desired.

# Creamy Chicken Noodle Soup

*serves four to six*

I feel like the commercial food industry owes chicken noodle soup an apology for calling the watery, tasteless stuff they put in cans "chicken soup." Nourishing broth packed with vegetables and real chicken is true soul food. I've made chicken soup with clear broth for years, but the addition of the roux takes this recipe to a whole new creamy level.

3 tablespoons extra-virgin olive oil

1 medium onion, diced

2 carrots, diced

2 stalks celery, diced

4 cloves garlic, minced

¼ cup all-purpose flour

2 bay leaves

2 tablespoons dried parsley

1 teaspoon paprika

1 teaspoon dried rosemary

½ teaspoon ground turmeric

½ teaspoon fine sea salt

¼ teaspoon freshly ground black pepper

6 cups chicken stock (page 236)

16 ounces dry egg noodles or pasta

1 cup whole milk or heavy cream

4 cups cubed cooked chicken

In a stockpot over medium heat, heat the olive oil and sauté the onion, carrots, celery, and garlic until the onion is tender, about 6 minutes.

Add the flour, along with all the seasonings, and cook for 3 minutes, stirring frequently.

Add the stock and pasta and bring to a boil. Simmer until the pasta is al dente (tender but firm). Stir in the milk and chicken and cook until heated through. Serve immediately.

*kitchen notes · This is my favorite meal to prepare the day after we eat the roast chicken on page 54. Before throwing all the bones and drippings into the stockpot, I pull any leftover meat from the bones and set it aside. The stock simmers all night, and then I use some of it, along with the reserved chicken, to make this soup.*

*If you'd rather use uncooked chicken instead of leftovers, substitute 4 cups raw, cubed chicken breast. Add the meat when you pour in the broth and cook, covered, for 15 minutes before adding the pasta.*

*If you're cooking for someone who is gluten- or dairy-free, the flour and milk or cream can be omitted from this soup and it will still be delicious.*

# Farmhouse Beef Stew

*serves six*

Beef stew graces our table in the dead of winter, when the crisp green vegetables of summer are long forgotten. A few of the potatoes and carrots from the larder are combined with homegrown, grass-fed beef in a rich sauce for a hearty meal that warms us inside and out. Don't let the slightly longer ingredient list of this rustic stew fool you—it's as easy as they come. The few extra seasonings just ensure your stew will be fully flavored, as bland beef stew is always so disappointing.

Serve with Crusty Dutch Oven Bread (page 160) for a hearty meal that's a perfect end to a cold day working outside. The leftovers only get better the second day, so make plenty!

2 pounds stew meat, such as chuck or round, trimmed of fat and cut into 2-inch cubes

1 teaspoon fine sea salt

½ teaspoon freshly ground black pepper

2 tablespoons extra-virgin olive oil

1 tablespoon unsalted butter

1 medium onion, diced

2 cups sliced mushrooms

4 cloves garlic, minced

1 cup dry red wine

3 cups chicken or beef stock (page 236)

2 tablespoons Worcestershire sauce

¼ cup tomato paste, or ½ cup tomato sauce (page 264)

2 bay leaves

1½ teaspoons dried marjoram

1½ teaspoons smoked paprika

6 red or Yukon Gold potatoes, cubed

2 cups sliced carrots

Season the meat with the salt and pepper. In a Dutch oven over medium heat, heat the olive oil and brown the meat in batches to avoid overcrowding the pan, adding more oil as needed and removing the meat to a bowl once it is browned on all sides. Set aside.

Melt the butter in the pan right on top of any browned bits left on the bottom. Add the onion, mushrooms, and garlic and cook for 5 minutes, or until the onion is soft.

Add the wine and simmer over low heat until it is reduced by half, about 12 minutes. Add the browned meat, stock, Worcestershire sauce, tomato paste, bay leaves, marjoram, and paprika. Cover, and simmer for 1½ to 2 hours, or until the meat is tender. Add the potatoes and carrots and cook, uncovered, for 30 minutes more, until the vegetables are tender and the broth is thickened to your liking.

# farm-style sides

*Jumping out of an airplane and building a* parachute on the way down. That's pretty much the perfect way to describe how I came into homesteading and learning how to cook from scratch. People assume I took a course, had family members who taught me the ropes, or went to some sort of homesteading school. Nope. My education was messier than that. I came into the world of homesteading knowing absolutely nothing. I wasn't raised around this lifestyle and I didn't have any local mentors to take me under their wing. It was trial by fire, right from the beginning.

I tapped into a hodgepodge of resources at first. I pored over various blogs, tattered books from the library, and YouTube videos as I wrapped my mind around something new. I tried to read a variety of voices and opinions on each topic in an attempt to stay well rounded, and then I unceremoniously jumped in. It was a haphazard progression of trial and error, but bit by bit I found my comfort zone expanding as I bumbled my way through milking a cow, baking bread, and crafting various staples from scratch. I also became adept at picking up the pieces and forging ahead after my many explosive mess-ups. (Literally. Once I exploded a bottle of blueberry kefir in the kitchen and was scraping blueberry bits off the ceiling for months.)

One of the things my unorthodox educational journey taught me was how obsessed I am about expanding skill sets, especially kitchen-related ones. I've kept a running list of experiences and skills we needed to master as we progressed on our journey, and I celebrated each time I crossed something off the list. Homemade fries with real potatoes? Check! Refried beans made from dry beans instead of from canned? Check! Coleslaw without bottled salad dressing? Check!

Only a few generations ago, the average person was impressively capable without really even trying. Most people had an innate understanding of how to grow, forage, and prepare foods, handle farm animals, and keep themselves alive in various situations. These skills weren't special or niche, they were just life.

Modern advances have brought us a long way, but in some aspects, they've also caused us to take a flying leap backward. I'm not completely dogging contemporary conveniences and industrialized food—there are definite benefits to both. But they've eliminated the need for most folks to know how to cut up a chicken, grow something edible, or turn cucumbers into pickles, among other things. Because of this, many miss out on the intoxicating satisfaction intertwined with producing, creating, and inventing. It's time to get back in our kitchens and expand our skill sets, and there's no better place to start than right here.

Side dishes don't have to be complicated. More often than not, the sides gracing our table are simple roasted vegetables, drizzled with butter or olive oil and sprinkled with sea salt. However, sides provide ample opportunity to expand your skills repertoire as well. In this chapter you'll find techniques and tips for turning basic dry beans into a savory company-worthy dish, transforming real cranberries into sauce instead of relying on a can, and taking cucumbers from your garden or farmers' market and turning them into the perfectly garlicky jar of refrigerator pickles.

It's empowering to create something new in the kitchen. It's exhilarating to master a task that previously felt intimidating and foreign. And most of all, it tastes incredible. It's time to skill up!

# Beet & Potato Mash

This recipe was born out of sheer desperation one evening when I had to have mashed potatoes, only to discover my potato bin was disturbingly sparse. After a brief moment of panic, I remembered the handful of golden beets that had been languishing in my refrigerator for a couple weeks. I tossed them in the pot with the cubed potatoes and was ecstatic to discover how perfectly the earthy sweetness of the beets married with the starchy smooth potatoes. I always select golden or Albino beets for this mash, but if you have adventurous eaters at your house who won't fret over pink potatoes, you can use red beets too.

3 medium golden or Albino beets, peeled and cubed

4 large red or Yukon gold potatoes, peeled and cubed

2 cloves garlic, slightly smashed

¼ cup (½ stick) unsalted butter

⅓ cup sour cream

¾ teaspoon fine sea salt

½ teaspoon freshly ground black pepper

Fresh chives, for garnish

In a stockpot, place the beets, potatoes, and garlic and cover with water. Bring to a boil over high heat, then reduce the heat to medium and cook until tender, about 30 minutes. Drain and place back into the hot pot. Stir for 1 to 2 minutes over low heat to evaporate any leftover water, then remove the pan from the heat. Mash with the butter, sour cream, salt, and pepper until smooth. Sprinkle with chives and serve.

*kitchen notes · I generally opt not to use an immersion blender when making regular mashed potatoes, as it can cause them to take on a strange gummy texture. However, I've found using the immersion blender for this recipe results in a smoother texture for the beets. Another option is to use a hand or stand mixer to whip everything together.*

# Crispy Potato Stacks

These friendly little stacks of Parmesan potato goodness make an elegant side dish or a simple appetizer. Admittedly, it's hard for me to be objective when it comes to potato dishes (I've yet to meet a potato I didn't devour), but these are *really* good. Like stand-by-the-stove-and-burn-your-tongue-eating-them sort of good. Like the kind of good where you are tempted to make them when the family is gone and you're home alone watching movies. (Those are all hypothetical situations, of course.)

2 tablespoons extra-virgin olive oil

⅔ cup freshly grated Parmesan cheese

2 teaspoons dried thyme

1 teaspoon fine sea salt

½ teaspoon garlic powder

¼ teaspoon freshly ground black pepper

5 medium red or Yukon Gold potatoes, unpeeled, sliced ⅛ inch thick

¼ cup (½ stick) unsalted butter, melted

Preheat the oven to 375°F and brush the bottoms of the cups of a muffin tin with the oil.

Combine half the cheese, the thyme, salt, garlic powder, and pepper in a small bowl. Put the potatoes in a large bowl and add the cheese mixture along with the melted butter. Toss to combine.

Stack the potatoes in the cups of the muffin tin, trimming any slices that are too big to fit, and sprinkle the remaining cheese on top, dividing it evenly among the stacks. Bake for 45 to 50 minutes, or until the potatoes are tender.

# Scalloped Potatoes

*makes one 9 x 13–inch pan*

The scalloped potatoes of my past were dehydrated potato slices topped with a "just add water" cheese sauce that had the most peculiar aftertaste. I've tried a number of scalloped potato variations over the years where I've just layered potato slices with cheese and bits of butter. Those were good, but the smooth white sauce in this recipe takes the dish to a whole new level. Russet potatoes are fine, but I prefer starchier reds or Yukon Golds for this recipe. Peels can be on or off, although I leave mine on for a bit of extra color and texture. I always make these potatoes to serve with the ham on Easter Sunday, but they show up on the table plenty of other times during the year too. They're just that tasty.

¼ cup (½ stick) unsalted butter

1 cup diced onion

2 cloves garlic, minced

¼ cup all-purpose flour

1¼ teaspoons fine sea salt

¼ teaspoon freshly ground black pepper

2 cups whole milk

½ cup chicken stock (page 236)

2 pounds red or Yukon Gold potatoes, sliced ⅛ inch thick

2 cups shredded cheddar cheese

⅓ cup freshly grated Parmesan cheese

Preheat the oven to 400°F and butter a 9 x 13–inch baking dish.

In a medium saucepan over medium heat, melt the butter and sauté the onion and garlic until tender, about 6 minutes. Add the flour, salt, and pepper and cook for 2 to 3 minutes, until slightly browned. Whisk in the milk and stock and cook, stirring frequently, until the mixture is thickened and bubbly, about 15 minutes.

Layer half the potatoes over the bottom of the baking dish. Spread half the white sauce on top, followed by 1 cup of the cheddar. Repeat the layers one more time before topping with the Parmesan. Bake for 45 to 50 minutes, or until the potatoes are tender and the sauce is bubbly.

# Zesty Oven Fries

I have no problem heating a vat of beef tallow and frying up a batch of French fries when the situation calls for it, but sometimes we are craving fries and I'm not in the mood to make a mess out of my stove top. (I love you, tallow, but you drip everywhere.) These seasoned oven fries come out perfect every time and are the ideal companion to the Wyoming Burger (page 62) or Sticky Honey Chicken (page 59).

3 pounds potatoes (5 or 6 medium to large potatoes), cut into wedges

¼ cup extra-virgin olive oil

2 tablespoons dried parsley

2 teaspoons fine sea salt

2 teaspoons paprika

2 teaspoons onion powder

2 teaspoons garlic powder

½ teaspoon freshly ground black pepper

Preheat the oven to 425°F.

Place the potatoes in a large bowl and add the remaining ingredients. Toss to coat, then arrange in a single layer on a baking sheet. I usually use two sheets since spreading the potatoes out a bit helps them to cook faster.

Bake for 30 to 40 minutes, or until the potato wedges are browned and crispy on the edges. You can flip or stir them once while they are in the oven, but if you forget, it's not the end of the world.

*kitchen notes · I've found a cheap apple slicer-corer tool to be the best way to slice potatoes into wedges. Place the potato on its end (you can slice a bit off the bottom so it stands up better), then place the tool over the top and press down firmly. It's faster than using a knife, which is helpful when you're trying to get the fries into the oven in a hurry.*

*I usually use russet potatoes here, but red or Yukon Gold potatoes work just as well.*

# Roasted Beets &
# Whipped Goat Cheese

Roasting concentrates the flavor of homegrown beets, and creamy, tangy goat cheese accentuates their smooth earthiness. I like to arrange the sliced beets on a platter and serve them as an appetizer, but you can chop the beet greens and toss them with the rest of the ingredients for a rustic salad too.

**4 medium beets**

**1 tablespoon plus 2 teaspoons mild-tasting olive oil**

**¾ teaspoon fine sea salt**

**¼ cup chèvre (page 247)**

**2 tablespoons whole milk**

**¼ to ½ cup Orange Poppy Seed Vinaigrette (page 269) or your favorite vinaigrette**

Preheat the oven to 400°F.

Scrub the beets and trim the tops short. Rub them with 1 tablespoon of the oil, sprinkle with ½ teaspoon of the salt, and set them on a baking sheet. Roast for 50 to 60 minutes, or until the beets are tender in the middle. Let them cool, then trim the roots and tops and slip off the skins. Slice the beets into ¼-inch slices.

In a small bowl, combine the chèvre, the remaining 2 teaspoons oil, the milk, and the remaining ¼ teaspoon salt and beat with a fork until fluffy.

Arrange the beet slices in a serving dish, top with dollops of the whipped cheese mixture, and drizzle with the vinaigrette. I prefer to serve this dish slightly warm, but cold works too.

*kitchen notes · To avoid stained fingers, slip on a pair of food prep gloves before you trim and slice the beets.*

# Browned Butter Skillet Corn

Sweet, crisp kernels basted in thyme-infused brown butter . . . You could seriously eat this stuff for dessert. It's hard to beat fresh corn on the cob, but this skillet corn gives it a run for its money.

3 tablespoons unsalted butter

Kernels from 4 ears of sweet corn

¼ teaspoon fine sea salt

Dash of freshly ground black pepper

1 tablespoon fresh thyme leaves

In a skillet with a light-colored bottom (so you can see the color of the butter as it changes), melt the butter over medium-low heat. Watch the butter closely and swirl the pan occasionally. The butter will foam and gradually change color to a golden brown. When you see light brown specks in the bottom of the skillet and the butter takes on a nutty, toasted scent (it's easy to burn it at this point—be careful), add the corn, salt, and pepper.

Cook and stir for 5 minutes, or until the corn is tender. Sprinkle with fresh thyme and serve hot.

# Parmesan Roasted Cabbage Steaks

I love growing cabbage. And all the bugs love it when I grow cabbage too. I engage in hand-to-hand combat against the formidable cabbage moth every year, and it's brutal. After lots of experimenting (and even paying my children to pick caterpillars from the leaves), I finally mixed up a homemade nontoxic spray (page 284) that does the trick. The key is spraying early and spraying often, but it's worth it. Celebrate winning the Battle of the Bugs with these buttery cabbage steaks generously sprinkled with Parmesan cheese.

1 medium head of cabbage

2 tablespoons unsalted butter, melted

¼ teaspoon freshly ground black pepper

¾ to 1 cup freshly grated Parmesan cheese

Preheat the oven to 350°F.

Remove any limp or discolored leaves from the cabbage and cut the head into ½-inch slices. Place the slices on a baking sheet, brush them with the melted butter, and season them with the pepper.

Sprinkle each steak with cheese and bake for 25 to 30 minutes, or until the cabbage softens and begins to brown around the edges.

# From-Scratch Cranberry Sauce

As a little kid, I remember standing next to the table and taking inventory of the waiting Thanksgiving feast. There was golden roasted turkey, buttery mashed potatoes, warm homemade rolls, spiced pumpkin pie . . . and a quivering cylinder of canned cranberry sauce. The ridged red mass always seemed slightly out of place, so I was thrilled the first time I stumbled across a recipe for real cranberry sauce. My quick version calls for orange juice and honey, which eliminates the need for white sugar and adds a pleasant pop of flavor, because oranges and cranberries are BFFs.

1 tablespoon orange zest

¾ cup orange juice

½ to ¾ cup honey

12 ounces whole cranberries

In a medium saucepan over medium heat, combine the orange zest, orange juice, and honey. Reduce the heat to low and gently simmer for 5 minutes. Stir in the cranberries and cook until they burst, about 15 minutes. Spoon the sauce into a mold or bowl and refrigerate for 6 to 8 hours, or until set.

# Garlic Dill Icebox Pickles

So many pickle options, so little time. There are the traditional canned ones, the fizzy fermented versions, and the so-fast-you-won't-believe-it refrigerator variety, which is what we're covering here. You'll find all three types of pickles stashed in various places on my homestead, but these icebox pickles are the winner when it comes to simplicity. They're also extremely handy when your plants torment you with only two cucumbers at a time for the first month or two, which makes canning pretty much impossible. Because they aren't cooked, these pickles not only have a fresher flavor, but their rawness contributes to extra crunch as well. Most refrigerator pickle recipes call for heating the vinegar and salt first, but I've found that to be an unnecessary step. Give your jars a good shake after you fill them, and you should be all set.

4 to 6 cucumbers, depending on the size (about 2 pounds)

2 cloves garlic, smashed

3 heads fresh dill, or 1 tablespoon dried dill seeds

1 tablespoon coarse sea salt

1 tablespoon yellow mustard seeds

½ teaspoon black peppercorns

1 bay leaf

1 cup white vinegar

Trim the blossom ends from the cucumbers and cut the larger ones into spears.

In a clean 1-quart jar, combine the garlic, dill, salt, mustard seeds, peppercorns, bay leaf, and vinegar, then pack the cucumbers on top. Fill the jar the rest of the way with cool water, taking care to cover the cucumbers completely.

Cap tightly and shake well. Icebox pickles can be eaten just a few hours after you make them, but the flavor vastly improves after at least 3 days in the fridge. These pickles will last about 3 months, but the garlic flavor will intensify and the pickles will increase in spiciness the longer they sit in the refrigerator.

# Fresh Garden Salsa

It's late summer. The tomatoes are ripe on the vine, the peppers swing expectantly among their waxy leaves, and the onions peek above the soil. If you listen, you can hear the garden practically begging you to make this bright salsa. Don't leave your garden hanging. Just do it.

5 plum (Roma) tomatoes, diced

½ cup finely diced red onion

½ jalapeño, seeded and minced (or leave the seeds in if you like spicier salsa)

1 to 2 poblano peppers or other mild chile peppers, seeded and diced

2–4 tablespoons minced fresh cilantro

1 clove garlic

1 teaspoon fine sea salt, plus more as needed

1 tablespoon lime juice

In a medium bowl, combine the tomatoes, onion, peppers, and cilantro. Cilantro is vital to this dish, but can also be overpowering, so start out on the conservative side and add more as needed.

Make a garlic paste by first mincing the clove, then sprinkling ½ teaspoon of the salt on top of the garlic and continuing to mince, alternating between mincing and using the edge of your knife to smash the garlic against the cutting board. Continue until the garlic has released its juices and you are left with a small pile of paste on your cutting board. Add this to the bowl, along with the remaining ½ teaspoon salt.

Add the lime juice, then taste and adjust the salt as needed.

Chill the salsa for at least 1 hour before serving to allow the flavors to mingle. It's best if eaten within 2 days. Serve with tortilla chips or use it to top nachos, tacos, or burritos.

# Restaurant-Style Refried Beans

Pasty, canned refried beans don't even remotely compare to this well-seasoned homemade version. I purchase pinto beans in bulk to make sure I always have plenty stashed away (they'll last about a year in storage) since bean quesadillas are one of my go-to meals when unexpected guests swing by the homestead for lunch. I use my pressure cooker to cook them up fast, then mash and season them to perfection. Use these homemade refried beans as a fast side dish or spread them on tortillas, sprinkle with cheese, and fry up for quick quesadillas.

3 tablespoons bacon grease or lard (page 251)

¾ cup chopped onion

4 cups cooked pinto beans, drained (see below)

3 cloves garlic, minced

2 teaspoons paprika

2 teaspoons ground cumin

1¾ teaspoons sea salt

½ teaspoon freshly ground black pepper

Cooking liquid from the beans or milk, to thin (optional)

1 cup shredded cheddar cheese

Heat the bacon grease in a large skillet over medium heat; add the onion and sauté until softened. Add the beans, garlic, paprika, cumin, salt, and pepper. Fry for 4 to 5 minutes.

Mash the beans with a potato masher, or use an immersion blender for a smoother consistency. For thinner refried beans, add several tablespoons of the bean cooking liquid or milk to the skillet as you mash. Taste and adjust the seasonings as necessary. If you are using lard, it's likely you'll want to add a bit more salt. Sprinkle with the cheese, let it melt, then serve with chips or tortillas.

*kitchen notes · Remember: 1 cup dry beans equals 3 cups cooked beans.*

## HOW TO COOK DRY BEANS

In a stockpot or Dutch oven, cover 1⅓ cups dry beans completely with water. Bring the water to a boil, then turn off the heat, cover the pot, and let the beans sit for 1 hour.

Drain the soaked beans and cover with fresh water. Add 2 teaspoons coarse sea salt, then simmer for 1½ to 2 hours, or until the beans are tender. (See page 97 for more bean cooking tips and why I break most of the rules when it comes to cooking beans.)

# Honey Whipped Carrots

This quick recipe turns the humble carrot into a serious showstopper. I've experimented with adding extras like cranberries, nutmeg, or cinnamon to this dish, but have returned to the simplicity of just these four ingredients every time. Use a blender, food processor, or stand mixer to whip the cooked carrots—manual potato mashers won't create the right texture for this recipe.

2 pounds carrots, cut into 1-inch chunks

3 tablespoons unsalted butter

1 tablespoon honey

¼ teaspoon fine sea salt

In a medium saucepan, cover the carrots with several inches of water. Bring to a boil, then reduce the heat to low and simmer until tender, about 8 minutes. Drain and transfer the hot carrots to a blender or food processor. Add the remaining ingredients and blend until smooth. (If using a blender, be sure to leave the lid slightly ajar to allow steam to escape.) Serve warm.

# Roasted Garlic Chickpea Dip

*makes about two cups*

(pictured on page 178)

A hot, heavy meal is the last thing we want after a day of toiling outside in triple-digit heat. A batch of this quick dip (it's similar to hummus, but doesn't require tahini, a sesame seed paste) alongside a platter of Sourdough Crackers (page 179) and watermelon wedges is my idea of the perfect light summer supper. And yes, the recipe calls for an entire bulb of garlic—it's not a typo. Roasted garlic is much more mellow than its raw counterpart, so use plenty to ensure the flavor comes through loud and clear.

**2 cups cooked chickpeas or white beans, drained but liquid reserved**

**1 tablespoon lemon juice**

**1 teaspoon ground cumin**

**1 teaspoon paprika**

**¾ teaspoon fine sea salt**

**½ teaspoon crushed red pepper flakes**

**1 bulb roasted garlic (see below)**

**2 tablespoons extra-virgin olive oil**

Combine the chickpeas, lemon juice, seasonings, and garlic in a food processor and process until the mixture is crumbly and well blended.

Slowly drizzle in the oil while the machine is running. For creamier dip, add a few tablespoons of the reserved cooking liquid until you get the texture you like.

Store in an airtight container in the refrigerator for up to 7 days. This dip will intensify in flavor the longer it sits, so it's best to make it at least the day before you plan to eat it.

## HOW TO ROAST GARLIC

I like to roast garlic when I'm cooking something else in the oven. But if you're roasting it all by itself, preheat the oven to 400°F. Peel the majority of the papery outer layers from the bulb, leaving just enough to keep the bulb intact. Cut ¼ inch off the pointy end of the bulb to expose the raw cloves inside. Place the bulb on a small square of foil, drizzle with ½ teaspoon extra-virgin olive oil, and bring the corners of the foil up, crimping them to form a little package. Place on a baking sheet and bake for 40 to 50 minutes, or until the cloves are soft. Squeeze the creamy roasted cloves onto fresh bread, or add to Roasted Garlic Chickpea Dip or compound butter (page 71).

# Summer Squash Gratin

No matter how hard I try, I never seem to be able to grow the perfect amount of squash. I either end up with sorry-looking squash plants that won't produce, or I have bucketloads of the stuff on the counter staring at me. This smooth gratin is a tasty way to serve zucchini, yellow squash (the ones with smooth skin or bumpy skin will both work), or flying saucer–shaped pattypans. I try to use smaller squashes for this recipe, since I prefer not to peel them first and I want the skins to be tender once cooked. That being said, what would a garden be without a few baseball bat–sized zucchini? Always grow at least a couple of those so you can make bread later in the season.

2 tablespoons unsalted butter

4 heaping cups ⅛-inch-thick slices zucchini or yellow squash (about 1 pound)

1 medium leek, sliced

2 teaspoons dried thyme

½ teaspoon fine sea salt

¼ teaspoon freshly ground black pepper

½ cup heavy cream

½ cup freshly grated Parmesan cheese

¼ cup breadcrumbs (page 262)

Preheat the oven to 400°F.

In a large skillet over medium heat, melt the butter. Add the squash, leek, thyme, salt, and pepper and cook for 5 minutes, stirring frequently.

Add the cream and cheese to the skillet and cook for 1 to 2 minutes more, until the cheese is melted.

Transfer to a baking dish and top with the breadcrumbs. (Alternatively, you could sauté everything in a cast-iron pan and transfer it directly to the oven.) Bake for 15 to 20 minutes, or until the squash is tender.

# Sesame Green Beans

Green beans are the standard kid snack around our homestead in the summer, so a large portion of our harvest rarely even makes it into the house. When I'm able to sneak a colander or two into the kitchen, green beans shine when combined with the nuttiness of sesame oil and the brightness of lemon juice. Regular green beans are dandy but the more colorful heirloom varieties, like Dragon Tongue, Purple Podded, or Golden Wax, make supper just a little more exciting.

1 tablespoon toasted sesame oil

3 heaping cups green beans with ends snapped off (about 1 pound)

1 tablespoon sesame seeds

¼ cup chicken stock (page 236)

2 teaspoons soy sauce or alternative of your choice

1 tablespoon lemon juice

In a medium skillet over medium heat, heat the sesame oil. Add the beans and sesame seeds and cook, stirring, for 5 minutes.

Add the stock and soy sauce and cover. Cook for an additional 5 to 10 minutes, or until the beans are crisp-tender. Toss with the lemon juice just before serving.

*kitchen notes · Frozen beans will work in a pinch if that's all you have, though you may need to add a few extra minutes to the cook time.*

# Fried Green Tomatoes

I grow tomatoes every single year, but I've officially given up on ending a season with anything but mostly green tomatoes. Despite my best efforts to start the seeds indoors extra early, I always struggle getting the fruit to turn red before the first hard frost hits. Thankfully, it's a cinch to coax tomatoes to ripen indoors (see "How to Ripen Green Tomatoes Indoors," opposite), not to mention that I *want* some of them to stay green so I can batter and fry them up. I love this buttermilk batter—it's easy to mix together and it eliminates the issue of "breaded fingers," which I never seem able to avoid when I make recipes with a multipart dredge.

Lard (page 251) or coconut oil, for frying

1 cup all-purpose flour

½ cup cornmeal

1 teaspoon paprika

1 teaspoon onion powder

½ teaspoon fine sea salt

½ teaspoon freshly ground black pepper

1¼ cups buttermilk (page 244), plus more if needed

4 firm green tomatoes, cut into ¼-inch slices

In a skillet over medium-high heat, melt the lard. (Aim for around ¼ to ½ inch of melted lard in the pan.) Heat it until it sizzles when a bit of flour is sprinkled into the pan.

In a medium bowl, combine the flour, cornmeal, paprika, onion powder, salt, pepper, and buttermilk. The mixture should resemble pancake batter—if it is too thick, add a bit more buttermilk. Dip the tomatoes in the batter, making sure each slice is coated on both sides, then fry them in the lard for 2 to 3 minutes, flipping once. They are done when the coating is crispy and deeply browned. Transfer to a plate lined with a paper towel to absorb any excess fat. Serve hot with a side of ketchup or buttermilk ranch (page 268) for dipping.

# how to ripen green tomatoes indoors

There are plenty of urban legends surrounding the topic of ripening green tomatoes off the vine. Some people swear by creating newspaper layers between the tomatoes and some folks even go as far as to wrap each one individually. (I'm not that patient.) I've tried them all, even the one that recommends pulling the entire plant out of the ground and hanging it upside down. (It didn't ripen any faster and it made a huge mess. Fail.)

I'm not one to fuss over details, so I usually just dump all of my greenies in a cardboard box and call it good. Sometimes I'll separate the layers with sheets of newspaper, but usually I skip that part because I'm lazy . . . er, efficient. I check the boxes several times per week so I can pull out ripe or rotten ones. They usually ripen gradually over the course of three to four weeks, although I suspect the temperature of the storage rooms plays a part in the exact time frame. (A cooler room = a longer ripening time.)

If you only have a few green tomatoes, just leave them on your kitchen counter and they'll gradually turn red in a few days.

# Herbed Potato Salad

When the herb garden is bursting with green and the potato plants are producing tender young potatoes under the dark soil, I opt out of heavy, mayonnaise-laden potato salads and turn to this light, herby option instead. The sour cream provides a tangy base that contrasts perfectly with the bright crunch of celery and scallions, and the fresh-picked herbs contribute a refreshing punch of flavor.

2 pounds small red potatoes, whole, or halved or quartered if bigger

3 stalks celery, chopped

⅓ cup sliced scallions

½ cup sour cream

2 tablespoons minced fresh dill

2 tablespoons minced fresh parsley

1 tablespoon Dijon mustard

1½ teaspoons lemon juice

½ teaspoon fine sea salt

½ teaspoon onion powder

¼ teaspoon garlic powder

In a stockpot over high heat, bring 2 quarts water to a boil. Cook the potatoes for 15 to 20 minutes, or until fork-tender. Drain and place them in a bowl with the celery and scallions.

In a small bowl, combine the sour cream, dill, parsley, mustard, lemon juice, salt, onion powder, and garlic powder. Pour the dressing over the warm potatoes. Toss to coat. Chill for at least 2 hours before serving to give the flavors time to mingle.

# Grilled Pear & Apple Salad

*serves four*

Make this late summer salad when it's sticky and hot outside and you don't feel like turning on the oven. Peppery arugula pairs beautifully with the sweetness of the warm fruit, but any selection of mixed greens will work as a base.

1 pear, cored and cut into ½-inch slices

1 apple, cored and cut into ½-inch slices

5 cups arugula or mixed greens of your choice

½ cup walnuts, chopped

⅓ cup freshly grated Parmesan cheese

Cider Vinaigrette (recipe follows)

Heat a griddle or grill pan over medium heat and grill the pears and apples for 30 to 60 seconds on each side, until golden brown with visible grill marks.

Arrange the grilled fruit on a bed of the greens, top with the walnuts and cheese, then finish with a drizzle of the vinaigrette.

# Cider Vinaigrette

*makes about a third of a cup*

2 tablespoons apple cider vinegar

2 tablespoons extra-virgin olive oil

1 tablespoon lemon juice

1 tablespoon maple syrup

Pinch of fine sea salt

In a small glass jar, combine all the ingredients. Place the lid on the jar and shake until well blended.

# Cilantro Slaw

serves six to eight

(pictured on page 76)

Am I allowed to admit I've never been the biggest coleslaw fan? Well, there. I said it. However, growing cabbage in the garden has necessitated that I cultivate a newfound appreciation for slaw, as there are only so many cabbage steaks (see page 123) a person can make. This is a mayo-free slaw I can get behind, thanks to its mellow dressing with a bright pop of flavor from the fresh cilantro. If you crave bolder salads, bump the vinegar or mustard up a bit. Just remember to add ingredients sparingly at first—the flavors will intensify as the slaw sits in the fridge.

4 cups shredded green cabbage (about ½ head)

2 carrots, shredded

⅓ cup roughly chopped fresh cilantro

⅓ cup sliced scallions

½ cup plain yogurt (page 48)

2 tablespoons apple cider vinegar

2 tablespoons honey

½ teaspoon fine sea salt

¼ teaspoon ground mustard

Pinch of freshly ground black pepper

In a medium bowl, combine the cabbage, carrots, cilantro, and scallions.

In a separate bowl, mix the yogurt, vinegar, honey, salt, mustard, and pepper, pour over the cabbage mixture, and toss to coat.

Cover and chill for at least 1 hour before serving to give all the flavors a chance to come together. Slaw is best served the day you make it. Serve alongside the Wyoming Burger (page 62) or Slow Cooker Pulled Pork (page 77).

*kitchen notes · Use the slicing (not the shredding) disc of a food processor for perfectly shredded cabbage in just a few seconds.*

# Warm Cherry Tomato Salad

*serves four*

*Slow* is the key word with this warm tomato salad. The low oven temperature and long roast time allow the tomato juices to caramelize and the sweet flavor of the tomatoes to intensify, so fight the temptation to increase the oven temperature or reduce the cooking time to speed things along. The good news? Beyond checking the oven occasionally, all you have to do is cut up the cheese and slice the basil, and you'll have an elegant summer side bursting with sweet tomato goodness. I highly recommend sourcing fresh mozzarella for this salad—those dry, flavorless bricks just won't cut it.

1½ to 2 pounds cherry tomatoes, halved

1 tablespoon extra-virgin olive oil

1 tablespoon balsamic vinegar

½ teaspoon fine sea salt

4 ounces fresh mozzarella cheese, cubed

¼ cup fresh basil leaves, cut into ribbons

Preheat the oven to 300°F.

In a large bowl, toss the tomatoes, olive oil, vinegar, and salt.

Arrange the tomatoes cut-side up on a baking sheet and roast them for 1½ to 2 hours, or until the juice thickens and turns slightly sticky. Remove from the oven and allow to cool for 5 minutes. Toss the warm tomatoes with the cheese and basil and serve immediately.

# Roasted Pumpkin Salad

*serves four*

This is the ultimate fall salad, and its savory pumpkin flavor keeps me from throwing temper tantrums when the summer bounty from the garden starts to lull. If you don't have fresh pumpkin handy, substitute butternut, Delicata, or acorn squash.

1 pound fresh pumpkin, peeled and cut into 1-inch cubes

2 tablespoons extra-virgin olive oil

2 tablespoons maple syrup

½ teaspoon ground cumin

½ teaspoon fine sea salt

¼ teaspoon freshly ground black pepper

6 cups spinach leaves or mixed greens of your choice

⅓ cup roasted pumpkin seeds (page 267)

⅓ cup dried cranberries

¼ cup crumbled chèvre (page 247)

Pumpkin Spice Dressing (recipe follows)

Preheat the oven to 400°F.

In a large bowl, toss the pumpkin, olive oil, maple syrup, cumin, salt, and pepper. Spread the pumpkin over a baking sheet. Roast for 35 to 40 minutes, or until the pumpkin is soft and golden brown.

Place the roasted pumpkin on a bed of the spinach and top with the pumpkin seeds, cranberries, and chèvre. Drizzle with the dressing and dig in.

# Pumpkin Spice Dressing

*makes about a half cup*

¼ cup mild-flavored olive oil or other cooking oil

¼ cup plain yogurt (page 48)

2 tablespoons red wine vinegar

1 to 2 teaspoons honey

¼ to ½ teaspoon pumpkin pie spice (see page 225)

Pinch of fine sea salt

In a small jar, combine all the ingredients. Cover the jar and shake well to blend.

# how to peel hard-boiled fresh eggs (without losing your mind)

Hard-boiling eggs from our chickens used to be the bane of my existence. Well-meaning friends would request I bring deviled eggs to various gatherings, because they knew we had plenty of eggs with our large flock of chickens, and I would inwardly groan because I knew what was coming.

If you've only ever purchased eggs from the store, you've probably never had the excruciating experience of attempting to chip eggshell from the flesh of a boiled egg. (I know my fellow homesteaders are nodding in solidarity right now.) It's enough to make one want to say some very choice words, especially when you have several dozen to chip—er, I mean, peel.

Truth be told, it's actually a good problem to have and is a testament to the freshness of the egg itself. The longer an egg is in storage, the more moisture it loses. This results in the air pocket inside the egg becoming larger, which in turn makes the shell easier to pull off. Since fresh eggs rarely have had much evaporation occur, the inner membrane remains tightly attached to the shell. And the results are ugly if hard-boiled eggs are on the menu.

There are numerous old wives' tales floating around that claim to have the magic trick to make eggs easier to peel, but I'm pretty sure they're all lies.

I tried leaving the eggs on the counter for a week prior to boiling. No change. I tried boiling the eggs with vinegar. I tried boiling them with salt. I tried boiling them with baking soda. Nope, nope, and nope. I tried shocking the hot eggs with cold water after I boiled them. Still miserable. I tried pricking the end of the raw eggs with a needle before boiling. That one didn't work. It was also an epic disaster.

Then one day I tried *steaming* my eggs. The heavens opened, the angels sang, and my life was changed forever. Here's how to do it.

YOU WILL NEED:

**Metal colander or steaming basket**

**Large pot with a lid**

**Fresh eggs**

Make sure the colander or basket can fit fully inside the pot without preventing the lid from sitting properly.

Fill the bottom of the pot with water. The exact amount isn't important—you just need enough to keep the pot from boiling dry *without* submerging the eggs.

Place the eggs in the colander (it doesn't matter how many—you can crowd them a bit if you like) and bring the water to a boil. Put the lid on the pot and steam the eggs for 20 minutes.

Lift the colander or basket from the pot and immediately rinse with cool water to halt the cooking process.

And now, my friends—bask in the experience of peeling a fresh egg without strife, frustration, or bad words. You're welcome.

# home bakery

*The process of coaxing bread from yeast, water,* flour, and salt now feels as natural as breathing to me, but it wasn't always that way. Homemade bread used to be my nemesis, and I churned out countless inedible loaves during our first years of marriage. I had an uncanny talent for making my loaves different every time, so our bread ran the Goldilocks gamut: too dense, too dry, too flat, too puffy, too raw, too burnt, too crumbly. I think I definitely got points for variety, though. (Also, this is why I can make homemade breadcrumbs, page 262, in my sleep.)

Then one day, after enough practice, it just clicked. The baguettes finally rose, the biscuits suddenly became flaky, and I stared in disbelief at the perfectly crusty loaf I pulled out of the oven one chilly evening. I'm not exactly sure what the tipping point was, other than that I finally learned how to read the dough, and perhaps that my trademark stubbornness allowed me to persevere. (Oh, and not killing the yeast with too-hot water. That helps too.) All this is to say, bread is an art, and like any art it takes time to master. But it's so very worth it.

I had a bread machine once, but I gave it away when I discovered I love the experience of making bread just as much as I love eating it. There's the feel of the dough on your palms as you knead, the thrill of watching it rise through the window in the oven door, and the unmistakable aroma as it bakes. My house feels warmer and more welcoming when it's filled with the scent of fresh loaves. Then there's the swell of pride you feel when you present a wooden cutting board topped with a crusty round loaf and a slab of butter to a table full of hungry people. Baking bread is an undertaking that engages all the senses.

So many of our meals feel incomplete without bread. The Crusty Dutch Oven Bread is served alongside Rustic Sausage Potato Soup (page 102), the Green Chile Cornbread almost always accompanies the Barn Raising Beans (page 96), and I wouldn't dream of serving my legendary sausage gravy (page 41) without a steaming platter of Sky-High Buttermilk Biscuits.

Crafting homemade bread makes a bold statement in a world of easily available store-bought loaves. It gives a nod to the old ways and proudly proclaims a purposeful choice of quality of life over convenience. If you're going to eat bread, then let it be good bread. And the recipes you'll find in this chapter are exactly that.

# Cast-Iron Skillet Bread

makes one 10-inch loaf

Two of my favorite things: homemade bread and cast iron. You're going to love this versatile recipe—it happily goes with whatever soup, stew, chili, or meat you may be serving and requires very little hands-on time. The rosemary and thyme can be swapped out for other herbs, so use whatever you have on hand.

2¼ teaspoons active dry yeast

2 teaspoons honey

2 cups warm water (95–110°F)

½ cup freshly grated Parmesan cheese

1 tablespoon dried rosemary

1 tablespoon dried thyme

1 teaspoon fine sea salt

4⅓ cups all-purpose flour

1 tablespoon extra-virgin olive oil

In a large bowl, stir the yeast and honey into the warm water until dissolved. Mix in ¼ cup of the cheese, the rosemary, thyme, and salt. Add the flour 1 cup at a time, stirring with a wooden spoon after each addition, then stirring in the remaining ⅓ cup. Mix until the dough forms a rough, sticky ball. This is a no-knead bread, so it will be much stickier than regular dough.

Cover the bowl and let the dough rise in a warm place for 1 hour. Remove the dough from the bowl—avoid punching it down or smooshing it as much as possible. Place the dough into an oiled 10-inch cast-iron skillet and gently press it into a disc. Let rise for 30 minutes more.

Preheat the oven to 400°F.

Drizzle the olive oil over the bread and slash it twice with a sharp knife to make an *X*. Sprinkle the remaining ¼ cup cheese on top and bake for 35 to 40 minutes, until golden brown. Let the bread cool in the pan for 15 minutes, then tip it out of the skillet onto a cutting board to slice.

152    The Prairie Homestead Cookbook

# caring for cast iron

I know of no other type of cookware surrounded by as much superstition as cast iron. I got my first cast-iron skillet years ago and was immediately petrified to use it after reading the list of don'ts I found online: Don't use soap! Don't scrub it too hard! Don't cook anything acidic in it! Don't touch it with metal utensils—it'll scratch! Good grief, I had no idea cast iron was so delicate.

But in reality? It's not delicate at all. You can take a skillet home from the antiques store and it put right back into daily use after a good cleaning—that by itself is a testament to the resiliency of this cookware.

Contrary to popular belief, the cast-iron police will not show up at your door if you use a bit of soap to clean your pans. Seasoning (the natural nonstick coating that forms on well-used cast iron) isn't merely a thin layer of oil sitting on top of the metal. When a pan is properly seasoned, the oil is baked onto the pan and becomes bonded to the metal. This makes it darn tough—a little bit of soap isn't going to bother it. Thank goodness. The same line of thought goes for metal utensils—occasionally using a metal spatula to flip your eggs shouldn't hurt the seasoning on your pan one bit.

## HOW TO SEASON (OR RE-SEASON) A PAN

There are a few occasions when it's wise to re-season your cast iron:

- If you were lucky enough to find an old skillet or pan at an antiques store or yard sale

- If your pans develop rust spots or start to feel sticky

- If the insides of your pans begin to lose their shine and take on a dull appearance

### (Re-)Seasoning: Step-by-Step

1. Wash the pan well with hot soapy water. If there is a lot of buildup, you can break out the steel wool (this is the only instance it's appropriate to use steel wool on cast iron, by the way).

2. Dry the pan completely. Coat it inside and out with a layer of melted lard or bacon grease. Flaxseed oil is also a good choice.

3. Place the skillet upside down on the middle rack of your oven. (Put a piece of foil on the rack underneath it to catch drips.) Bake it at 350°F for 1 hour. Turn off the oven and let the skillet cool inside.

This process can be repeated several more times to build layers of seasoning if the pan was stripped or previously abused.

### To Clean Cast Iron after Normal Use

Always skip the dishwasher and don't let cast-iron cookware soak in water. Rust develops more quickly than you might imagine, so dry immediately after washing and apply a light coat of cooking oil inside and out before you put it away.

If I'm using a well-seasoned pan and haven't cooked anything especially messy in it, I just wipe it out with a soft cloth and call it good. If bits of food are stuck on or I cooked something with strong flavors, I use hot water and a bit of soap to clean it. Remember—if the pan is seasoned correctly, soap won't hurt it.

Cast iron can be stored in the cupboard like any other cookware, but I personally prefer to hang mine on the wall for a bit of extra homestead kitchen charm.

There's nothing to be scared of when it comes to cast iron. With the tiniest bit of consideration, your cast-iron skillets and pans will quickly become cherished parts of your kitchen toolbox to be passed on to future generations. Now get out those pans and put them to work!

# Cranberry Orange Soda Bread

*makes one 10-inch loaf*

Since it doesn't require any rising time, soda bread always comes through for me when I decide we need a loaf of bread but I haven't done a great job of planning ahead. This loaf is lightly sweetened with cranberries and a splash of orange, which makes it perfect for breakfast, but it's just as easily served alongside supper too.

3¾ cups all-purpose flour

2 tablespoons sugar, preferably organic whole cane sugar

1½ teaspoons baking soda

¼ cup (½ stick) cold unsalted butter

1 cup dried cranberries

1 large egg

1 teaspoon orange zest

1 cup orange juice

¾ cup buttermilk (page 244)

Preheat the oven to 375°F.

In a large bowl, combine the flour, sugar, and baking soda. Cut in the butter using a pastry blender or two knives (you can also use a food processor) until pea-sized crumbs form in the dough, then stir in the cranberries.

In a separate bowl, mix the egg, orange zest, orange juice, and buttermilk, then add them to the dry ingredients. Stir until a shaggy, sticky dough forms.

Scrape the dough onto a baking stone covered in parchment and form it into a 10-inch round mound. (Use floured fingers to lightly shape the dough, if needed. Sometimes it's sticky.) Cut a deep *X* in the top using a serrated knife. Bake for 45 to 55 minutes, or until a toothpick inserted into the center comes out clean. Let the loaf rest on a wire rack for 30 minutes before slicing.

# Maple Oat Sandwich Loaves

*makes two 9 x 5–inch loaves*

Sandwich bread is a hot topic in home-baking circles. Most homemade breads are perfect for serving alongside soups or acting as a vehicle for a giant slab of butter, but if you've ever tried to choke down a peanut butter and jelly sandwich made with two dry slices of 100 percent whole wheat bread, you know the experience is less than palatable. Not only do homemade sandwich breads tend to dry out much faster than their store-bought counterparts, many of them are nearly impossible to slice thinly without creating a crumbly mess. I've wrestled with this issue for years, so I was thrilled when my dear friend and author of *Sweet Maple: Backyard Sugarmaking from Tap to Table*, Michelle Visser, offered to let me try—and share!—her maple sandwich bread recipe. These mildly sweetened oat-filled loaves are soft and smooth with the most delectable hint of real maple syrup. Plus, they work beautifully for sandwiches—hallelujah! My search is finally over.

1 cup rolled oats

½ cup maple syrup

¼ cup (½ stick) unsalted butter

1 tablespoon honey

2½ teaspoons fine sea salt

1 teaspoon ground cinnamon

2 cups boiling water

1 tablespoon active dry yeast

5½ cups all-purpose flour

In a large bowl, combine the oats, maple syrup, butter, honey, salt, and cinnamon. Add the boiling water and let sit for 15 minutes. Stir in the yeast and flour to form a soft dough. Knead for 8 to 10 minutes, or until the dough is smooth and satiny. Cover and let rise for 1 hour in a warm place.

Divide the dough in half, shape it into two loaves, and place each loaf into a greased 9 x 5–inch loaf pan. Let the loaves rise until they poke up about an inch above the rims of the pans, 1 to 1½ hours.

Preheat the oven to 350°F. Bake the loaves for 35 to 40 minutes, until golden brown, covering the pans lightly with a sheet of foil for the last 15 minutes of baking to keep them from becoming too brown.

Let them cool slightly, about 5 minutes, then remove the loaves from the pans to cool. They will keep for 3 to 5 days in an airtight container on your counter. Or you can wrap them tightly in plastic wrap and freeze them for later.

# Homemade French Bread

The original French bread recipe I posted on the blog has more than 150 comments from readers who've tried it and loved it. The most common complaint I get from folks who've made the recipe is that the loaves never seem to make it to the table because the family generally mows them down as soon as they come out of the oven. I've served these chewy baguettes to many guests at our table, and they never disappoint. Eat slices hot with butter, or sprinkle with garlic and Parmesan cheese and broil for garlic bread.

1½ cups warm water (95–110°F)

1½ teaspoons active dry yeast

1 teaspoon fine sea salt

3 to 3½ cups all-purpose flour

1 large egg, beaten with 1 teaspoon water

In a large bowl, combine the water and yeast and stir until the yeast is dissolved.

Using a wooden spoon, mix in the salt and enough flour to form a stiff dough. Switch to your hands and knead on a lightly floured surface for 7 to 8 minutes, or until the dough is smooth and no longer sticking to your fingers.

Return the dough to the bowl, cover with a towel, and let rise in a warm place for 1 hour, or until it has doubled in size. Divide the dough into two equal pieces. Form each piece into a rough 8 x 10–inch rectangle. Fold the rectangle in half lengthwise and pinch the seams together very well. Fold it in half lengthwise again and pinch once more. Pinch the ends and form a long, thin loaf. (If the seams won't stay together, rub a little water over them and smooth with your fingers.)

Place a baking stone on the center rack of your oven and a metal pan on the rack underneath. Preheat the oven to 450°F.

Place the loaves on a sheet of parchment and slash each loaf several times with a serrated knife. Let rise in a warm place for 15 minutes. Lightly brush each loaf with the egg wash.

Transfer the loaves on the parchment to the hot stone. Pour 1 cup hot water into the metal pan and quickly shut the oven to trap the steam inside. Bake for 15 to 20 minutes, until golden brown. Let cool a little before slicing.

# Crusty Dutch Oven Bread

These homemade loaves are hearty, wholesome, rustic, crusty, and every other adjective I can think of that describes a supremely satisfying loaf of bread. Perfectly crusty round loaves eluded me for years until I realized it's less about the ingredients and more about the baking method. Using a Dutch oven (a heavy pot with a lid) for this free-form loaf creates a steamy baking environment that yields a crispy exterior resembling those of the artisan loaves at your favorite bakery. I think every kitchen needs at least one Dutch oven anyway, but for the purpose of making this recipe alone, it's worth the splurge if you don't already own one. Immediately transfer the finished loaf to a rack and you might even hear the much-sought-after crackling noise of the loaf as it cools. If you don't want to make two loaves at once, store the leftover dough in an airtight container in the refrigerator and bake the second loaf in a day or two. Bonus: The dough improves in flavor as it ages.

1 teaspoon active dry yeast

1 tablespoon fine sea salt

3 cups warm water (95–110°F)

6 cups all-purpose flour

In a large bowl (I use a food-safe plastic tub with a lid since I usually make one loaf at a time and refrigerate the rest of the dough for later), dissolve the yeast and salt in the warm water.

Stir in the flour to form a loose, sticky dough. Cover the bowl and let rise on the counter for 3 to 5 hours, until at least doubled in size. Because of the lengthier rising period, I don't worry about putting this dough in a warm place like I do with other yeast breads.

At least 45 minutes before you plan to bake, place a 5-quart Dutch oven with the lid on into the oven and preheat the oven to 475°F.

Divide the dough in half and gently shape each piece into a ball. (Avoid punching or kneading it—we want to keep as many air pockets in the dough as possible.) Slash the top of the dough balls several times with a serrated knife. Set the dough balls on separate pieces of parchment and let sit at room temperature for 40 minutes while the oven heats.

When you are ready to bake, very carefully remove the Dutch oven lid and lower the parchment and one loaf inside. Replace the lid and bake for 30 minutes. Remove the lid and bake for an additional 15 minutes. You are looking for the crust on this bread to be deeply browned, much more so than a typical loaf. The first time I made it, I was certain I had burned it to smithereens, but it ended up being perfect.

Remove the finished loaf from the Dutch oven and cool on a wire rack. It's best if you can wait at least 30 minutes before slicing, although I haven't had much success keeping my family away from these loaves, so I wish you luck.

Return the Dutch oven to the oven for 10 minutes to reheat, then bake the second round of dough. Or, if you'd rather bake the other loaf later, store the dough in the refrigerator for up to 1 week. Before baking, allow the cold dough to sit on parchment for 2 hours after shaping, but otherwise, the baking process will be the same as for the first loaf.

*kitchen notes* · *If you don't have a Dutch oven, you can still make this bread with a baking stone, although the crust won't be quite as crispy. Place a baking stone on the middle rack of the oven and preheat to 450°F. Place a small oven-safe baking dish on a lower rack of the oven. Once the oven and stone have heated for at least 45 minutes, transfer the dough to the hot stone. Pour 1 cup hot water into the dish and quickly shut the oven door. Bake for 40 minutes, or until the crust is a deep brown.*

# Herbed Crescent Rolls

I am convinced those canned "pop-n-bake" biscuits are the adult equivalent of a jack-in-the-box—I used to jump every single time I opened one of the darn things. But my fear of exploding biscuits isn't the only reason I abandoned the rolls of cardboard-wrapped dough in favor of this recipe. These buttery homemade crescents have a softer, fluffier texture, not to mention that they're missing that lovely chemical aftertaste I've always noticed in the canned variety. I serve these on special occasions and the addition of fresh herbs makes them even more extraordinary. (If you don't have fresh herbs handy, substitute 2 tablespoons dried herbs instead.)

2¼ teaspoons active dry yeast

½ cup warm water (95–110°F)

⅓ cup plus 3 tablespoons unsalted butter

½ cup whole milk

⅓ cup sugar, preferably organic whole cane sugar

1 teaspoon fine sea salt

1 large egg

3½ to 4 cups all-purpose flour

½ cup chopped fresh herbs (my favorites are rosemary, thyme, and parsley)

In a large bowl, dissolve the yeast in the warm water. In a medium saucepan over low heat, heat ⅓ cup of the butter, the milk, sugar, and salt, stirring until the butter is just barely melted. Cool for 5 minutes, then stir into the yeast mixture. Add the egg and mix until fully incorporated.

Mix in the flour ½ to 1 cup at a time just until a soft dough forms. Knead the dough on a floured surface for 6 to 8 minutes, or until the dough is elastic and smooth.

Place in an oiled bowl and let rise until doubled, about 1 hour. Punch down the dough and divide it in half. Roll each half into a 12-inch round.

Melt the remaining 3 tablespoons butter. Brush each round with 1 tablespoon of the melted butter and sprinkle with half the herbs. Cut each round into 12 wedges and roll up each wedge, starting at the wide end and pinching the pointed end in place to keep it from unrolling while it bakes. Place the rolls on a greased baking sheet and let rise in a warm place for 30 minutes.

Preheat the oven to 375°F.

Brush the rolls with the remaining 1 tablespoon melted butter and bake for 10 to 12 minutes, or until golden brown. Serve warm.

# Butter Pie Crust

I'm horribly picky about my pie crust. If I'm going to indulge in pie, I want a tender (not tough) crust. No burnt, overcooked edges, please. Once upon a time, lard was king when it came to the ultimate pie pastry, but it fell out of favor once vegetable shortenings hit the scene. When I first began my journey into eating more whole foods, I promptly tossed all the tubs of hydrogenated vegetable shortenings in the trash, which left me wondering how I'd make pie moving forward. At that time, I didn't have a great source for lard, so I started using butter and never looked back. Butter crusts are light and flaky, and have the best flavor of all the pie-making fat options.

1¼ cups all-purpose flour

¼ teaspoon fine sea salt

5 tablespoons cold unsalted butter

5 to 6 tablespoons ice-cold water

In a medium bowl, mix the flour and salt. Cut in the butter using a pastry blender or two knives. You can also use a food processor to make short work of pie dough.

When the butter chunks resemble coarse crumbs, add the water 1 tablespoon at a time until the dough just starts to form a ball; you may not need to add all the water. Press the dough until it comes together, but don't knead it, or the heat from your hands will melt the butter and result in tough crust.

Wrap the dough in plastic wrap and chill for 30 minutes.

Generously flour the countertop and roll the dough into a circle several inches larger than the diameter of a 9-inch pie pan. You may need to dust the top of the dough with flour as you roll to prevent sticking or tearing.

Fold the circle in half and then in half again for easy transfer into the pan. Unfold the dough and trim the edges if needed, leaving a slight overhang around the edge of the pan. Crimp the edges or press them with a fork.

Fill with your favorite pie filling and bake as directed. If your recipe calls for pre-baking the crust, follow the directions in "How to Pre-Bake a Crust" (opposite).

*kitchen notes · If you have a good source for pastured lard, you can absolutely use it in place of some or all of the butter in this recipe for a wonderfully flaky crust. I do recommend using leaf lard for pies to avoid any risk of pork flavor coming through in your sweet pies, although that won't be as much of a concern with savory fillings. Skip the hydrogenated lards at the grocery store—they've been processed and contain unhealthy trans fats.*

## HOW TO PRE-BAKE A CRUST

After placing the crust in the pan and finishing the edges, pop it into the freezer for 20 minutes. Preheat the oven to 375°F. When ready to pre-bake, place a sheet of parchment inside the chilled crust and fill the lined crust with pie weights, dry beans, or rice to help it hold its shape as it bakes. Bake for 20 minutes, then remove the weights and parchment and prick the crust with the tines of a fork. Bake for an additional 10 minutes, then fill and bake as directed.

# Pumpkin Pan Rolls

Truth be told, you can make these with any sort of pureed winter squash, including butternut, acorn, or Delicata. No matter what sort of puree I use, I always call them "pumpkin rolls" to avoid any protests at the dinner table. The only thing that gives away the hidden ingredient of these melt-in-your-mouth rolls is the slight orange color. If you prefer a bit more pumpkin flavor, add 2 teaspoons pumpkin pie spice (see page 225) to the dough. Otherwise, enjoy these light and fluffy pan rolls as is. This is also the perfect way to use up any leftover pumpkin puree after you make Honey Pumpkin Pie (page 189).

2½ teaspoons active dry yeast

¾ cup warm milk (95–110°F)

¼ cup sugar, preferably organic whole cane sugar

¼ cup (½ stick) plus 1 tablespoon unsalted butter, melted

¾ cup pumpkin puree (page 267)

1 large egg

1 teaspoon fine sea salt

3½ to 4 cups all-purpose flour

In a large bowl, dissolve the yeast in the warm milk, then mix in the sugar, ¼ cup of the butter, the pumpkin, egg, and salt. Add enough flour, 1 cup at a time, to form a slightly sticky dough. Knead for 6 to 8 minutes on a lightly floured surface, until the dough is smooth and elastic.

Place the dough in an oiled bowl and let rise in a warm place until doubled in volume.

Preheat the oven to 350°F and grease a 9 x 13–inch pan.

Punch down the dough and divide it into 15 pieces. (Dust your hands with flour if it starts to get sticky—it's a slightly gooey dough.) Shape each piece into a small ball and place it in the prepared pan.

Let rise for 30 minutes, then brush the tops with the remaining 1 tablespoon melted butter. Bake for 20 to 25 minutes, or until golden brown.

# Chive & Cheddar Mounds

*makes twelve to fourteen biscuits*

Sometimes I'm in the mood to pat buttery dough on the counter and cut out circles with my crinkly vintage biscuit cutter. And then other times, *just give me biscuits, darn it!* These cheesy mounds are the perfect plop-and-bake option for when you're short on time and nothing but biscuits will do. You can also swap out the chives for fresh thyme or substitute Swiss for the cheddar if you're so inclined.

2 cups all-purpose flour

1 tablespoon baking powder

½ teaspoon fine sea salt

1 teaspoon garlic powder

2 tablespoons minced fresh chives

5 tablespoons cold unsalted butter

1 cup shredded cheddar cheese

¾ cup plus 2 tablespoons whole milk

Preheat the oven to 400°F.

In a large bowl, combine the flour, baking powder, salt, garlic powder, and chives. Cut in the butter using a pastry blender or two knives (you can also use a food processor) until the mixture resembles coarse crumbs.

Stir in the cheese, then add the milk and stir until the mixture forms a wet, sticky dough. Drop ¼ cup mounds of the dough onto an unlined baking sheet or stone and bake for 18 to 20 minutes, or until golden brown.

# Sky-High Buttermilk Biscuits

I have high standards when it comes to biscuits—I can't help it. I like 'em tall, fluffy, and golden brown. As long as you keep the butter chunky and cold and don't overwork the dough, these biscuits will live up to their name and rise high with flaky layers of buttery goodness. Mix (don't knead) the dough just until the ingredients come together and you'll be golden. Or rather, your biscuits will be golden. But you get the idea.

3½ cups all-purpose flour

1 tablespoon baking powder

1 teaspoon fine sea salt

2 tablespoons sugar, preferably organic whole cane sugar

½ cup (1 stick) cold unsalted butter, cubed

1½ cups cold buttermilk (page 244)

Preheat the oven to 450°F.

In a large bowl, combine the dry ingredients, then cut in the butter using a pastry blender or two knives (you can also use a food processor) until pea-sized crumbs form in the dough; this will ensure that the biscuits turn out flaky and light. Add the buttermilk and stir until the dough just comes together; don't overmix.

Lightly flour the countertop and pat the dough to ¾ inch thick. Using a 2-inch biscuit cutter or the rim of a drinking glass, cut the dough into rounds. Place on a baking sheet or stone and bake for 12 to 14 minutes, or until lightly browned.

*kitchen notes · Serve these with Old-Fashioned Sausage Gravy (page 41) for the best biscuits 'n' gravy you've ever put in your mouth.*

*If you open your refrigerator in the midst of making these biscuits only to discover you're out of cultured buttermilk, you can mix up this quick substitute instead: Put 1½ tablespoons lemon juice or vinegar in a 2-cup measuring cup, then fill with milk to the 1½-cup line. Stir until you see small curdled bits on your spoon, then add to the recipe.*

# Soft Flour Tortillas

Be prepared—it's extremely hard to go back to store-bought tortillas after tasting homemade ones. I started making tortillas at the very beginning of my homestead journey, back when I was still stocking the cupboards with margarine, boxed mac 'n' cheese, and cans of cream of chicken soup. Thankfully, I've come a long way since then, and so has my tortilla technique. The only downfall of the homemade variety is that they dry out rather quickly. Place them in a resealable plastic bag lined with paper towels while they are still hot to increase their shelf life, then briefly reheat in a skillet to restore them to their original, freshly made glory when ready to serve.

2 cups all-purpose flour

1 teaspoon fine sea salt

3 tablespoons lard (page 251) or coconut oil, melted

¾ cup hot water (100°F), plus more if needed

In a medium bowl, mix together the flour and salt. Mix the melted lard into the flour until the mixture is crumbly. Add the water and knead for 2 to 3 minutes, or until the dough comes together and is smooth and pliable. (Add another 1 to 2 teaspoons of water if the dough seems too dry and crumbly.) Form the dough into a ball, wrap in plastic wrap, and let rest for 30 minutes at room temperature.

Divide the dough into eight evenly sized balls and roll each one as thinly as possible. My tortillas are never perfectly round—thankfully, irregular shapes don't affect the taste at all. You can sprinkle a little flour on the counter if they start to stick, but I find I rarely need to do that.

Preheat a skillet or griddle over high heat. Cook each tortilla for 30 seconds on each side, or until a few light brown spots show.

Remove from the heat, wrap in a clean kitchen towel, and serve warm. If storing for later, place the warm tortillas on a paper towel inside a resealable plastic bag. If the tortillas become stiff, reheat them for several minutes in a hot skillet until they soften.

*kitchen notes* · *Add some shredded cheese and refried beans (page 129) to these tortillas for tasty homemade quesadillas.*

# Ham & Cheese Pockets

*makes eight pockets*

Ever had one of those hams that just won't quit, no matter how much you eat? When you can't swallow any more ham sandwiches or ham soups, toss the remaining bits with some cheese and make these gooey pockets. Honestly, they really should be called *leftover pockets* because they are the perfect way to use up bits of this and that in the fridge and still get happy cheers from the family. I've made dozens of batches of these with regular pizza crust, but discovered we prefer this soft dough made with milk and butter instead.

2¼ teaspoons active dry yeast

½ cup warm water (95–110°F)

½ cup whole milk

¼ cup (½ stick) unsalted butter

¼ cup sugar, preferably organic whole cane sugar

¾ teaspoon fine sea salt

2 large eggs, beaten separately

3½ to 4 cups all-purpose flour

2⅔ cups cubed cooked ham

2⅔ cups shredded cheddar cheese

In a large bowl, combine the yeast and water and stir until dissolved.

In a small saucepan over low heat, combine the milk, butter, sugar, and salt and heat until the butter is just barely melted. Cool for 5 minutes, then mix in the dissolved yeast.

Mix in 1 beaten egg, then the flour ½ cup at a time. Knead for 6 to 8 minutes, or until the dough is smooth and elastic. Cover and let rise in a warm place for 1 hour.

Preheat the oven to 400°F.

Punch down the dough and divide it in half. Divide each half into four evenly sized balls. On a lightly floured surface, roll each ball into a 7-inch round. Spoon about ⅓ cup each ham and cheese onto half of each circle. Fold the other half of the dough over the filling and crimp to seal the edges. Brush each pocket with the remaining egg. Bake for 15 to 20 minutes, until golden brown.

To freeze for later, let cool completely, then wrap in foil and freeze in a resealable plastic bag. To reheat from frozen, place foil-wrapped pockets in a preheated 350°F oven for 15 to 20 minutes, or until heated through.

## Filling Variations

Pockets can be filled in an almost infinite number of ways. Let your imagination run wild! Here are a few variations we're fond of at our house:

• Pepperoni or sausage and mozzarella

• Leftover steamed broccoli and cheddar

• Mushrooms and Swiss cheese

• Leftover scrambled eggs and pepper Jack cheese

# Green Chile Cornbread

At our house, cornbread is a nonnegotiable companion to chili or the Barn Raising Beans (page 96), and we love how the chiles and cheddar elevate this cornbread to a whole new level. If you're like me and never seem to have cornmeal on hand when you need it, make your own by grinding regular unpopped popcorn kernels in a grain mill or high-powered blender. I use mild peppers for the kiddos, but if you prefer extra spice, use hot chiles or ½ cup finely diced jalapeños instead of the green chiles. For extra cool-homesteader points, definitely bake this in a cast-iron skillet.

1 cup all-purpose flour

1 cup cornmeal

1 tablespoon baking powder

¾ teaspoon fine sea salt

1 cup whole milk

2 large eggs

2 (4-ounce) cans mild green chiles, drained

¼ cup (½ stick) unsalted butter, melted

3 tablespoons honey

1½ cups shredded cheddar cheese

Preheat the oven to 400°F and butter a 10-inch cast-iron skillet or a 9-inch square pan.

In a large bowl, combine the flour, cornmeal, baking powder, and salt. In a separate bowl, mix the milk, eggs, chiles, melted butter, and honey. Stir the wet ingredients into the dry until barely combined, then fold in the cheese. Scrape the batter into the prepared pan.

Bake for 25 minutes, or until a toothpick inserted into the center comes out clean.

*kitchen notes · If you'd prefer to use fresh chiles instead of canned, substitute 6 to 8 diced roasted and peeled green chiles (such as poblano, Hatch, or Anaheim). Find instructions for roasting chile peppers below.*

## HOW TO ROAST CHILE PEPPERS

Heat the broiler to high and spread the peppers on a baking sheet. Broil for 5 to 10 minutes, flipping them once halfway through, until the majority of the skin is charred and bubbled for easiest peeling. Place immediately in a resealable plastic bag and close tightly, letting the peppers steam for 20 minutes. The skins should rub off easily. Cut the peppers in half and scrape out the seeds (wear rubber gloves when you do this—even mild peppers can burn your skin!). Roasted peppers can be frozen or kept in the refrigerator for up to 5 days.

# Soft Pretzels

Sunday is the day we press pause on our hectic homestead life. Generally I'm not in the mood to cook elaborate suppers on Sundays, although everyone still wants to eat. (Funny how that works.) In the winter, pretzels are our ritual. I mix up the dough and let it rise while we nap, then the kids and I shape the twists and boil them in the baking soda slurry later in the afternoon. They're chewy, salty, and satisfying, and you must try dipping them in cheese sauce (page 259). Seriously, you MUST.

2¼ teaspoons active dry yeast

2 tablespoons sugar, preferably organic whole cane sugar

1½ cups warm water (95–110°F)

1 teaspoon fine sea salt

3½ to 4 cups all-purpose flour

½ cup baking soda

2 tablespoons unsalted butter, melted

Coarse sea salt, for topping

In a large bowl, dissolve the yeast and sugar in the warm water. Mix in the fine salt and enough flour to form a soft dough that doesn't stick to your hands as you work it. Knead the dough on a floured surface for 6 to 8 minutes, or until smooth and elastic, before placing it in an oiled bowl. Cover and allow the dough to rise in a warm place for 45 minutes.

Preheat the oven to 400°F.

Line a baking sheet with parchment or put a baking stone in the oven to preheat. In a medium saucepan over high heat, bring 4 cups water and the baking soda to a boil.

Punch down the dough and divide it into 12 evenly sized pieces. Roll each piece into a 12-inch rope and twist it into a pretzel shape. Immerse the pretzels one at a time in the boiling water for 30 seconds, then place them on the prepared baking sheet or stone.

Bake the pretzels for 14 minutes, or until they are a rich shade of golden brown.

Brush with melted butter immediately after you remove them from the oven and sprinkle with coarse salt. These pretzels are best if eaten warm from the oven, but are definitely still edible the following day if kept in an airtight container overnight.

*kitchen notes · It's hard to beat pretzels topped with coarse salt, but a cinnamon-sugar topping is a close second. Mix ¼ cup packed brown sugar with 1 tablespoon ground cinnamon. Sprinkle this onto the pretzels after brushing them with butter.*

# Sourdough Crackers

My children lurk in the kitchen like hungry sharks when they discover I'm making these crackers. Even the littlest one manages to snatch them off the cooling rack, though she can barely reach the countertop. I don't make a lot of snack foods, so when I do, they must be no-fuss and something I can easily pop into the oven while I'm doing dishes or stirring something on the stove. These fit the bill on both accounts, and I love them even more for using up my ever-abundant excess sourdough starter. I've tried quite a few sourdough cracker recipes that left me with results resembling the hardtack I've read about in history books. After lots of experimentation, I discovered adding the smallest bit of baking soda makes all the difference and I finally got the crispy wafers I'd been searching for.

1 cup all-purpose flour

1 teaspoon packed brown sugar, preferably organic whole cane sugar

½ teaspoon baking soda

¼ teaspoon fine sea salt

1 cup sourdough starter (page 256)

¼ cup extra-virgin olive oil

Coarse sea salt, for topping

Place a baking stone (a regular baking sheet will work in a pinch) in the oven and preheat the oven to 350°F.

In a medium bowl, combine the flour, sugar, baking soda, and salt. Stir in the starter and oil.

Divide the dough into four evenly sized balls. Place the first ball on a piece of parchment and roll it as thinly as you can (about ¹⁄₁₆ inch thick). Sprinkle a bit of flour on top if the dough threatens to stick to the rolling pin.

Use a pizza cutter or sharp knife to cut the dough into squares. Mine are usually around 2 inches square, although I don't get too picky about the size or the ragged edges.

Lightly sprinkle the tops of the crackers with coarse salt and transfer the parchment to the hot baking stone. Bake for 12 to 14 minutes, or until the crackers are beginning to brown slightly and the center ones are crisp. Remove immediately to a rack to cool. These will keep for up to 2 days in an airtight container at room temperature, but are the very best if eaten the day you make them.

*kitchen notes · Using whole wheat flour instead of all-purpose creates a slightly coarser cracker with a nuttier taste. Depending on the type of whole wheat flour you use, you may need to add 1 or 2 tablespoons water to keep the dough pliable.*

*For herbed crackers, add 1 tablespoon of your favorite dried herbs to the dry ingredients. My suggestions would be rosemary, thyme, or herbes de Provence.*

# five tips for consistently better bread

For me, the most frustrating part of learning to make yeast bread was my continually inconsistent results. After dozens of failed attempts, I finally realized there are a few details that are more important than they seem at first glance. Once I started paying attention to these little things, perfect loaves suddenly weren't as mysterious as they once were.

Here are a few of the tips I've picked up after many, many tries. Hopefully these will shorten your learning curve just a bit and you won't end up having to make quite as many batches of breadcrumbs as I did.

## 1. Good Yeast Matters

The cute little envelopes of yeast in the baking aisle? Skip 'em. I've always had the most inconsistent results using those. I suspect the yeast loses its punch faster in the envelopes, so I prefer to purchase active dry yeast in 1-pound packages and store it in the freezer. I've had yeast sit in the freezer for years past its expiration date, but still be perfectly usable. If you are concerned your yeast is no longer active, proof it before you add flour. To do this, mix the yeast with the warm water or other warm liquid called for in the recipe. Let the mixture sit for 10 minutes. If you see frothy bubbles, you have happy yeast and you can proceed with the rest of the recipe. If the mixture looks no different after 10 minutes, it's a good indication the yeast is dead. Some cooks proof the yeast for every single batch of bread they make, but I don't. If I'm reasonably sure my yeast is good, I just go for it. What can I say? I like to live on the edge.

## 2. Warm (Not Hot!) Water

Most bread recipes call for starting with warm water. This activates the yeast and prepares it to do its thing once you add the rest of the ingredients. Aim for the water to be between 95 and 110°F. If you dip your fingertip into the water it should feel like very warm bathwater. If it is uncomfortably hot, let it cool before you mix in the yeast. I don't know exactly how many batches of yeast I've killed with hot water, but it's been a bunch. Don't be like me. Let your yeast live.

### 3. Add Just the Right Amount of Flour

. . . except I can't really tell you what that is, because it depends on the recipe, your climate, and the flour you're using. That's helpful, huh? If I could, I'd have you come over and we'd practice kneading so you could feel the difference. The best way I can describe it is that you'll know you have it right when the dough starts to feel soft and satiny. It will be pliable and smooth, without sticking to your hands too much—it almost feels as though it's alive. If the dough feels overly dense and heavy, it's likely you added too much flour. This is just one of those things that takes practice. Accept that you'll probably have some dry loaves here and there, and just roll with it.

### 4. Warm House = Happy Dough

Most bread recipes call for an initial 1-hour rise, which works best if the dough can be in an environment around 75 to 80°F. My house is usually cold, so I have to manipulate the process a bit. If I'm in the kitchen and using my stove top for other things, I'll set the covered bowl of dough near my cooktop where the radiating heat will keep it happy. Otherwise, I preheat my oven to 350°F for several minutes, then shut it off and place the covered dough inside to rise. *(This is really important—make sure you shut it off!)* This ensures my rises happen in a reasonable amount of time, and as long as I don't forget the bowl is inside and turn on the oven to bake something else, all is well.

### 5. Cool Before Slicing

Yes, I realize this is a cruel rule. If you have the willpower to avoid cutting into a hot loaf right away, the texture and flavor will be better. I'm not saying I always follow this rule, but I figured I should do my duty and share it with you nonetheless.

# old-fashioned sweets

*When I first awakened to the notion of home-*steading, there were so many factors that appealed to me. I loved the idea of fresh, homegrown food, I was fascinated with the quality of life I envisioned it providing, and I was drawn to the thought of raising my future children in a lifestyle that promoted old-fashioned values and work ethic.

Fast-forward ten years, and here we are with a barn full of animals, a garden, and three wild prairie children. Watching them embrace the lifestyle as their own has been priceless, and I love the constant opportunities for growth and learning homesteading provides. They have an innate confidence and connection with animals I never did at that age and can identify every herb and vegetable we grow by sight and taste. At chore time, they have turned into quite the helpers and some days they even water, feed, and harvest the garden without me. Since they play such an active role in helping to grow our food, they love watching it transform into all sorts of tasty recipes, and all three frequently accompany me in the kitchen. They love talking about which components of each meal we grew here on the homestead as they crack eggs for Prairie Cream Puffs, crank the handle of our stovetop popper as it pops the corn for Honey Caramel Corn, and watch in eager anticipation as the ice cream maker churns Blueberry Cheesecake Ice Cream.

But before I wax too poetic and you think our days are filled with perfect, rosy-cheeked children picking green beans in the garden and baking cookies, hang on just a minute. This homesteading with children thing—it's also chaotic, and crazy, and so very dirty.

Floors without tiny muddy boot prints everywhere? Not an option. Forgetting to add the sugar to the gingerbread cake recipe because you're being peppered with questions about how it rains, why flour is spelled *f-l-o-u-r* and not *f-l-o-w-e-r* (I have no idea why, by the way), and why gingerbread cookies are crunchy and gingerbread cake is not? Oh, yes. Turning around while you're cooking to see a little boy standing in your kitchen holding a (live) chicken? Absolutely. A bowlful of cracked eggs, complete with countless bits of eggshell? All. The. Time.

For every day my children wander the garden in idyllic poses or look adorable as they watch the Lemon Whey Pie browning through the oven window, there are ten other days filled with stop-and-start projects and utter chaos. I don't have the perfect formula for homesteading with children. We just do it the best we can. Some days are more productive than others, and some days I just give up on accomplishing anything on my list. But memories are being made, lessons are being ingrained, and I wouldn't have it any other way.

My kids happily devour all the recipes in this chapter, but their very favorites are Honey Pumpkin Pie—they like to select the perfect pumpkin from the patch; Chocolate Frozen Yogurt—I give 'em a bowl and send 'em outside; and Fudgy Sourdough Brownies—easy for little hands to help mix and bake. The recipes in this chapter are prairie-tested and proven to satisfy any sweet tooth, young and old alike.

# Lemon Whey Pie

*makes one 9-inch pie*

Whey isn't an ingredient we hear much about these days, though if you make your own cheese, you're probably intimately familiar with it. I found the original recipe for this pie in an old cookbook as a way for enterprising housewives to substitute a common, everyday ingredient (whey) for a harder-to-find, more expensive one (lemon juice). In our modern times, the tables have turned and now lemon juice is easier for most of us to source than whey. However, I'm rooting for whey to make a comeback—it's a handy ingredient to have around (see page 250 for a list of uses). This charming farmhouse pie takes a little extra time to put together, so I usually save it for special occasions, but the pile of golden brown meringue and tangy whey filling is worth every bit of effort.

### FILLING

1 cup organic white sugar

¼ cup cornstarch

½ teaspoon fine sea salt

1½ cups whey

5 large egg yolks, beaten

¼ cup lemon juice

2 tablespoons unsalted butter, melted

### MERINGUE

⅓ cup cool water

1 tablespoon cornstarch

5 large egg whites, at room temperature

1 teaspoon vanilla extract (page 261)

½ cup organic white sugar

½ teaspoon cream of tartar

1 baked pie crust (page 164)

Preheat the oven to 350°F.

Make the filling: In a medium saucepan over medium-low heat, combine the sugar, cornstarch, and salt, then slowly whisk in the whey. Bring the mixture to a simmer and cook, stirring often. Once the mixture is thickened and bubbly, cook for 2 minutes more.

Slowly drizzle the hot mixture into the beaten egg yolks, whisking constantly, then pour it all back into the saucepan and bring to a gentle boil. Reduce the heat to low and cook for 2 minutes more. Remove from the heat and stir in the lemon juice and butter. Keep the filling hot while you prepare the meringue.

Make the meringue: In a small saucepan over medium heat, whisk together the cool water and cornstarch. Cook, stirring until it thickens, remove it from the heat and set aside. This cornstarch paste will help keep the meringue from sagging or weeping.

*(continued)*

In a medium bowl, use a handheld mixer on high speed to beat together the egg whites and vanilla until foamy, about 1 minute. In a separate bowl, combine the sugar and cream of tartar, then add to the egg whites, 1 tablespoon at a time, beating continuously.

Once stiff peaks have formed, test the meringue to see if the sugar has dissolved by rubbing a bit between your fingers. If it's smooth, it's ready. If it feels gritty, keep beating. When the sugar is completely dissolved, reduce the mixer speed to low and beat in the cornstarch paste, 1 tablespoon at a time, beating continuously.

Pour the hot filling into the pie crust. Spoon the meringue on top of the filling, starting with the edges. Make sure the meringue has contact with the edge of the crust and forms a solid layer. Heap the rest in the middle and use the back of a spoon to make swirls or peaks. Bake for 15 to 20 minutes, or until the tips of the meringue are golden brown. Cool completely before slicing and serve at room temperature.

*kitchen notes · To prevent weeping meringue (that annoying phenomenon where liquid pools between the two layers of the pie), be sure the filling is piping hot before you spread the meringue on top. Unfortunately, this crucial tidbit tends to leave one doing a bit of a dance while attempting to make both components at once. I suggest setting out all your meringue ingredients before beginning the whey filling. Keep the filling in the saucepan once it is done and gently reheat it over low heat for several minutes once the meringue is whipped. This way, you can pour the filling in the waiting pie shell, spread on the meringue, and bake immediately.*

*If you're dying to make this pie but don't plan on making cheese anytime soon, collect whey by draining 4 cups plain yogurt (page 48) in a piece of cheesecloth or linen. Use the whey for this pie and spread the resulting yogurt cheese on bread, bagels, or crackers.*

*This is one of the rare instances where I use an organic version of a more refined white sugar. My heartier, molasses-filled whole cane sugar options tend to muddy the delicate flavor of the curd and meringue more than I like.*

FARM JOURNAL'S COMPLETE

PIE cookbook

700 BEST DESSERT AND MAIN-DISH PIES
IN THE COUNTRY . . . . . EDITED BY
Nell B. Nichols FIELD FOOD EDITOR
WITH THE ASSISTANCE OF THE FOOD STAFF
OF *FARM JOURNAL* · PHOTOGRAPHY SUPER-
VISED BY AL J. REAGAN, ART DIRECTOR
OF *THE FARMER'S WIFE*

& COMPANY, INC.
EW YORK

*ournal*
Y COOKBOOK
COUNTRY COOKBOOK
ING COOKBOOK

# Honey Pumpkin Pie

makes one 9-inch pie

As much as I love our brined and roasted homegrown turkeys, pumpkin pie is still my favorite part of Thanksgiving dinner. I've tried bunches of different recipes over the years, but this one is heads and tails above the others. Three eggs instead of just two takes the custard texture to a whole new level, and swapping out the usual sugar for honey and the canned milk for real cream creates the smoothest, most decadent pumpkin pie you've ever had in your life. If you happen to be short on pie spice, there's a recipe to make your own on page 225.

2 cups pumpkin puree (page 267)

¾ cup honey

1 teaspoon vanilla extract (page 261)

½ teaspoon fine sea salt

1 tablespoon pumpkin pie spice

¾ cup heavy cream or half-and-half

3 large eggs, lightly beaten

1 unbaked pie crust (page 164)

Preheat the oven to 375°F.

In a large bowl, combine the puree, honey, vanilla, salt, and pumpkin pie spice. Mix in the cream and gently beat in the eggs. Pour the mixture into the pie crust. Cover the edges of the crust with a pie shield (or strips of foil) and bake for 30 minutes. Remove the shield and bake for another 35 to 40 minutes, or until a knife inserted into the center of the pie comes out clean.

Cool for 2 hours before serving. Top with a generous dollop of whipped cream (page 248). I like pumpkin pie to be well chilled, so I make pies a day ahead of time and keep them in the refrigerator overnight. However, it's perfectly acceptable to serve room temperature pie too—just be sure to pop the leftovers in the fridge.

Old-Fashioned Sweets    189

# Apple Molasses Pie with Cheddar Crust

*makes one 9-inch pie*

Molasses is an old-fashioned sweetener that plays beautifully with crisp apples. A childhood spent watching my dad melt generous slabs of cheddar over hot apple pie inspired the shreds of sharp cheddar mixed into the crust. Ten cups of apples creates a hefty mound, so use a deep-dish pie pan (mine is 2 inches deep), or reduce the apples to 8 or 9 cups if you only have a regular pan.

CRUST

2¼ cups all-purpose flour

1½ cups shredded cheddar cheese

½ teaspoon fine sea salt

½ cup (1 stick) cold unsalted butter

10 to 12 tablespoons ice-cold water

FILLING

8 to 10 medium apples, cored and sliced ½ inch thick (about 10 cups)

1 tablespoon apple cider vinegar

⅓ cup packed brown sugar, preferably organic whole cane sugar

¼ cup all-purpose flour

¼ cup molasses

1 teaspoon ground cinnamon

¼ teaspoon fine sea salt

1 tablespoon unsalted butter, cut into small cubes

1 large egg, beaten with 1 teaspoon water

Make the crust: In a large bowl, combine the flour, cheese, and salt and cut in the butter using a pastry blender or two knives (you can also use a food processor) until pea-sized crumbs form in the dough. Mix in the water 1 tablespoon at a time just until the dough sticks together and forms a ball. Wrap the dough in plastic wrap and chill for 30 minutes.

Make the filling: In another large bowl, toss the apples, vinegar, sugar, flour, molasses, cinnamon, and salt until the apple slices are well coated.

Preheat the oven to 425°F.

Divide the chilled dough in half. Generously flour the countertop and roll half the dough into a round several inches larger than the diameter of a 9-inch pie pan. You may need to dust the top of the dough with flour as you roll to prevent sticking or tearing.

Fold the dough round in half and then in half again for easy transfer into the pan. Unfold the dough and trim the edges if needed, leaving a slight overhang around the edge

of the pan. Spoon the filling into the crust and dot with butter. Roll the second half of the dough into a slightly smaller round.

Place the second dough round over the filling and seal the top and bottom crusts' edges together, fluting them or crimping with a fork. Cut several slits in the top crust so the pie can vent and brush the top with egg wash.

Transfer the pie to the oven and bake for 20 minutes. Reduce the oven temperature to 375°F and bake for 40 to 60 minutes more, or until the apples are tender and the filling is bubbly. Cool on a wire rack. Served topped with ice cream or whipped cream (page 248).

*kitchen notes · Everyone has a favorite pie apple, but I like to use a combination of sweet and tart varieties. Some of my favorites are Pink Lady, Fuji, Golden Delicious, Honeycrisp, Gala, McIntosh, Rome, and Jonathan. Skip the ever-present Red Delicious—they tend to be mushy and bland once cooked.*

*I usually don't peel pie apples. Baking softens the skins enough that I barely notice them.*

# Fried Cinnamon Apples with Cream

*serves two*

"Apples for dessert?" I could see the disappointment on my children's faces when I announced what our much-anticipated weekend dessert would be. It only took one bite of these cinnamon-dusted apples drizzled with cream to change their mind. You can skip the cream and ladle the warm apples over vanilla ice cream if you'd prefer.

2 tablespoons unsalted butter

2 large apples, peeled, cored, and sliced

2 teaspoons packed brown sugar, preferably organic whole cane sugar

Pinch of ground cinnamon

Pinch of ground nutmeg

2 tablespoons heavy cream

In a large skillet over medium heat, melt the butter. Add the apples, sugar, cinnamon, and nutmeg. Cook the apples for 5 minutes, or until they are tender and starting to brown. Drizzle with the cream and serve warm.

# Minted Strawberry Tart

Mint and strawberries usually arrive in the garden around the same time, so it only makes sense to eat them together. Herbaceous mint leaves elegantly complement the bright sweetness of strawberries and they both shine when wrapped in a flaky pastry crust. While not overly sweet, this light, rustic tart is the perfect early summer dessert and tastes even better if eaten while sitting on the front porch with a glass of iced tea nearby.

CRUST

1¼ cups all-purpose flour

1 teaspoon sugar, preferably organic whole cane sugar

¼ teaspoon fine sea salt

6 tablespoons cold unsalted butter, cut into cubes

4 to 6 tablespoons ice-cold water

FILLING

2½ cups sliced strawberries

¼ cup fresh mint leaves, chopped

¼ cup sugar, preferably organic whole cane sugar

1 tablespoon organic cornstarch

1 teaspoon vanilla extract (page 261)

1 tablespoon unsalted butter

1 large egg, beaten, for wash

Make the crust: In a large bowl, combine the flour, sugar, and salt, then cut in the butter using a pastry blender or two knives (you can also use a food processor) until the mixture resembles coarse crumbs. Add 4 tablespoons of the water and mix, adding the remaining water if necessary, until the dough comes together and forms a ball. Press it into a disc, taking care not to overwork the dough. Wrap the disc in plastic wrap and chill in the refrigerator for at least 1 hour.

Make the filling: In another large bowl, combine all the filling ingredients except the butter and allow the flavors to meld for at least 20 minutes. Drain off any liquid that accumulates in the bottom of the bowl.

Preheat the oven to 400°F.

Generously flour the countertop, remove the disc from the plastic wrap, and roll it into a 12-inch circle on a piece of parchment. Spread the strawberry filling in the center of the circle, leaving 2 inches of dough uncovered around the outer edge. Dot the top of the filling with the butter to give it a glossy shine when it comes out of the oven.

Fold the edges up one section at a time, overlapping as you go. Brush the edges of the crust with the egg, and place the parchment with the tart onto a baking sheet or stone. Bake for 30 minutes, or until the crust is golden brown and the filling is bubbly. Cool for 30 minutes and serve at room temperature.

# Roasted Peaches & Cream

When I've been digging in the garden all morning and I suddenly remember I have company coming for supper, these honey-glazed peaches save the day. They look impressively fancy for only four ingredients, and guests fall in love at first bite. If you have fresh basil growing in your garden, tear up a handful of leaves and sprinkle them on top of the warm peaches for a burst of herby flavor. No one will know you threw this elegant dessert together last minute—your secret is safe with me.

**4 peaches, ripe but not squishy, halved and pit removed**

**4 tablespoons (½ stick) unsalted butter**

**4 tablespoons honey**

**Heavy cream or vanilla ice cream, for serving**

Preheat the oven to 400°F.

　　Place the peaches cut side up in a baking dish large enough to fit them in a single layer. Place ½ tablespoon of the butter on top of each peach half and drizzle each with ½ tablespoon of the honey.

　　Bake for 15 to 20 minutes, or until the peaches soften and turn golden brown. If you want a deeper golden color, turn on the broiler for the last 2 to 3 minutes. Remove from the oven. If there is cooking liquid in the bottom of the baking dish, spoon it over the tops of the peaches. Cool slightly, then serve with a generous drizzle of cream or a scoop of ice cream.

# Strawberry Shortcake Squares

The strawberries we grow here on the homestead are one of our most precious harvests. We only have a small patch and the robins love them as much as we do, so each and every strawberry we are able to pluck from the plants is a treasure. Our berries are smaller than the ones you find at the store, but they are a vibrant shade of red and they burst with the purest strawberry flavor I've ever tasted. This play on traditional shortcake is my dessert of choice for early summer picnics and barbecues. In-season strawberries are a classic choice, but blueberries or raspberries are just as delicious on top of these fluffy bars.

SHORTCAKE

½ cup (1 stick) unsalted butter, softened

½ to ¾ cup sugar, preferably organic whole cane sugar

2 large eggs

¾ cup whole milk

1 teaspoon vanilla extract (page 261)

1¼ cups all-purpose flour

1 teaspoon baking soda

¼ teaspoon fine sea salt

TOPPING

8 ounces cream cheese (page 245), softened

¼ cup maple syrup

1 tablespoon vanilla extract (page 261)

½ cup heavy cream, whipped

3 cups sliced strawberries

Preheat the oven to 350°F. Grease a 9 x 13–inch pan.

Make the shortcake: In the bowl of a stand mixer, beat the butter until fluffy. Add the sugar, eggs, milk, and vanilla and beat until smooth, about 2 minutes.

In a small bowl, combine the flour, baking soda, and salt and add to the creamed butter mixture, mixing on medium speed until well incorporated and stopping to scrape down the sides of the bowl as necessary.

Pat the dough into the prepared pan. Bake for 12 to 15 minutes, or until a toothpick inserted into the center comes out clean. Cool completely.

Make the topping: In the bowl of a stand mixer, beat the cream cheese at medium speed until fluffy, about 1 minute. Add the maple syrup and vanilla and mix until incorporated. Fold in the whipped cream and spread over the cooled shortcake.

Top with the berries and serve immediately. The shortcake will keep, tightly covered, in the fridge for up to 2 days.

# Old-Fashioned Gingerbread with Caramel Sauce

*makes one 9-inch square pan*

Every happy holiday memory you've ever had is wrapped up in a bite of this spicy vintage cake. The warm gingerbread and caramel will instantly bring to mind cozy crackling fires, baking cookies with Grandma, and fuzzy flannel blankets. And don't you dare skip the caramel sauce—it's nonnegotiable.

2 cups all-purpose flour

1 teaspoon baking soda

1½ teaspoons ground ginger

1 teaspoon ground cinnamon

½ teaspoon fine sea salt

½ cup (1 stick) unsalted butter, melted

½ cup packed brown sugar, preferably organic whole cane sugar

2 large eggs

¾ cup hot water (100°F)

¾ cup molasses

Caramel Sauce (recipe follows)

Preheat the oven to 350°F. Grease a 9-inch square pan.

In a large bowl, combine the flour, baking soda, ginger, cinnamon, and salt. In a separate bowl, mix the butter, sugar, and eggs until well combined, then whisk in the hot water and molasses. Add the molasses mixture to the dry ingredients and stir until just combined.

Pour the batter into the prepared pan. Bake for 40 minutes, or until a toothpick inserted into the center comes out clean. Serve warm, with the sauce drizzled over the top. The gingerbread will keep, tightly covered, in the refrigerator for up to 2 days.

## Caramel Sauce

½ cup packed brown sugar, preferably organic whole cane sugar

1 tablespoon organic cornstarch

⅓ cup heavy cream

1 tablespoon unsalted butter

1 teaspoon vanilla extract (page 261)

In a small saucepan over medium heat, whisk together the sugar and cornstarch, then stir in ¼ cup water and whisk until smooth. Add the cream and butter and cook until the sauce is thickened and bubbly. Remove the pan from the heat and stir in the vanilla. Serve immediately or store in an airtight container in the fridge for up to 3 days. To reheat, warm in a small saucepan over medium heat until heated through.

# Butterscotch Pudding

*serves six*

Chocolate is great, and vanilla is a crowd-pleaser, but given the choice, I'll always pick butterscotch. I've never understood the fascination with boxed pudding mixes—it doesn't take all that much effort to make your own pudding from real ingredients. The only thing missing from this silky, from-scratch dessert is the fake butterscotch flavoring you get from the instant varieties, which really isn't anything to miss, of course.

3 cups whole milk

¼ cup organic cornstarch

½ teaspoon fine sea salt

6 tablespoons (¾ stick) unsalted butter

1 cup packed dark brown sugar, preferably organic whole cane sugar

5 large egg yolks, beaten

2 teaspoons vanilla extract (page 261)

In a large bowl, combine the milk, cornstarch, and salt and set aside. In a medium saucepan over medium heat, melt the butter, then stir in the sugar. At first the mixture will be granular, then it will go through a stage of separating before it finally comes together into a smooth, shiny, cohesive mixture. Stir it continuously throughout this whole process.

Once the mixture comes together and starts to barely bubble, slowly stir in the milk mixture. You'll see some chunks of sugar in the milk at first, which is fine. Continue to whisk and stir until all the sugar dissolves and the mixture thickens.

Pour a small amount (about ¼ cup) of the thickened mixture into the eggs, whisking continuously, to heat the eggs gradually without scrambling them. Repeat until you've incorporated several cups of the hot mixture into the eggs, then pour the heated egg mixture back into the saucepan. Bring to a boil and boil for 1 minute, stirring continuously.

Remove the pan from the heat, stir in the vanilla, and strain through a sieve into a large, clean bowl to catch any rogue bits of egg. Spoon into small bowls or ramekins and chill for at least 2 hours before serving. Top with whipped cream (page 248), if desired.

*kitchen notes · There are two points in this recipe where I start to doubt myself every time. The first is when I start whisking the butter and sugar—it tends to separate in a weird way that makes you think it'll never blend together. But then, suddenly, it does. The second is when the milk is initially added and the sugar creates small chunks. The answer in both situations? Keep whisking and don't give up! Eventually and somewhat magically, it all comes together.*

# Blueberry Cheesecake
# Ice Cream

There's blueberry ice cream, and then there's *this* blueberry ice cream that gets all fancy and special with bits of cream cheese and the rich tang of buttermilk. If you plan to make homemade ice cream a part of your routine, I recommend investing in a machine with a refreezable bowl. I know, it's not as old-fashioned as a hand-crank machine, but it makes the process so much simpler. You don't need bags of ice and boxes of salt to stand between you and homemade ice cream bliss.

2 cups fresh or frozen blueberries

¾ cup sugar, preferably organic whole cane sugar

8 ounces cream cheese (page 245)

1 cup buttermilk (page 244)

1 cup whole milk

1 tablespoon vanilla extract (page 261)

¼ teaspoon lemon zest

Pinch of sea salt

2 cups heavy cream

Crushed graham crackers, for serving (optional)

In a small saucepan over medium-low heat, combine the blueberries, sugar, and 1 tablespoon water and bring to a simmer. Cook for 7 to 8 minutes, or until the berries soften and the sauce begins to thicken. Remove from the heat and allow to cool for 10 minutes.

In a blender, combine the cooled blueberry sauce, cream cheese, buttermilk, milk, vanilla, lemon zest, and salt. Process on high until completely blended and smooth, about 1 minute.

Pour the blueberry mixture into a large bowl and stir in the cream. Cover tightly and chill in the refrigerator for 2 hours. Freeze in a 2-quart ice cream maker according to the manufacturer's instructions.

Serve immediately or, if you prefer firmer ice cream, cover tightly and place in the freezer for at least 1 hour to harden up a bit. When ready to serve, scoop into dessert dishes or small bowls and sprinkle with graham cracker crumbs, if desired.

*kitchen notes · This recipe is one of the rare occasions when I don't soften the cream cheese first. Adding it cold from the refrigerator results in little bits of cream cheese remaining in the finished ice cream. Yum.*

# Chocolate Frozen Yogurt

Believe it or not, froyo on the homestead is even easier than homemade ice cream. For the very best results, only use high-quality whole-milk yogurt (preferably the kind with the cream top). Skip Greek yogurt (it's too tangy) and definitely avoid skim or low-fat yogurts (they create too many ice crystals). Or just make your own yogurt using the instructions on page 48. If chocolate isn't your thing, omit the cocoa powder and mix in 1 cup pureed fresh berries for a fruity frozen yogurt.

**4 cups plain whole-milk yogurt**

**½ cup sugar, preferably organic whole cane sugar**

**¼ cup cocoa powder**

**2 tablespoons maple syrup**

**1 teaspoon vanilla extract (page 261)**

In a large bowl, mix together all the ingredients until the sugar and cocoa are mostly dissolved (a blender is especially handy for this). Taste the mixture and add more sugar if needed. I've found frozen yogurt tends to fade in sweetness after you freeze it, so add more sugar at this stage if you are craving a sweeter dessert. Freeze in a 2-quart ice cream maker according to the manufacturer's instructions.

We like our frozen yogurt soft-serve style, but you can also transfer it to a container with a lid and keep it in the freezer for later. The texture won't be as smooth, but it'll still be yummy.

# Lavender Honey Custards

The sweet floral notes of lavender mingled with honey make this smooth baked custard nothing short of dreamy. If you have them, duck eggs add an extra degree of silkiness. At the moment, I have three male ducks and no females, which is less than handy when you need duck eggs. You can bet there will be ducklings coming to the homestead this spring to remedy that situation.

| | |
|---|---|
| 2 cups whole milk | ⅓ cup honey |
| 1 tablespoon dried lavender buds | 1 teaspoon vanilla extract (page 261) |
| 4 duck or chicken eggs | ¼ teaspoon fine sea salt |

Preheat the oven to 325°F.

In a medium saucepan over low heat, combine the milk and lavender and bring to a very gentle simmer, stirring frequently, for about 10 minutes, to allow the lavender to infuse into the milk. Strain the milk and discard the lavender.

In a separate medium bowl, beat the eggs, honey, vanilla, and salt. Slowly whisk in the lavender milk a little bit at a time. Divide the custard among four custard cups or ramekins.

Place the cups in a baking dish and fill the dish with hot water to halfway up the sides of the cups to create a water bath. Bake for 60 to 70 minutes, or until the custards are set but still loose. I check by touching the top lightly—a little jiggle is fine, but they should not still be liquid.

Remove the cups from the water bath and cool on a wire rack for 30 minutes before serving, or cover and refrigerate the cooled custards for at least 3 hours for a chilled dessert. Custards will keep tightly covered in the refrigerator for up to 2 days.

# Fudgy Sourdough Brownies

If you have any sourdough skeptics in your life, you can easily convert them with these brownies. It may seem like an unlikely combo at first glance, but sourdough and chocolate go together like peanut butter and jelly. The richness of the chocolate plays beautifully with the tanginess of the sourdough, making these brownies a sweet way to keep excess starter from (literally) going down the drain.

1½ cups packed brown sugar, preferably organic whole cane sugar

1¼ cups coconut oil, melted

3 large eggs

1½ cups sourdough starter (page 256)

2 teaspoons vanilla extract (page 261)

½ cup all-purpose flour

½ cup cocoa powder

½ teaspoon fine sea salt

1 cup chocolate chips

Preheat the oven to 375°F. Grease a 9 x 13–inch pan.

In a large bowl, combine the sugar and oil, then mix in the eggs, sourdough starter, and vanilla.

In a separate bowl, mix together the flour, cocoa powder, and salt and add to the wet ingredients, stirring until just combined.

Pour the batter into the prepared pan. Bake for 20 to 25 minutes, or until a toothpick inserted into the center comes out clean. Remove from the oven and immediately sprinkle with the chocolate chips and let them sit for a few minutes to soften before spreading them evenly across the top of the brownies.

Cool for 30 minutes, then transfer them to the freezer for 1 hour. Let the brownies sit at room temperature for 20 minutes and slice before serving. Store tightly covered at room temperature for up to 2 days.

*kitchen notes* · *Either semisweet or milk chocolate chips will work for these brownies. And of course, the chocolate chip layer is optional, but really . . . who wants to omit chocolate chips?*

*The freezer step might sound strange, but it has a magical way of making brownies extra fudgy. Trust me. Skip it at your own risk.*

# Prairie Cream Puffs

Cream puffs are usually considered a slightly fussy dessert. I don't do fussy, so this is my rustic homestead version. These are best eaten the day you make them, as they tend to get a bit soggy on the second day. (Don't worry, though—leftovers never seem to be a problem.) These puffs will happily hold pudding or pastry cream mixtures, but I love the lightness of the cocoa whipped cream.

½ cup (1 stick) unsalted butter

1 cup all-purpose flour

¼ teaspoon fine sea salt

4 large eggs, at room temperature

Cocoa Cream Filling (recipe follows) or filling of your choice

Powdered sugar or cocoa powder, for serving (optional)

Preheat the oven to 425°F. Line a baking sheet with parchment paper.

In a medium saucepan over low heat, heat the butter and 1 cup water until the butter is melted. Add the flour and salt, stirring with a wooden spoon until the mixture forms a soft ball. Transfer to the bowl of a stand mixer fitted with a paddle attachment and beat in the eggs one at a time on medium speed until the mixture is glossy and smooth.

Drop the dough in 12 evenly sized mounds onto the prepared baking sheet. Bake for 15 minutes, then reduce the oven temperature to 375°F and bake for an additional 10 minutes, until the tops are golden brown.

Cool the puffs completely, about 30 minutes, then split them in half crosswise, scoop out the inner flesh, and fill with cocoa cream filling or other filling of your choice. Put the tops of the cream puffs back on and dust with powdered sugar or cocoa powder, if desired.

## Cocoa Cream Filling

1 cup cold heavy cream

3 tablespoons cocoa powder

3 tablespoons maple syrup

2 teaspoons vanilla extract (page 261)

Pinch of sea salt

In the bowl of a stand mixer fitted with the whisk attachment, combine all the ingredients and beat on high speed until stiff peaks form, about 7 minutes.

# Honey Caramel Corn

Caramel corn is always a hit at gatherings, and I love that this version doesn't use corn syrup like so many other recipes. It comes together in a flash, so it's my emergency dessert when I've committed myself to bringing something to a potluck or party and then have promptly forgotten until a few hours before heading out the door. When you're ready to combine the popped kernels and caramel sauce, use a bigger bowl than you think you'll need—the popcorn likes to fly out of the bowl when you're mixing everything together.

¾ cup unpopped popcorn kernels

½ cup (1 stick) unsalted butter or coconut oil

⅓ cup honey

½ cup packed brown sugar, preferably organic whole cane sugar

Pinch of sea salt

½ teaspoon baking soda

1 teaspoon vanilla extract (page 261)

Pop the popcorn on the stove top or in an air-popper and place it in a large bowl. (Use a bigger bowl than you think you'll need so you have plenty of room for mixing.)

In a medium saucepan over low heat, melt the butter with the honey, sugar, and salt. Bring to a gentle simmer and cook for 5 minutes, stirring continuously.

Remove the pan from the heat and stir in the baking soda and vanilla. It will foam up and then settle down as you stir. Pour the caramel sauce over the popped corn. The sauce will rapidly begin to harden, so work quickly with a wooden spoon to fully coat all the popcorn with the sauce.

For slightly less sticky caramel corn, spread the coated popcorn on baking sheets and bake at 250°F for 30 minutes, stirring two or three times during baking to make sure it cooks evenly. We don't mind sticky caramel corn, so I usually skip the baking step.

Cool for 15 minutes before serving. Store in an airtight container for up to 2 days.

# homestead sips

*Burnout.* *In a world with so many options and* an increasingly fast pace, it's a phenomenon with which we're all intimately familiar. Jam-packed calendars, activities every night of the week, and a never-ending stream of commitments have the potential to create the perfect cocktail of stress and exhaustion that leaves us not caring about much of anything. I've been there more than once—it's not fun and it takes a long time to recover. For many, including myself, the pursuit of simple living is an antidote for burnout, but I've discovered that if I'm not careful, it can creep into an old-fashioned lifestyle too.

Outwardly, the small farm routine looks romantic. There are chirping yellow chicks, vibrant spreads of homegrown vegetables, and newborn calves with velvety noses. And I would argue that it *is* romantic. At times. There are plenty of days where I'm overcome by the quaint magnificence of our little homestead. But behind the colorful vegetables and fuzzy farm animals, there's a whole lot of work. Plain, dirty, gritty, unromantic, and sometimes monotonous work.

Homesteading can be a backbreaking journey requiring the blood, sweat, and tears of anyone who dares to pull on their muck boots and venture into the world of home food production. Animals don't take vacations or observe holidays, which means sometimes we don't get to either. The ice on the water tank must be chopped and hay must be fed to hungry mouths, regardless of whether you are sick in bed or it's Christmas Day and you have a houseful of guests waiting for the ham to come out of the oven.

Spring brings with it a level of hustle my city-dwelling friends can barely fathom. New calves hit the ground precisely at the same time you bring home the irresistible yellow chicks from the feed store, and the garden somehow transforms from completely dormant to urgently requiring prepping and planting overnight. It's sheer insanity.

Summer starts, and with it comes the slightest lull. For a while you get to settle comfortably into a routine of weeding, watering, and tending the growing babies. But then harvest season hits you in the face and you find yourself lugging basket upon basket of produce into the house with barely enough time to deal with one day's harvest before the next finds its way to your countertops.

It may surprise you, but ten years into this homesteading gig, I have yet to wish away the workload. Do I get tired? Most definitely—exhausted might even be a more accurate description during certain times. But I still crave the rhythm of the seasons and the work that comes with it.

That said, homestead burnout is very real. One of the ways I have learned to combat it is with intentional self-care, which is something that looks different for everyone. For some, it equates to bubble baths and pedicures, while for others, it might be a stroll down a country road at dusk, or taking a moment to pause, breathe, and enjoy a cold glass of mint iced tea. Practicing self-care and maintaining intentional rest periods has made all the difference in my personal battle against burnout, both as a homesteader, and as a mom and business owner. I know if I have a good book and a cup of chai waiting for me at the end of a frigid day of chopping ice and chipping frozen cow patties from the barn, I stay more motivated. Or I punctuate a long day raking, hoeing, and pushing seeds into fresh garden soil with a midday pause and a frosty glass of Honey Lemonade in my hand. As you craft your own routine of self-care, I hope the drinks in this chapter fill your cup (both literally and figuratively), no matter what sort of pressure your daily schedule may bring. Drink up, my friends.

# Honey Lemonade

You know that final phase of summer where you find yourself perpetually sweating, the grass is brown and ugly, and the flies attempt to attach themselves to your face? This lemonade is precisely for those times. Let's pour ourselves a tall glass, sit in the shade, and dream of snow, shall we?

**1 cup fresh lemon juice (from 6 to 8 lemons)**

**½ cup honey**

**Lemon slices, for garnish (optional)**

In a 2-quart pitcher, combine the lemon juice and honey, then stir 5 cups water. Chill for 3 hours. Serve over ice with a slice of lemon as a garnish, if desired.

*kitchen notes · This recipe works just as well with limes as it does with lemons, if you have a hankering for limeade.*

*If you don't have access to fresh lemons or limes, organic bottled juice will work in a pinch.*

*As written, this recipe isn't sugary sweet. It's easy to swirl in more honey if you'd prefer it a tad sweeter.*

# Real Cream Soda

*serves one*

It was late. I was tired. I was craving something sweet and creamy, but alas, there wasn't much in the refrigerator. A carton of fresh raspberries, a dab of cream, and some sparkling water later, I was kicking up my feet with this drink in my hand. Not only was my craving satisfied, I accidentally created one of my favorite drinks of all time. Necessity is the mother of invention when you live 40 miles from the grocery store, and it's even better when the invention involves velvety, fizzy sweetness.

½ cup ice cubes

¼ cup Fruit Syrup (recipe follows)

¼ teaspoon vanilla extract (page 261)

¾ cup sparkling water

3 tablespoons half-and-half

In a tall glass, place the ice cubes and add the fruit syrup. Then add the vanilla and sparkling water and finish with the half-and-half. Admire the layers of color before stirring and sipping.

# Fruit Syrup

*makes two to three cups*

2 cups fresh or frozen strawberries, raspberries, or blueberries

1 cup sugar, preferably organic whole cane sugar

In a small saucepan over low heat, combine the fruit, sugar, and 2 cups water. Bring to a gentle simmer and cook for 10 minutes. Remove from the heat and mash the berries with a fork to release their juices.

Pour the mixture through a sieve and cool. (Save the mashed fruit to add to smoothies or to spread on biscuits or toast.) Store the syrup in an airtight container in the refrigerator for up to 2 weeks.

# Watermelon Basil Cooler

Bonus points if you grow your own watermelons *and* basil. However, if you don't, just follow in my footsteps and grab a watermelon or two from the farmers' market to complement the basil growing in your herb garden. Basil and watermelon may seem like an unlikely combination at first glance, but they actually tango beautifully. This herby slush is the perfect reward after a sweaty day of summer homestead projects.

**4 heaping cups 1-inch chunks cold watermelon**

**1½ cups ice cubes**

**¼ cup roughly chopped basil leaves**

**1 teaspoon lime juice**

In a blender, combine all the ingredients and process on high until the basil is thoroughly chopped, about 1 minute. Serve immediately.

*kitchen notes · Watermelons vary in sweetness, so if your melon is a bit bland, add 1 or 2 teaspoons honey to the mix.*

# Haymaker's Punch

I was completely intrigued the first time I heard mention of haymaker's punch, also known as switchel. It's an old-fashioned version of our modern-day sports drink that was favored by haying crews in colonial times. Historic recipes contained vinegar, ginger, and molasses, which just so happen to be considerable sources of potassium—a mineral we lose as we sweat. The vinegar lends a tangy flavor to the punch, making it surprisingly satisfying on hot sweaty days. I like to mix mine with a bit of sparkling water for an even more refreshing drink.

3 tablespoons honey

3 tablespoons apple cider vinegar

1 tablespoon lemon juice

1 teaspoon ground ginger

sparkling water (optional)

In a 2-quart pitcher, combine all the ingredients with 4 cups water, stirring thoroughly to make sure the honey dissolves completely. Chill for at least 2 hours before serving so the flavors have a chance to mingle. Serve over ice or combine 2 parts punch to 1 part sparkling water.

# Homemade Mint Syrup

Sometimes I just want to be a rebel and not follow the rules. So when they said, "Be sure to only plant mint in pots," I threw caution to the wind and planted it right in my herb garden. And then of course, it attempted to completely overthrow the rest of the plants in said herb garden. Whoops. Thankfully this easy syrup recipe will help cover a multitude of mint-planting sins.

**1 cup sugar, preferably organic whole cane sugar, or ¼ cup honey**

**1 cup mint leaves, roughly chopped**

In a small saucepan over low heat, bring the sugar and 1 cup water to a boil. Add the mint and simmer for 15 minutes, stirring occasionally. Remove the pan from the heat and strain the syrup; discard the mint. Pour the syrup into a glass jar with a lid, cool slightly, and store in the refrigerator for up to 1 month.

*kitchen notes* · *To make iced tea, add ½ cup mint syrup, or to taste, to 2 quarts brewed iced tea. Stir well and serve.*

*I often grow a variety of mint plants, including spearmint, and I add them all to this recipe. It's good no matter which variety of mint you use.*

*You can use unrefined cane sugars, coconut sugar, or even just regular white sugar if that's all you have. Unrefined sugars will result in a darker, stronger-tasting syrup, while honey or white sugar will produce a lighter-colored result.*

*I usually double, triple, or quadruple this recipe when I make it. Mint is crazy-growing stuff, man.*

# Pumpkin Pie Milkshakes

Once upon a time, the advertisements in town for pumpkin milkshakes would turn my head, but now I just drive home and make this instead. The magic of this creamy shake comes from freezing the mixture in ice cube trays before tossing it back into the blender for a final whirl. The consistency is deliciously close to soft-serve ice cream, and tastes surprisingly rich for only having a few tablespoons of maple syrup.

2 cups whole milk

¾ cup pumpkin puree (page 267)

¼ cup maple syrup

2 teaspoons vanilla extract
(page 261)

1½ teaspoons pumpkin pie spice
(recipe follows), plus more for
garnish

⅔ cup whipped cream (page 248),
for serving

In a high-powered blender, combine all the ingredients except the whipped cream and process on high until incorporated, about 1 minute.

Pour the mixture into two ice cube trays and freeze for at least 2 hours. Place the cubes back into the blender and blend until smooth, about 1 minute, then pour into glasses. Top with a dollop of whipped cream and a dash of pumpkin pie spice. Serve immediately.

*kitchen notes · You can make and freeze the cubes well in advance, but I've found the best consistency comes from cubes that are slightly soft. I usually freeze mine for only 2 hours. If they are frozen solid, I let them sit at room temperature for 15 to 20 minutes, or until slightly softened, before blending for the creamiest texture.*

# Pumpkin Pie Spice

¼ cup ground cinnamon

4 teaspoons ground nutmeg

1 tablespoon ground ginger

1 tablespoon ground cloves

In a small bowl, combine all the ingredients and mix well. Store in an airtight container at room temperature for up to 1 year.

# Chai Concentrate

When the horses start getting a little extra fuzz around their chins and the breeze carries that unmistakable crispness, it's time to break out the chai. This spicy, sweet concentrate is worth the effort it takes to gather the spices. I usually buy them in bulk from my local health food store as they are more affordable that way, and I can get many batches of chai from each purchase. If you're feeling extra sassy, add a splash of cream with the milk.

½ cup honey or packed brown sugar, preferably organic whole cane sugar

1 (2-inch) knob fresh ginger, peeled and sliced into medallions

5 cinnamon sticks

3 star anise pods

15 whole cloves

10 allspice berries

2 teaspoons cardamom seeds

8 black tea bags

2 tablespoons vanilla extract (page 261)

Milk of your choice

In a medium saucepan over low heat, heat the honey and 6 cups water until the honey is dissolved. Add the ginger, cinnamon sticks, star anise, cloves, allspice, and cardamom and simmer for 20 minutes, stirring occasionally. Remove from the heat, add the tea bags, and steep for 10 minutes. Strain to remove the spices and tea bags and stir in the vanilla. Store the finished concentrate in the refrigerator for up to 3 weeks.

To serve, mix 2 parts concentrate to 1 part milk. Gently warm over low heat before pouring into mugs.

*kitchen notes · Chai is pretty flexible, so if you are missing one or two of the spices in the ingredient list, make it anyway—you'll still end up with a pretty darn awesome tea.*

# Creamy Eggnog

I think we should start a petition to normalize year-round eggnog consumption. It's just as tasty in the summer as it is around the holidays, not to mention that it has *homesteader* written all over it when you consider it uses a generous share of fresh eggs and milk. If I have a source of clean, farm-fresh eggs, I have no problem making raw eggnog. Otherwise, I stick to this thick, rich, cooked version.

6 large egg yolks

2 cups whole milk

1½ cups heavy cream

½ cup maple syrup

½ teaspoon ground cinnamon

½ teaspoon ground nutmeg

Pinch of fine sea salt

2 teaspoons vanilla extract (page 261)

In a small bowl, whisk the yolks and set aside.

In a medium saucepan over low heat, combine the milk, cream, maple syrup, cinnamon, nutmeg, and salt and heat until small bubbles form around the edges.

Slowly whisk about half the heated milk mixture into the yolks. This will gradually increase the temperature of the eggs without scrambling them (hopefully).

Pour the heated egg mixture back into the saucepan and cook it over very low heat until the eggnog is thick enough to coat a spoon.

Remove from the heat and stir in the vanilla. If you see little bits of egg floating on top, strain the nog through a sieve. Otherwise, pour it into a jar or pitcher, cover, and chill for at least 6 hours or overnight before serving.

*kitchen notes · For uncooked (and quicker) eggnog, combine all the ingredients in a blender and mix thoroughly. To make raw eggnog thicker, reserve ½ cup of the cream and, in the bowl of a stand mixer fitted with the whisk attachment, beat the cream with the unused egg whites on high speed until stiff peaks form, about 7 minutes. Chill as above before serving.*

*For boozy eggnog, stir 4 to 8 ounces of rum, bourbon, or brandy into the chilled eggnog.*

# Salted Caramel Coffee Creamer

Sometimes I wish I were one of those tough girls who drinks black coffee so stiff a spoon will stand up in it, but alas, I love cream far too much. I won't tell you exactly how much of this salted caramel creamer I add to my cup, but let's just say my coffee is far more on the light side than the dark.

1 cup packed brown sugar, preferably organic whole cane sugar

1 cup heavy cream

¾ cup whole milk

1 teaspoon vanilla extract (page 261)

¼ teaspoon fine sea salt

In a small saucepan over medium heat, bring the sugar and ½ cup water to a boil and simmer for 5 minutes. (Watch the pot closely—this mixture likes to boil over!) Remove from the heat and stir in the cream, milk, vanilla, and salt.

Store in an airtight container in the refrigerator for up to 2 weeks. Add as much to your coffee as you like—I won't tell.

# From-Scratch Mulled Cider

Someday I'll have a cider press and an apple orchard, but it might be a ways down the road considering I killed my only two apple trees within three months of planting them. Whoops. In the meantime, I'll enjoy this homemade cider recipe with organic apples and a handful of autumn-inspired spices. It'll make your house smell divine as it cooks, so I absolutely recommend simmering it before friends come over to visit on crisp October days. I like to add a bit of extra sweetener to mine, but depending on what type of apples you use, you may be able to skip it altogether.

8 to 10 apples, quartered (there's no need to core them)

1 orange, sliced

⅓ to ½ cup packed brown sugar, preferably organic whole cane sugar

1 (1-inch) knob fresh ginger

3 cinnamon sticks, plus more for stirring

1 teaspoon whole cloves

3 star anise pods

In a stockpot over high heat, combine the fruit, sugar, spices, and 14 cups water. Bring to a boil, reduce the heat to low, cover, and simmer for 2 hours.

Mash the apples with a potato masher to help them release their juices and cook for 1 hour more. Strain out the solids and donate them to your chickens or compost bucket. Serve the cider warm or chilled with a cinnamon stick for stirring. Store covered in the refrigerator for up to 7 days.

*kitchen notes · A mix of apple varieties often makes the best tasting cider, so don't be afraid to use several different types of apples in your batch. I like a mix of sweet and tart varieties. Homemade cider is also the perfect way to use up wrinkly or less-than-crisp fruit.*

*To make cider in a slow cooker, place all the ingredients in the slow cooker, cover, and cook on high for 4 hours, mash, then cover and cook on high for 1 hour more. Proceed as above to remove the solids and serve.*

# prairie pantry staples

*When you open my fridge, the first thing that* catches your eye will be the jars. So many jars. The largest ones are filled to the brim with raw milk from Mabel or Oakley, our Brown Swiss cows, while others proudly display yellowish whey, cultured yogurt, or thick homemade buttermilk. The quarts of home-rendered lard and skimmed cream are neighbors, and it's hard to tell them apart until you give the jars a gentle shake. Pickles, kimchi, sauerkraut, and raw vinegar live on the top shelf, with homemade chicken or beef stock residing somewhere in the middle. There are smaller jars in various stages of consumption tucked in the corners, filled with homemade jams and jellies, salsa, salad dressings, and cooked beans and a little blue bucket stocked with cheese cultures and rennet sitting on the bottom shelf.

The kitchen counters follow the same theme, featuring a jar of bubbling sourdough starter, baskets of just-collected eggs, ferments in various stages of fermenting, and the occasional jar of kombucha with a giant SCOBY floating on top.

A peek inside our freezers in the barn will reveal hundreds of packages of homegrown meat tightly wrapped in white butcher paper and stacked with Tetris-style precision. Bags bursting with garden green beans or corn are stashed in the doors and corners, with containers of homemade ricotta and butter tucked away in between.

You see, among all the jars and packages lies the secret of from-scratch cooking. That homemade pesto with fresh pasta? The pesto was created in large batches three months ago and frozen, leaving only the pasta to be made the day of serving. The creamy chicken noodle soup? The chicken was roasted for a meal two days prior, and the broth was simmered a day after that, which makes it a cinch to sauté a few veggies and throw the rest of the dish together on a cool fall evening after chores are done.

Homestead cooking is about creating in phases and squirreling away homemade ingredients here and there. A little bit of time devoted to developing your ingredient stockpile each week will result in a refrigerator, pantry, and freezer ready to aid you in creating impressive from-scratch goodness at a moment's notice. Use the recipes in this chapter to fill your freezer, fridge, and pantry with homemade ingredients and you'll be well on your way to cooking like a homesteader.

# Nourishing Homemade Stock

*makes three to four quarts*

If there's one pantry staple I can't live without, it's homemade stock. I haven't purchased broth from the store in over seven years. On the rare occasions I do run out, you'll find me in full panic mode until I have a fresh pot simmering away on the stove. I add it to as many recipes as possible, not only for its rich nutrients (protein, minerals, and collagen, just to name a few), but also for the amazing depth of flavor it brings to every dish. (You will especially love the richness it adds to the French Onion Soup, page 98, and Chicken Poblano Chowder, page 105.) Once you start cooking with from-scratch broth, you'll never be satisfied with the watery, store-bought stuff again.

2 to 3 pounds beef bones, or
1 leftover roasted chicken carcass

2 carrots, coarsely chopped

2 stalks celery, coarsely chopped

1 large onion, coarsely chopped

6 cloves garlic

3 tablespoons apple cider vinegar (optional)

2 tablespoons dried rosemary

2 tablespoons dried oregano

2 tablespoons dried thyme

1 tablespoon fine sea salt

10 black peppercorns

3 bay leaves

Preheat the oven to 350°F.

If you are using beef bones, roast them in the oven in a shallow roasting pan, flipping them once so they brown on all sides. If you're in a hurry, you can skip this step, but roasting adds an amazing depth of flavor, so I recommend it if you have time. The bones don't need to be completely cooked, you're just looking for that pretty brown crust on all sides.

In a slow cooker or stockpot, combine the bones, veggies, vinegar (if using), and seasonings and cover with 4 to 6 quarts cool water. Let sit for 30 minutes.

Set your slow cooker or burner on low, cover, and simmer, checking after 1 hour and skimming any scum or impurities from the surface. Simmer for 12 to 36 hours more.

Strain the finished stock into jars and store tightly covered in the fridge for up to 2 weeks. For long-term storage, freeze for up to 12 months or pressure can it.

*(continued)*

*kitchen notes* · *Any beef bones will work for stock, but a mixture of meaty bones and joints (like knucklebones) are the best combination if you're looking for maximum flavor and collagen.*

*For chicken stock, my favorite trick is to roast a chicken for supper, pull all the meat from the bones, then toss the bones and skin right back into the pot with the cooking juices. I add random veggies, extra herbs, and water, and simmer it all night for the best chicken stock you've ever had.*

*You can keep a "broth bag" in your freezer and fill it with random accumulated veggie scraps—celery tops, carrot tops, and onion ends, for example. These bits and pieces can be tossed into your next batch of broth, which makes it even more cost-effective.*

*I actually rarely follow this recipe exactly as written. Surprise! Homemade broth is extremely forgiving, and I generally just dump whatever I have into a pot without bothering to measure. The bones and water are really the most important components here—everything else can be swapped or easily omitted. (Although I would argue the salt is key as well—unsalted stock is pretty blah.)*

*The salt content of homemade stock will vary from batch to batch. It's easy to add too little or too much salt or seasoning to a recipe if you are just following the directions, so always taste-test any recipes made with homemade stock and adjust the seasoning as needed.*

# my broth looks like Jell-O!

Congratulations! You've achieved the ultimate goal of every home broth maker: gelled broth. A jar of jiggling broth is proof that the collagen in the bones was successfully extracted. Collagen is an abundant protein in the body and has health benefits for joints, gut, skin, hair, and more. It's earning a lot of accolades in health circles lately, and many folks even add collagen supplements to their diets. In short, it's a really good thing. Even though I've been simmering stocks for years, I can't help but get giddy when I peek into my latest batch and see a gorgeous mass of gelatin. Just wait—you'll be dancing around the kitchen the first time it happens to you too.

However, thanks to all the buzz about gelled broth, I get lots of emails from home cooks who are afraid they've ruined their broth when it stays liquid. The good news is, gel or no gel, homemade broth is still outrageously good for you.

(P.S. Broth only gels after it completely cools—so don't expect to see any jiggling while it's still hot.)

If you've been chasing the elusive gel factor, here are some tips to increase your chances.

## 1. Use More Joints

The connective tissue and cartilage in joints make them your best bet for collagen-rich beef stock. Use meaty bones (like oxtails, short ribs, or soup bones) along with knucklebones or joints for the best-tasting stock with the greatest odds of jiggling. Whole chicken carcasses will yield the richest chicken stock, which is another reason to skip buying packages of individual parts and purchase whole birds instead. And if you're feeling extra-adventurous, adding several chicken feet (peel them first) to the pot will greatly increase your chances of gelled stock.

### 2. Soak in Vinegar

Adding a splash of apple cider vinegar jump-starts the process of extracting minerals from the bones. To do this, put all the ingredients in your stockpot and add several tablespoons of vinegar. Let the pot sit for 30 to 60 minutes before turning on the heat. Don't worry—you won't be able to taste the vinegar in the finished product.

### 3. Simmer Longer

I usually simmer stock for around 12 hours, but hard-core bone broth enthusiasts will cook for 24 to 72 hours to maximize gelatin amounts. The longer the stock simmers, the more concentrated it will be. (You may need to add more water at some point, so keep an eye on the pot.) If you're not sure how long you should simmer, let taste be your guide.

### 4. Use a Pressure Cooker

Slow cooker, stove top, pressure cooker—if there's a way to make stock, I've tried it. While I still regularly use my slow cooker and stove top for making stock, I've found the greatest occurrences of gelatin to occur when I use my electric pressure cooker (stovetop pressure cookers work too). I'm not sure if it's the high heat of the cooker or the fact I usually have a higher bone-to-water ratio in the smaller pot, but I love how it takes less time (only 60 to 90 minutes, plus time to cool) and produces plenty of jiggly broth.

### 5. Reduce the Water

I suspect overdilution to be the most common reason stock doesn't gel. Aim for 3 to 4 pounds of bones for every gallon of water, although I never actually measure mine. If your stock cools completely and is still liquid, you can always put it back in the pot with the bones and cook it awhile longer, allowing more water to evaporate.

# Sweet Cream Butter

*makes about one pound (yield varies)*

I have a serious obsession with the processes of transforming milk into all sorts of fascinating things. A jar of white liquid turning into a golden-yellow solid is just about as miraculous as it gets. Homegrown, home-churned butter is one of the main reasons I feed, care for, and milk a 1,200-pound milk cow throughout the year, including in the dead of winter. Fresh butter has a richer, deeper flavor and is usually a richer shade of yellow than the anemic white sticks from the store. Butter is the fat I use the most in my cooking, which makes it worth every frigid early morning milking. Not to mention you just can't beat home-churned butter on a warm slice of homemade bread. Three cheers for butter!

**1 quart heavy cream (or a gallon, or a bucket, or whatever—you can't have too much butter)**

**Fine sea salt**

An hour or two before you plan to make butter, pull the cream from the refrigerator and let it warm to room temperature on the counter. (I always have better luck with room-temperature cream than I do with chilled.)

In a food processor, blender, or stand mixer fitted with the whisk, process the cream on high speed. First the cream will thicken and form stiff peaks, then it will turn into a chunky version of whipped cream, and finally it will "break." This is when the butterfat separates from the buttermilk. Pour off the bulk of the buttermilk and reserve it for later, and transfer the butter clumps to a bowl.

Run cool water over the butter while using a wooden spoon or paddle to press the clumps together and squeeze out the remaining buttermilk. The more buttermilk you remove, the harder the butter will be, and the longer it will last in the fridge.

Once you've kneaded and pressed out as much buttermilk as possible and the water is running clear, knead in a pinch or two of salt. Place the butter in an airtight container or wrap it tightly in plastic wrap and store in the fridge for up to 5 days or freeze for up to 9 months.

*kitchen notes · If you don't have a milk cow, no worries. Store-bought heavy cream (either raw or pasteurized) will work just fine for this recipe.*

*Homemade butter is utterly delicious spread on a hunk of homemade bread, or use it to add extra flavor to recipes like the Baked Eggs with Cream & Chives (page 28) or Browned Butter Skillet Corn (page 121).*

## BUTTER EQUIPMENT

Butter making can be as simple or as high-tech as you'd like. Agitated cream makes butter, so as long as you're agitating the cream, you'll get there eventually. It just depends how long you want it to take. While you can purchase electric and hand-powered versions of the classic butter churn, I often use a food processor to make mine. Another option is a stand mixer fitted with the whisk—just be sure to cover the bowl with a towel while you're mixing so you don't fling cream all over your kitchen. (This is the voice of experience talking.)

# Cultured Buttermilk

*makes one quart*

Poor buttermilk. Often relegated to random corners of the dairy case at the store, it just doesn't get the press it deserves. Homestead chefs know real cultured buttermilk is a gold mine for making tangy, mouth-watering pancakes, buttermilk biscuits (page 168), salad dressing (page 268), marinades, or mashed potatoes. And now you can have a jar of your very own in the fridge at all times.

**4 cups whole milk (either raw or pasteurized)**

**1 packet direct-set buttermilk starter culture (see Resources, page 348)**

In a quart-size glass jar, gently stir together the milk and starter culture. Loosely cover the jar with a clean towel and secure with a rubber band.

Culture the milk at room temperature for 12 to 24 hours, until the buttermilk is thick and has a delicious, tangy smell. Store the finished buttermilk in the fridge for up to 3 weeks.

*kitchen notes · If you are in a hurry to make buttermilk but don't have any starter culture hanging around, you can use store-bought buttermilk (as long as it has live, active cultures) to get your batch going in a pinch. Combine 1 cup store-bought cultured buttermilk with 3 cups whole milk and proceed as above.*

*Once you make one batch of buttermilk, you can use it to create future batches. You can usually repeat this three or four times before the cultures get "tired" and you need to create a fresh batch.*

## CULTURED VERSUS OLD-FASHIONED BUTTERMILK

Did you know there are two types of buttermilk? The recipe above helps you create cultured buttermilk—the thick, tangy liquid we love to add to biscuits, dressings, and pancakes. However, there's also old-fashioned buttermilk, which is what's left over after churning the butter on page 242. Cultured and old-fashioned buttermilk *cannot* be used interchangeably in most recipes, but you can substitute old-fashioned buttermilk for the water in many bread or biscuit recipes for a little extra tang.

244    The Prairie Homestead Cookbook

# Fluffy Cream Cheese

Too much cream . . . is there such a thing? (The answer is no, just in case you were wondering.) When our cow is in milk and I'm drowning in cream, I absolutely love to culture jars of cream on my counter to make this decadent treat. It's fantastic on bagels or toast, or use it when you make Strawberry Shortcake Squares (page 199) and Blueberry Cheesecake Ice Cream (page 204). Or you can just eat it by the spoonful. Your secret is safe with me.

2 cups heavy cream

2 cups whole milk

1 package cream cheese starter culture, or ⅛ teaspoon mesophilic starter culture

Fine sea salt (optional)

In a quart-sized glass jar, combine the cream and milk and gently stir in the starter culture.

Loosely cover the jar with a clean towel, secure with a rubber band, and set aside at room temperature for 8 to 12 hours, until the mixture thickens and resembles yogurt. If it's not thickened within 12 hours, leave it out for several hours longer.

Pour the thickened cream into a piece of clean cheesecloth and tie the ends together to form a bag. Loop the bag over a cabinet knob and place a bowl underneath to catch the whey. Let the whey drip out for 6 to 8 hours (the longer it drips, the firmer the cheese will be).

Scrape the drained cheese out of the cheesecloth and lightly salt to taste if desired and stir in until mixed. The salt is optional, but adds flavor and helps the cream cheese last longer in the fridge. Store the finished cream cheese in an airtight container in the refrigerator for up to 10 days.

*kitchen notes · This recipe will work with either raw or pasteurized milk.*

# Chèvre

As exotic as it may sound, *chèvre* is simply the French word for "goat." This isn't the only type of cheese you can make from goat's milk, but it's definitely one of the most-loved, and pairs perfectly with roasted beets (page 120). You can totally make this with cow's milk too—but then you might want to call it *vache* instead, which is the French word for "cow," because calling it *chèvre* would be weird. Just sayin'.

**1 gallon raw goat's milk**

**1 packet direct-set chèvre culture (see Resources, page 348)**

In a stockpot over low heat, warm the milk to 72°F. Sprinkle the starter culture on top and gently stir. Cover and set aside at room temperature for about 12 hours. If your house is chilly, the curd may not form properly, so keep it in a spot in your home where the temperature stays around 72°F.

After culturing, the milk should resemble thick yogurt. There may even be yellow whey rising to the top, which is just fine. Pour the contents of the jar into a clean tea towel or cheesecloth and tie the ends together to form a bag. Loop the bag over a cabinet knob, place a bowl underneath, and hang for 6 hours, or until the whey has finished dripping out.

Store the finished cheese in an airtight container in the fridge for up to 1 week. Serve homemade chèvre with crackers and fruit, use it in place of ricotta or cream cheese, or freeze it in small logs, tightly wrapped in plastic wrap, for up to 3 months. You can also mix in fresh herbs, nuts, or honey; the combinations are endless.

*kitchen notes* · *If you don't have chèvre starter culture, substitute ¼ teaspoon mesophilic culture plus 1 drop liquid rennet dissolved in ¼ cup cool water.*

*Use the leftover whey to make Lemon Whey Pie (page 185) or for any of the other uses on page 250.*

# Simple Whipped Cream

(pictured on page 188)

*makes two cups*

I grew up eating dollops of "whipped topping" on all our desserts, so the first time I made real whipped cream for a homemade pie, I was absolutely certain I had crossed over into Julia Child territory. But here's the secret—making your own whipped cream is hardly any more work than pulling those tubs of fake stuff out of the freezer. Plus, it tastes heaps better and contains plenty of good, healthy fat.

**1 cup chilled heavy cream (either raw or pasteurized)**

**1 to 2 teaspoons maple syrup**
**½ teaspoon vanilla extract (page 261)**

In a medium bowl, if using a handheld mixer, or in the bowl of a standing mixer fitted with the whisk attachment, combine all the ingredients. Beat on high speed until stiff peaks form, about 7 minutes. Serve immediately.

*kitchen notes · If you don't have maple syrup, substitute 2 teaspoons organic powdered sugar or 2 teaspoons honey instead.*

*Homemade whipped cream is especially decadent when served atop homemade Butterscotch Pudding (page 203), Honey Pumpkin Pie (page 189), or an ice-cold Pumpkin Pie Milkshake (page 225).*

## THE BEST CAKE FROSTING

Whipped cream is one of my very favorite cake frostings. It's lighter than buttercream frosting, yet still adds a wonderful decadence to homemade cakes. If you plan to serve a cake immediately, use the above recipe as is. If the cake will be sitting for a day or two before serving, stabilize it with a bit of gelatin so the cream doesn't get all flat and sad: In a small, oven-safe bowl, sprinkle ½ teaspoon unflavored powdered gelatin over 1 tablespoon water. Let sit for 5 minutes.

Place the bowl containing the gelatin mixture into a saucepan filled with several inches of water and bring to a boil until the gelatin is completely melted. Cool completely, about 10 minutes, add to the unbeaten cream when you add the maple syrup and vanilla, and proceed as in the recipe above. Frost your cake immediately. Stabilized whipped cream will keep for up to 2 days in the refrigerator.

# Whole-Milk Ricotta

Ricotta is a beautiful blank slate that can go sweet or savory—the choice is up to you. Traditionally, ricotta is made from reheating leftover whey, but I personally prefer to make this whole-milk version since it produces a greater yield. And who doesn't want more fresh ricotta in their life? Take your homemade ricotta for a test drive in the Tomato Basil Galette (page 92).

**8 cups whole milk**
**¼ cup lemon juice**

**½ teaspoon coarse sea salt**

In a large stockpot over medium heat, combine the milk, lemon juice, and salt and heat to 190°F, stirring frequently.

Remove from the heat and let sit for 10 minutes, or until you see the fluffy white ricotta cheese clouds separating from the yellowish whey in the pot.

Place a colander inside a bowl and line the colander with a clean tea towel or several layers of cheesecloth. Pour the mixture through the towel. Bring up the corners of the towel and tie them together to form a bag. Loop the bag over a cabinet knob, place a bowl underneath, and hang the bag until the whey stops dripping out. (This usually takes several hours.) Store finished ricotta in an airtight container in the fridge for up to 2 weeks or in the freezer for up to 6 months.

*kitchen notes* · *Lemon juice isn't your only option for creating curds. You can also use ¼ cup apple cider vinegar or 1 teaspoon citric acid dissolved in ¼ cup cool water. There's lots of room to play around—as long as you end up with curds at the end, you're on the right track.*

*To make traditional ricotta using only whey, heat 1 to 2 gallons whey to 195°F. When you see the cloudy little curds forming in the pot, remove it from the heat and strain through a piece of cheesecloth. Keep in mind that the yield from whey will be considerably less than for ricotta made from whole milk.*

# how do i use all this whey?

Before venturing into the world of homemade dairy, I never gave much thought to whey, other than mentioning it in the occasional nursery rhyme recitation. Little did I know how inundated I'd become with the stuff once I started experimenting with homemade cheese. Whey is the sticky, yellow liquid that is left over after milk curdles. It's packed full of protein, vitamins, minerals, and enzymes, and is a valuable addition to any kitchen. It's far too precious to pour down the drain, so here are a few ways you can put it to good use around the homestead.

- Substitute whey for water or milk in bread, pancake, waffle, biscuit, roll, or tortilla recipes.

- Add it to smoothies or shakes.

- Use it in marinades.

- Make Lemon Whey Pie (page 185).

- Pour it on your compost pile.

- Dilute it with equal parts water and pour it around plants as fertilizer.

- Feed it to your chickens or pigs.

- Use whey instead of water to cook rice.

- Use it as a substitute for vinegar or lemon juice in homemade vinaigrettes.

- Some people say whey makes an excellent face wash. I haven't tried that yet, but thought I'd throw it out there.

# Rendered Lard

Looking to create some buzz at the water cooler? Just casually mention that you spent your weekend rendering lard—it produces entertaining reactions every single time without fail. Rendering lard or tallow takes a bit of time up front, but you'll be rewarded with jars of amazing cooking fat for months afterwards. The homemade French fries and pie crusts are worth it—promise. The yield varies depending on the amount and type of fat you use.

**Cold or partially frozen leaf fat
(kidney fat) from pigs (any amount
will work)**

Trim any meat or kidney bits from the fat, then chop the fat into small pieces. You can also run it through your food processor or meat grinder. The smaller the bits of fat, the faster it will melt down. If you do use a food processor, be careful not to overprocess the lard, as it has a tendency to heat up and turn into a giant fat ball. (If this does occur, simply break apart the mass as much as possible and proceed with the rest of the recipe.)

Place the small fat pieces and ¼ cup water in a slow cooker set on low or a large stockpot over low heat. Cover. The key is to keep the temperature extremely low. If you render the fat too quickly, it's apt to end up with more of a "piggy" taste and brownish color. It will still be usable, but will likely be too strongly flavored for pastries or pie crusts.

Allow the fat to render for several hours, stirring and checking frequently. You are looking for the bits of meat and gristle to rise to the top, leaving a clear, liquid fat underneath. Avoid boiling the fat or allowing it to burn or stick to the edges, which may result in a stronger flavor in the finished product.

Strain the liquid fat through a piece of fine cheesecloth and store it in glass jars. Some folks keep their rendered lard at room temperature, but I prefer to store it in the refrigerator or freezer long term. It will last many months in cold storage, and I've kept jars in my fridge for well over a year without spoilage.

Use lard for sautéing or frying. Or, if you cooked it carefully and it is mild and white, lard makes beautifully flaky pie crusts and pastries.

*kitchen notes · Use your home-rendered lard to add flavor to any recipe requiring sautéing or frying, such as Foraged Frittata with Potato Crust (page 27), Maple-Glazed Pork Chops (page 74), or the Saucy Spiced Beef & Onions (page 65), just to name a few.*

*If you don't butcher your own pigs, ask your local butcher to save kidney fat for you. They are often happy to either give it away or sell it for a nominal fee.*

*(continued)*

*Start out with cold fat. Trust me on this one—it makes the process much less messy.*

*On butchering day, I usually place the buckets of fat in the fridge to be dealt with later. You can even freeze the raw fat, and then let it partially thaw before you begin to chop it.*

*The process of rendering beef tallow is almost identical to that of rendering lard. Using kidney fat is also advisable with tallow, as it produces a milder end product.*

*Yes, the smell that fills your kitchen while rendering is normal. I've tried to think of a way to describe the aroma, but it's hard to explain it until you've experienced it. The best I can do is say it's a bit meaty with a hint of unpleasant barnyard. It's not my favorite part of the process, but thankfully the finished tallow or lard doesn't hold on to that scent or taste.*

*My tallow is usually much harder than my lard, so I prefer to store it in bars versus in mason jars. (It's nearly impossible to chip cold tallow out of a jar.) To make bars, pour the liquid tallow into a baking dish lined with parchment and let it cool before cutting it into bars the size of a bar of soap. Keep the bars in a large air-tight container in your freezer and pull them out to thaw when you are ready to make French fries, soap, candles, or whatever!*

## THE MYSTERY OF THE MISSING PIG FAT

I was so ready. It was our first hog-butchering day and my buckets were clean and waiting to capture all the luscious fat I planned to turn into lard. The steer we had harvested the year prior gave us many pounds of fat for tallow, so I assumed our pigs would be no different. After it was all said and done, I ended up with just a measly few pounds of fat. I was baffled. Where on earth did all my pig fat go? It wasn't until a chat with a butcher that I learned there are "bacon pigs" and "lard pigs." Many of our more modern breeds have been bred exclusively for lean meat production, especially as lard fell out of favor. So if you desire mountains of fat for rendering, your best bet will be to seek out one of the heritage breeds like the American Guinea hog to avoid disappointment on butchering day.

# Homestead Greens Pesto

*makes three quarters of a cup*

Greens, y'all. So many greens. Mustard, rainbow chard, arugula, beet tops, kale, and the list goes on. When we can't take any more green smoothies, Eggs 'n' Greens (page 33), or sautéed greens and butter, this pesto recipe is my secret weapon. It quickly uses whatever sort of green stuff we have hanging around and produces gourmet results every time. It's also the star ingredient in Pesto Cream Sauce (see page 82).

**2 cups packed roughly chopped stemmed greens (collard greens, mustard greens, chard, or kale will all work)**

**½ cup nuts (sunflower seeds, pine nuts, walnuts, or cashews)**

**¼ cup freshly grated Parmesan cheese**

**1 clove garlic**

**3 tablespoons extra-virgin olive oil**

**Fine sea salt and freshly ground black pepper**

In a food processor, combine the greens, nuts, cheese, and garlic and pulse until the mixture is finely minced. Drizzle in the olive oil while the machine is running and process until the mixture breaks down into a paste. Season to taste with salt and pepper.

Spread over a slice of crusty bread, add to a sandwich, serve alongside grilled meats, or toss with fresh pasta. Store in a jar in the fridge for up to 10 days.

*kitchen notes · This pesto freezes beautifully, which is especially handy considering greens don't keep very well otherwise. It should last for up to 4 months in an airtight container in the freezer.*

*You might think about doubling this recipe—or multiplying by ten if you plant as many greens as I do. You can safely scale up using this recipe and still get good results.*

# Savory Herb Salt

*makes three quarters of a cup*

I get so spoiled in the summer with our herb garden just steps from my kitchen. I always go through fresh-herb withdrawal after the first hard frost each year. This herb salt is my very favorite way to preserve an excess of herbs from the garden. It might not be quite as good as a bunch of parsley or basil picked fresh from the plant, but it's pretty darn close.

**3 cups loosely packed fresh herbs (see notes)**      **½ cup coarse sea salt**

Wash the herbs and remove coarse stems and discolored leaves. Dry thoroughly.

In a food processor, combine the herbs and salt and pulse until you have a coarse, uniform mixture. (Avoid overprocessing or you will end up with a paste.)

Place the herb mixture in a glass jar and refrigerate for 7 to 14 days to allow the flavors to meld, giving the jar a shake every day or so. The salt in this recipe acts as a preservative, so your herbs should last 6 months or even longer. (I recently found a 2-year-old jar hiding in my fridge—it's still good.)

*kitchen notes · Try parsley, dill, mint, oregano, marjoram, sage, thyme, cilantro, rosemary, or basil in this recipe. You can also mix and match for a variety of combinations. Sage and thyme is my current favorite combo.*

*Don't have a food processor? No worries. Just use your knife and chop like crazy until the herbs and salt form a uniform mixture.*

*Use this herb salt in any recipe benefitting from an extra punch. Rub it on roasts, steaks, or chops. Sprinkle it in stews, add pinches to your homemade stock, slather it on your chickens before roasting them (see page 54). Shall I go on? It's basically good for everything.*

# Sourdough Starter

*makes about two cups*

Nothing says "old-fashioned homestead" like a crock of bubbling sourdough starter. When I first began to research sourdough years ago, I was completely turned off by the complicated methods and tutorials I found. However, I've since realized maintaining a starter is much easier than I originally thought. I figure if the pioneers could handle keeping sourdough in their covered wagons, we should easily be able to fit it into the rhythms of our modern homesteads, don't you think?

½ cup whole wheat flour

Non-chlorinated water

All-purpose flour for maintaining the starter

Glass jar

To begin: Start the process by adding ½ cup whole wheat flour and ¼ cup water to the jar. Stir thoroughly and cover with a towel and rubber band. Let sit for 24 hours at room temperature. (Try to keep it in an area of your house that is somewhat warm. Very cool rooms tend to slow the action of a starter.)

The first feeding: After 24 hours, check the mixture for bubbles. If you see some, add ½ cup all-purpose flour and ¼ cup water. If you don't see bubbles, give it a stir and let sit 24 more hours.

The second feeding: After 24 hours, check for bubbles again. If you still don't see any, dump out the mixture and start over. If you do see bubbles, discard half of the starter, add ½ cup all-purpose flour and ¼ cup water and stir thoroughly. Let sit 24 hours.

The third feeding: Discard half of the starter, and feed with ½ cup all-purpose flour and ¼ cup water, stirring thoroughly. Let sit 24 hours.

Continue this routine until the starter is consistently bubbling and doubling in size within 8 hours of each feeding. At this point, you can store the starter in the refrigerator and feed it about once per week. When you plan to use the starter, pull it out of the refrigerator 24 hours in advance to feed it and allow it to warm up and grow.

*kitchen notes · If you've repeatedly attempted sourdough starters with dismal results, it could be that, depending on where you live, the wild strains of yeast floating in the air may not be well suited to sourdough. You can easily overcome this hurdle by purchasing a dried commercial starter for a minimal fee. Cared for properly, your starter should last for many, many years.*

*If you have other ferments or cultures in your kitchen, keep your starter at least several feet away from them to prevent cross-contamination.*

Have chlorinated tap water? Simply set the water out in an uncovered container for 24 hours before using it to feed your starter. This allows the chlorine to evaporate so it won't kill the little yeasties.

Once the starter has fully matured, you can share some of the daily discarded starter with your sourdough-loving friends.

Use your starter to make Sourdough Flapjacks (page 44), Sourdough Crackers (page 179), or Fudgy Sourdough Brownies (page 209).

# Brown Gravy

Repeat after me: "I solemnly swear to never buy those little packets of instant gravy at the store ever again." Because you're about to learn how to make the real deal, which only takes a few minutes and tastes so good you'll be licking it off the pan. Those little gravy envelopes don't even remotely compare to a well-seasoned homemade sauce with layers of hearty flavor made with the juices from the Saturday Night Roast Beef (page 73) or Simple Roast Chicken (page 54).

**2 tablespoons unsalted butter or fat drippings reserved from cooking meat**

**3 tablespoons all-purpose flour**

**2 cups pan juices from cooking meat, or stock (page 236)**

**Fine sea salt and freshly ground black pepper**

In a medium saucepan over medium heat, melt the butter, then whisk in the flour. Cook for 1 to 2 minutes, until the flour is browned. While whisking, gradually pour in the pan juices and cook, whisking, for 5 to 8 minutes, or until the gravy has thickened. Taste and add salt and pepper as needed. Serve immediately.

*kitchen notes · Separate the fatty drippings from the pan juices by pouring all the juices into a jar and allowing the fat to rise to the top.*

*I can't stress enough the importance of tasting the gravy before serving so you can add more salt if needed. Bland gravy = bad gravy.*

*If you are cooking for a gluten-free crowd, try substituting organic cornstarch for the flour.*

258    The Prairie Homestead Cookbook

# Cheese Sauce

(pictured on page 177)

The fake nacho cheese sauce that comes in jars is a sorry substitute for this gooey cheese sauce made with real cheddar and milk. I don't make this as often as you might think, but only because when I do, I don't have the willpower to stop myself from eating it by the spoonful until it's gone. We particularly enjoy it with Soft Pretzels (page 176) or drizzled over homemade nachos. Switch up this basic sauce with different types of cheese or spices—I love adding roasted chile peppers to mine.

2 tablespoons unsalted butter

2 tablespoons all-purpose flour

1 cup whole milk

1½ cups shredded sharp cheddar cheese

½ teaspoon prepared mustard

¼ teaspoon paprika

¼ teaspoon fine sea salt

In a small saucepan over low heat, melt the butter. Stir in the flour and cook for 2 minutes, or until the flour is lightly browned. Stir in the milk and cook, whisking continuously, until the mixture is slightly thickened and smooth, about 3 minutes.

Add the grated cheese, mustard, paprika, and salt. Stir over very low heat until the cheese is barely melted. Remove from the heat and allow the residual heat of the sauce to finish the melting process.

Serve with soft pretzels, baked potatoes, nacho chips, roasted vegetables, or hot pasta for quick mac 'n' cheese. This cheese sauce will keep in an airtight container in the fridge for up to 2 weeks, although it becomes rather gelatinous when it's cold. Reheat in a saucepan with a drizzle of milk to restore to its former creaminess.

*kitchen notes · If your sauce ends up with a grainy texture, it's likely because the cooking temperature was too high. Keep the burner at the lowest setting and don't overcook for the smoothest, creamiest sauce. (Grainy sauce is still 100 percent edible, though.)*

*For best results, skip the pre-shredded cheeses. They have added starches or cellulose that will mess up the texture of your finished sauce.*

# Vanilla Extract

*makes one quart*

Every homesteader needs a giant jar of homemade vanilla sitting in his or her cupboard. It only requires two ingredients, tastes a thousand times better than the imitation stuff, and is easy as pie to throw together. What's not to love? Pour the finished vanilla into small jars, tie a ribbon and tag on it, and give it as a gift. You'll be the coolest friend ever.

**8 whole vanilla beans**                                    **4 cups vodka**

Split the beans lengthwise and chop them into 3-inch pieces. Place the pieces into a quart-sized glass jar and fill it to the top with vodka.

Cover the jar and set aside to steep for at least 2 months or for up to 9 months. Remember, the longer it sits, the better it gets.

*kitchen notes · A mid-grade vodka works well for this recipe and produces the most neutral-tasting extract. However you can also use bourbon, rum, or brandy for variety.*

*Homemade vanilla doesn't really have an expiration date, since the alcohol acts as a preservative. I've kept jars in my pantry for years. This is also why you should most definitely make at least a quart at a time—it won't go bad and you'll end up using it more than you think.*

*I've lost count of how many recipes in this cookbook contain vanilla extract, but it's an important player in the Apple Cinnamon Puff Pancake (page 42), Simple Berry Sauce (page 50), and Lemon Whey Pie (page 185), just to name a few.*

# Homemade Breadcrumbs

*yield varies*

They're extremely useful, easy to make, and almost free—there's really no reason to buy breadcrumbs ever again. Plus, if you're learning how to make bread, this is a brilliant way to put any less-than-desirable loaves to good use. The yield varies depending on how much day-old or not-quite-presentable bread you have on hand, but generally 5 slices of bread makes 2 cups of crumbs. You can also make just the amount you need for a specific recipe. Use homemade crumbs for Cheddar & Herb Meatloaf (page 64) or Summer Squash Gratin (page 133).

**Leftover bread, cut into**
**1- to 2-inch cubes**

If the bread you are using isn't already dry, you can speed up the process by baking it: Preheat the oven to 300°F. Arrange the cubes on a baking sheet in a single layer. Bake for 10 to 15 minutes, or until the cubes are dry and crunchy. Cool them completely. Place the dry bread cubes in a food processor and pulse them into coarse crumbs. Store in an airtight container in the refrigerator for up to 3 weeks or in the freezer for up to 6 months.

# Sweet & Tangy BBQ Sauce

(pictured on page 76)

I seem to have a problem remembering to stock barbecue sauce in my fridge, which has resulted in a kitchen emergency more than once when I've found myself in the middle of a recipe needing a bit of barbecue flavor. I've served this slightly sweet and tangy sauce to a number of guests, and it receives ample compliments every time. It's best friends with Slow Cooker Pulled Pork (page 77), so you'll definitely want to serve them together.

2 cups tomato sauce (page 264), or 1 (14.5-ounce) can

1 (6-ounce) can tomato paste

⅓ cup apple cider vinegar

3 tablespoons maple syrup

3 tablespoons molasses

2 tablespoons Worcestershire sauce

1 teaspoon garlic powder

1 teaspoon paprika

1 teaspoon Dijon mustard

½ teaspoon onion powder

½ teaspoon fine sea salt

½ teaspoon freshly ground black pepper

⅛ teaspoon cayenne pepper

In a medium saucepan over medium heat, combine all the ingredients and bring to a simmer. Simmer for 10 to 15 minutes, stirring occasionally, until slightly thickened.

Transfer to a jar or other airtight container and store in the refrigerator for up to 2 weeks, or in the freezer for up to 4 months.

# Rustic Fresh Tomato Sauce

*makes two cups*

Tomato sauce is usually a commitment, and an all-day simmer is traditionally required for the richest, thickest sauces. There are plenty of days in the late summer where I do exactly that, but this fast, rustic sauce is the best when I'm craving tomato sauce in a hurry. It has a bright flavor and takes a fraction of the time to cook. It's beautiful for pouring over pasta or spooning onto the pizza crust on page 85. For the meatiest tomatoes with less juice to simmer away, choose a paste variety like Roma, San Marzano, or Amish Paste.

2 cloves garlic, minced

2 tablespoons extra-virgin olive oil

4 cups quartered fresh tomatoes

2 tablespoons fresh basil, or
2 teaspoons dried

2 tablespoons fresh oregano, or
2 teaspoons dried

½ teaspoon fine sea salt

½ teaspoon sugar, preferably organic
whole cane sugar

¼ teaspoon freshly ground
black pepper

In a medium saucepan over low heat, heat the garlic in the olive oil for several minutes until fragrant. Add the remaining ingredients and simmer for 10 to 15 minutes, or until the tomatoes have softened. Puree the sauce with an immersion blender, or transfer to a regular blender and blend with the lid slightly ajar to allow steam to escape, or puree in a food processor. I like to leave my fresh sauce a little bit on the chunky side, but you can puree it to your liking. Toss this fresh sauce with homemade pasta (see page 81) or use it as a topping for pizza.

*kitchen notes* · *Sometimes I'll seed the tomatoes and drain some of the juice from them before adding them to the pan to help the sauce thicken faster, but usually I don't bother.*

*You can use frozen tomatoes in place of the fresh if you like—they'll just need a little extra simmer time.*

# how to freeze tomatoes

In a perfect world, all the tomatoes in the garden would be perfectly ripe at the exact same time. But that never happens. They generally prefer to torment you and ripen one at a time, which makes gathering enough to make a batch of sauce excruciatingly slow. When the tomatoes are coming into the house at a trickle, my freezer saves the day.

WASH – Rinse the tomatoes and trim off the ends and any bad spots. Some people blanch them to remove the skins, but I hate blanching and I avoid it whenever possible. The skin doesn't bother me and it mostly disappears once you make sauce anyway.

CUT – Cherry tomatoes can be left whole, but it's best to cut medium to large fruit into halves or quarters.

SCRAPE – Seed the tomato pieces by running your thumb and forefinger down the inner portion of the tomato to scrape out the juice and seeds. (Chickens love tomato guts, by the way.) Don't worry about removing every last bit—just get the bulk of it. This will keep the frozen tomatoes from becoming a solid mass of juice in the freezer.

BAG – Place the tomato chunks into a resealable gallon-size freezer bag. If you're worried about the pieces sticking together, you can flash freeze them on a baking sheet for 30 minutes first. (I'm lazy and usually skip that part.)

FREEZE – Keep tomatoes in the freezer for up to 10 months. Save them until you have enough to make a big batch of slow-simmered sauce, or pop a few handfuls at a time into a saucepan to make the fast fresh sauce (opposite).

# Pumpkin Puree

*yield varies*

I make a point to go on a pumpkin binge each fall. We eat pumpkin everything for several months, until around January, when the mere sight of an orange squash makes my stomach turn. On the years when my garden patch doesn't produce well, I pick up organic pie pumpkins from our local farm store. They are richer in flavor and texture than the regular jack-o'-lantern variety, and make much better pies. The yield will depend on the size of the pumpkin.

**1 pumpkin, homegrown or otherwise**

Preheat the oven to 350°F and set one of the racks in the middle.

Put the pumpkin on a baking sheet and place it in the oven. (Yes, the whole pumpkin!) Bake until the pumpkin is soft, 30 minutes to 2 hours, depending on the variety and size of the pumpkin. You'll know it's done when you can easily pierce the skin with the tip of a knife.

Remove the pumpkin from the oven and let it cool. Cut out the top, just like you are carving a jack-o'-lantern, and scrape out the strings and seeds. (Save the seeds for roasting later; see below.)

Cut the pumpkin into sections and scrape the flesh into a food processor or high-powered blender. Discard the skin. Puree the flesh until smooth. The puree can be stored in an airtight container in the refrigerator for about 1 week, or freeze it for up to 8 months for later use.

*kitchen notes · If you find the pumpkin isn't baked enough when you cut into it, no worries. Simply place the chunks back in the oven until they are softened sufficiently.*

*Pumpkin guts are much easier to remove from a baked pumpkin than a raw one. Thank goodness.*

*Use homemade puree in Honey Pumpkin Pie (page 189), Pumpkin Pie Milkshakes (page 225), or Pumpkin Pan Rolls (page 166).*

## HOW TO ROAST PUMPKIN SEEDS

Preheat the oven to 350°F. After removing the strings from the seeds, rinse the seeds in a bowl of water, drain, and pat dry with paper towels. Toss with a drizzle of olive oil and a sprinkle of sea salt and spread on a parchment-lined baking sheet. Roast for 5 to 15 minutes, stirring every 5 minutes, until the seeds are golden brown.

# Buttermilk Ranch Dressing

*makes one and a half cups*

As much as I would like to pretend my family favors fancy gourmet salad dressings, that's just not the case. Like most Americans, we eat ranch more than anything else. But instead of relying on those jugs of dressing filled with MSG and partially hydrogenated vegetable oils, this easy buttermilk ranch recipe is our salad topping of choice. You can use fresh parsley and dill if you like, but I'm often throwing together dressing at the last minute, so dried herbs are usually easiest for me. Make your own buttermilk for this dressing with the instructions on page 244.

1 cup sour cream

½ cup buttermilk

1 tablespoon dried parsley, or 2 tablespoons finely chopped fresh

1 tablespoon dried dill or 2 tablespoons finely chopped fresh

1 teaspoon lemon juice

½ teaspoon garlic powder

½ teaspoon onion powder

½ teaspoon fine sea salt

⅛ teaspoon freshly ground black pepper

In a glass jar, combine all the ingredients and stir well. Cover and chill for at least 1 hour before serving so the flavors have time to come together and intensify.

Serve as a dip for vegetables or as a dressing for salads. (For a thinner, more pourable consistency, add an additional 2 to 3 tablespoons buttermilk.) Your ranch should keep for about 2 weeks in the jar in the refrigerator.

# Orange Poppy Seed Vinaigrette

Have you ever had the pleasure of eating a bowlful of just-picked spinach? It has hearty, substantial flavor that makes grocery-store spinach seem horribly boring and bland. Spinach doesn't tolerate heat very well, so I try to plant mine as early as I possibly can to get lots of harvests to enjoy with this tangy vinaigrette before the plants can go to seed. It's also a component in Roasted Beets & Whipped Goat Cheese (page 120).

2 tablespoons orange juice

2 tablespoons extra-virgin olive oil

1 tablespoon lemon juice

1 tablespoon poppy seeds

2 teaspoons honey

1 teaspoon Dijon mustard

¼ teaspoon fine sea salt

Pinch of freshly ground black pepper

In a glass jar, combine all the ingredients, cover the jar, and shake vigorously. This vinaigrette will keep in the jar in the refrigerator for up to 4 days, if not longer.

*part two*

# HOMESTEADING

## GROWING YOUR OWN INGREDIENTS

*Growing your own food
is like printing your
own money.*

—RON FINLEY

*If you only take away one piece of advice from* this cookbook, let it be this: If you are drawn to the homesteading way of life, *don't wait* until you have a perfect little farm to start learning new skills and cooking wholesome food—there's no reason you can't start now.

I believe the process of growing and preparing food was meant to feed our souls just as much as our stomachs. Although once so common it wasn't given a second thought, having an intimate connection with the foods we eat has become increasingly foreign. An invisible wall standing between producers and consumers has become so commonplace we rarely think to question it. The food on our plate is simply there to fill our stomachs—it no longer has a story. While there are times I am absolutely thankful to have modern food options available to us, I believe it's crucial to reconnect with our food sources any time we can. And the good news? Everyone can grow *something*, no matter where they live.

## Why It's Worth It to Grow Your Own Food

Why add another commitment to your already busy life when you can easily drive to your neighborhood market and pick up a dozen eggs and a gallon of milk? I'm so glad you asked.

### *It's Healthier*

When you grow your own food, you have complete control of what the animals are fed, what goes into the soil, and what is sprayed on your crops. My kids love to graze in the garden and pluck green beans right from the plant, and I love not having to worry about pesticides going into their mouths.

### *It's Green*

No fossil fuels are required when you're growing food right outside your back door. Not only will you be able to feed your own family a more local diet, you can share the bounty with your family and friends, enabling them to eat better too.

# It Can Be More Frugal

This is one question I hear frequently: Is it *really* cheaper to grow your own food? Well, the answer is yes *and* no. For example, if you consider the cost of raising chickens as compared to a cheap carton of regular store-bought eggs, then homegrown eggs are definitely more expensive.

However, if you compare your chicken costs with a carton of organic, free-range eggs that have been fed a completely natural diet, then it becomes much more comparable. Plus, things like *truly* free-range eggs or raw milk are not easily available in many areas, so in those instances, the only option is to grow them yourself.

# It's More Humane

I'm not a fan of the way most conventional meat, dairy, and eggs are produced. The system is set up to maximize profits, but it's not always humane to the animals involved. When we raise our own animals for food or buy from local producers instead of from factory farms, I know each animal was cared for in the most natural and compassionate way possible. It matters.

# It Tastes Good

Imagine ripe red raspberries picked seconds before landing on your tongue, blue and brown eggs with vibrant orange yolks, and rich raw milk with a cream line that takes up nearly half the jar as it waits to be transformed into golden butter. Shall I go on?

# It Boosts Self-Sufficiency

Homesteaders naturally have extra food on hand, thanks to bountiful gardens and this strange addiction we have to canning and putting stuff in jars. (It just comes with the territory—you won't be able to avoid it, no matter how hard you try.) It doesn't matter who you are or where you live, increasing your self-sufficiency can be extremely reassuring, whether you're concerned about a small emergency (losing the power for a few days) or a big one (uh, zombies . . .).

We're far from doomsday-style preppers, but we always have plenty of food tucked away that could last us many months if it needed to. Plus, the homestead skills we've naturally added to our repertoire over the years give me confidence we'd be better equipped than most folks in an extreme survival scenario.

# What If I Don't Have a Homestead?

Maybe you don't have a yard. Or your homeowners' association restricts what you can do. Or you just don't have the ability to build a chicken coop at this point in time. Regardless of your situation or roadblocks, there are plenty of ways to upgrade your pantry so you can start eating better-tasting food that's nourishing your body at the same time. Think outside of the box (and the grocery store) with some of these ideas.

## Grow Indoors

Indoor growing efforts can extend far beyond herbs—no greenhouse required. With a few considerations and some sunny windows, there are plenty of edibles that can be grown inside, including lettuce, kale, mushrooms, tomatoes, scallions, and even some dwarf fruit trees!

## Visit the Farmers' Market

There's no better place to connect with your local foods movement than a farmers' market. Browse locally grown vegetables, fruits, meats, and more and support small farms in the process. Plus, it's just plain fun to walk through a market with a basket on your arm and soak in the atmosphere.

## Join a CSA

Community-Supported Agriculture programs, also known as CSAs, are a fantastic way to bring farm ingredients to your table. Even with our large garden, I still participate in them occasionally to expand our vegetable options. CSAs allow members to purchase shares of vegetables, fruits, and sometimes other foods from local producers. Payments are made at the beginning of the year, and shares are delivered weekly or biweekly throughout the growing season. Your dollars go straight to local farmers and you have the freshest ingredients possible—it's a win-win for everyone. Participating in our local CSA also helped me to break out of my vegetable rut and try greens and root vegetables I never would have thought of purchasing prior to joining.

## Rent, Lease, or Share

Do you have friends or family with vacant garden plots or pastures? Who do you know who might want to partner on a food-growing adventure? Perhaps you can bring the labor and they will provide the space. I've even heard of older farm couples searching for energetic younger folks to work their land for them. With a little strategy and ingenuity, the possibilities here are endless.

## Use Technology to Your Advantage

Our milk cow came from craigslist.org and we've purchased tractors and chickens from Facebook groups. The Internet can be a fabulous tool for connecting with other homesteaders, finding local producers, and sourcing supplies. Many areas have local homesteading groups on social media, which can be wonderful for finding new likeminded friends and getting the scoop on the best local ingredients in your region. You can also check out localharvest.org to find markets, farms, CSAs, and producers in your area.

## Volunteer with Local Producers

Research is great, but nothing beats hands-on experience. Sharpen your skills and learn new ones by volunteering to help at local farms. Not all farmers will be open to this, so respect people's time and space, but it never hurts to ask. Good things come to those who are willing to get their hands dirty.

## Join (or Start!) a Community Garden

Community gardens come in all shapes and sizes, but generally involve a group of people coming together to grow fruit and vegetables on a shared lot. I cannot think of a better way to get your feet wet in the world of home food production than by gardening alongside a group of folks who love vegetables just as much as you do. Many community gardens also donate portions of their harvest to local food banks, so they are making a difference in more ways than one.

## Ready for the Next Step?

I'll never forget the first time we sat down to supper plates filled only with food grown on our 67 acres. The most soul-satisfying sense of contentment infused every fiber of my being as I mentally accounted for the food in front of us. There was the grass-fed beef roast from a cow raised on the prairie land in our backyard, creamy Yukon Gold potatoes hand-dug from our soil and mashed with butter from our family cow, and heirloom beans plucked from the vine just hours prior by my three-year-old daughter and me. It was the accumulation of many hours, if not years, of work, which made it a meal I'll never forget.

Growing the majority of your own food is dirty, hard, all-consuming, frustrating, and absolutely worth it. It's empowering to conquer a new skill, to play a role in cultivating the food you put into your mouth, to be a producer instead of just a consumer, and to set a goal and see it through until the end. Whether you're starting your own homestead, considering installing a chicken coop in the backyard (see page 299), or tending herbs sprouting on the windowsill (see page 290), there are plenty of ways you can experience the satisfaction of raising food for your own table.

# herbs & veggies

*If there is one place on the homestead I've* struggled more than any other, it's the garden. While some homesteaders seem to naturally possess the gift of coaxing breathtaking blooms and vibrant vegetables from raw soil, I do not. I can grow eggs and milk and meat all day long, but when it comes to the vegetable garden, I've had some absolutely spectacular fails. There have been years I've completely lost the battle with pests of all kinds, years when (thanks to poor compost) I've ended up seeding the plot with a literal lawn of grass, and years when I've poisoned the whole darn thing by unknowingly applying hay mulch that had been sprayed with a potent herbicide. If it's possible to mess something up in the garden, I've done it.

But I've never been one to quit after falling flat on my face, so onward I march. Each spring, I order a fresh batch of seeds, dust off the hoe, pull on my gloves, and try again. With a decent amount of blood, buckets of sweat, and most definitely tears (yes, I've cried over vegetables), I've slowly turned my brown thumb into one that's the faintest shade of green.

Despite the tough years, lately I seem to have (sort of) found my gardening groove and my battle-hardened garden is now one of the most picturesque parts of our homestead. The lushest time in our growing season is late summer, and it's hard to stay away from my little fenced plot that time of year. Dusk is the most enchanting part of the day and I relish the chance to sit on the crooked blue bench in the corner and soak it all in. The abundance is overwhelming. The bushy bean plants sway with a dense crop of heirloom pods, the heavy heads of cabbage sit tidy and expectant in their rows, the potato plants fill every square inch of their bed with leafy stems and dainty white flowers, and the copious squash vines curl up the sides of the gate, framing the entrance in a way that makes the space feel almost sacred.

If you've ever found yourself reeling after a miserable garden year and wondered if it was worth trying again, let me tell you: *it is.* Shake off the failure and start again. Your persistence will eventually pay off (I'm proof of that!), and the rewards are beautiful and oh-so-tasty.

Maybe you haven't yet mustered up the nerve to take the plunge and start digging around in the dirt. Maybe you're waiting until you know enough or until the moment arrives when you feel totally ready. My advice? *Dive in.* Plant that first seed, get your hands dirty, know you'll eventually mess something up, and then? Well, you'll simply learn from your mistakes and keep on trucking, because that's what homesteaders do.

There are few experiences that top the feeling of hooking a woven basket over your arm and heading outside to "shop" for ingredients—walking between the rows, plucking plump tomatoes from the vine, snapping waxy peppers from their stems, and clipping bunches of crisp lettuce from the cool, wet soil. Then once the basket is full, you'll carry it all back to the house and craft it into a home-cooked meal. It's one of the best feelings this crazy homestead life has to offer, and I cannot wait for you to experience it.

## Gardening: Three Ways

### In-Ground Gardens

When most of us think of vegetable gardening, this is the method that comes to mind. It's classic, it's simple, and it requires minimal prep and equipment. I had a traditional in-ground garden for years and it served me well. Each spring we would till the plot, mark the rows, and plunge seeds into the earth when the soil warmed. It was humble and it worked. We built a wire panel fence around the perimeter the first year we were on our homestead (if you have dogs, deer, or free-range chickens, a fence is not optional). But besides the purchase of a tiller, those few items were the extent of our initial garden investment.

Like most gardeners, my biggest complaint with my in-ground plot was the weeds. The task of pulling weeds from between the rows and seedlings was never-ending and in order to keep up with it, I needed hours in the day I couldn't seem to find. Each year, I'd start with the best intentions but end up losing the battle by mid-July. I inadvertently discovered most vegetables grow surprisingly well even if they are surrounded by weeds, but I still lost plants each year as they were choked out by lamb's-quarter and bindweed. While many homesteaders use tillers between their rows to help manage weeds, our garden wasn't laid out in a way that made that possible, which left my hoe and me to do the dirty work.

One year in a stroke of providence, I was rummaging through a pile of musty books and found an unassuming little volume titled *The Ruth Stout No-Work Garden Book*. Ruth Stout was a visionary who pioneered the deep-mulch method—a revolutionary technique that involves laying a heavy sheet of mulching material over the entire garden before planting. She swore by the way the deep layers of organic matter nurtured the soil and kept it from drying out, and she maintained this was the design nature intended all along. I was utterly intrigued. I was completely fed up with weeding at that point, so I figured I had nothing to lose. I convinced Christian to bring a half-ton bale of hay over to the garden after we tilled it that spring so I could begin my initial mulch layer. He thought I was crazy, the neighbors thought I was crazy, and even I began to question my sanity as I forked mounds of hay over the freshly worked soil.

By the time I was done, the layer was nearly 10 inches deep, which is what Ruth recommended. I marked my rows and spread the hay so I could plant my seeds directly into the soil. As the seedlings popped up, I pulled the mulch around the base of each plant to block future weeds from springing up alongside them.

And it worked! The soil under the mulch stayed loose and damp, and was filled with more earthworms than I'd ever seen in my life. My plants grew beautifully, and while the garden was not completely impervious to weeds, the time I had to devote there each day was drastically reduced. Instead of hours spent on my hands and knees weeding, I'd spend 10 to 15 minutes a day adjusting mulch and adding more hay to any sparse patches. As long as I kept the layer thick enough, the seeds in the hay didn't germinate and the weed seeds in the soil didn't have enough light to grow. It was a dream.

Unfortunately, our mulch gardening adventure ended abruptly when I unknowingly used herbicide-tainted hay in my garden. This mistake cost me an entire growing season and subsequently made our soil unfit for growing vegetables for several years, until the herbicide residue finally broke down. However, the silver lining in this whole mishap was that it directed me toward a new method: raised beds.

## Raised Beds

Raised beds are especially trendy right now, but that's not the reason we chose them. We had toyed with the idea for years, but considering the scope of the project, it always was relegated to the back burner. That is, until we were left with no other options. Our original plot was fairly small, not to mention there was a sizable tree growing right smack in the middle of it—it was time to start over. We took out the tree, leveled the ground, and more than doubled the footprint of the garden by adding twenty raised beds.

I was attracted to the idea of raised beds for a number of reasons:

- **Raised beds can help the soil warm up sooner in the spring.** Our winters last a long time, so I was especially excited about this possibility.

- **It's often easier to manage weeds in beds, thanks to clearly defined walkways and no rows to weed between.**

- **Higher beds prevent soil compaction** by keeping kids, dogs, and random humans from traipsing across the soil and packing it down.

- **Raised beds provide better drainage.** This wasn't something I was necessarily concerned about here in drought-prone Wyoming, but if you live in a wet climate this could be a considerable perk.

- **It's easier to keep raised beds tidy, and I love the organized aesthetic of a well-executed raised bed garden.** I've also found I want to spend more time out in my garden when it doesn't feel like constant chaos. Funny how that works.

Raised beds aren't without their challenges, however. We found the most formidable aspect of beds to be the amount of work it takes to build them, as well as the cost of materials.

There are dozens of different material options, and after many rounds of rousing debate, we personally settled on heavy-duty steel bridge decking panels with redwood 4x4s at the corners. Overkill? Perhaps. But these babies will last until Armageddon. Thanks to years spent rebuilding projects that quickly fell apart, Christian and I have learned our lesson and make it a point to create things that will last.

Wood is the most common material for raised beds. Building with less expensive, untreated lumber was tempting, but we quickly determined we had no desire to rebuild the beds every several years when the boards began to decompose. Redwood and cedar are hardier, naturally rot-resistant options, but they are prohibitively expensive if you plan to build more than one or two small beds.

We looked at lots of photos of gardens built with galvanized panels, which we pondered for a while. However, because the panels are thin, you must build an entire frame out of wood to support them so they don't bow out. That equals more cost in purchasing lumber and in labor building the frames, so

bridge decking ultimately made the most sense for us. (Check steel suppliers or building companies, as typical building stores won't carry these.)

Each bed is 4 x 10 feet and there are twenty beds total. The metal panels on each one are 18 inches high. Christian cut the panels to size with a plasma cutter (they are thick!) and then screwed the corners to the redwood 4x4s. We installed a drip system with a timer in each bed, which makes watering (my least-loved summer chore) a breeze.

Do I think raised beds are for everyone? Nope. But they were definitely the answer for us, and our first growing season with them was one of the best I've had so far. I'm hooked.

## Container Gardening

Even with 67 acres at our disposal, I still love growing things in various pots and containers on our deck and covered porch. If you live in a place with limited garden space or you're without a garden altogether, container gardening might be the answer. Dozens of favorite vegetables, including tomatoes, beans, squash, potatoes, and herbs, can thrive in containers, and even the starkest apartment balcony has the potential to become a lush forest of food with a collection of pots.

Containers can range from flowerpots to recycled five-gallon buckets to plastic bins. Lately, my favorite trick is to scour yard sales and thrift stores for old pots and pans and then plant my flowers and herbs in those. There is the tendency for vegetable plants to not produce as prolifically in pots as they do in the ground, so use high-quality organic potting soil and a good plant food or fertilizer throughout the season to keep plants as productive as possible.

## HOMEMADE ORGANIC GARDEN SPRAY

Use this DIY spray instead of toxic pesticides to battle the bugs in your garden.

Combine 1 onion, 4 cloves garlic, 2 cups mint leaves, 2 tablespoons cayenne pepper, and 1 cup water in a blender and blend until smooth. Pour the mixture through a mesh strainer into a 1-gallon jar. Add enough water to fill the jar to the top and mix in 2 tablespoons natural liquid soap (I use mild castile soap or natural dishwashing soap).

To use, pour some of the liquid into a spray bottle and spray on affected plants two to three times per week or after a heavy rain. This spray is best used within seven days.

# Starting Seeds Indoors

I usually don't plant much of anything in my garden until May (we have an annual Mother's Day blizzard around here), but I start my seeds in the house much earlier than that.

Starting seeds takes effort, but it's definitely worth it. Not only can it save you hundreds of dollars (vegetable seedling costs add up quickly if you have a large garden), but the sky's the limit when it comes to variety—you'll be able to grow whatever organic, heirloom varieties strike your fancy. (And you can show off your purple tomatoes and exotic peppers that the local garden store doesn't have.)

I've tried a number of DIY and repurposed seed-starting setups over the years, but simple plastic greenhouse trays and small seed-starting pellets remain my favorite. I prefer coconut coir pellets to peat, since coir is a more sustainable material. Simply soak the pellets in water for several minutes and they're ready to go.

Seeds don't need light until they germinate—a warm room will suffice for the first few days until you see their teensy leaves peeking from the soil. After that, good light is crucial, so set your seedlings in a sunny window or use grow lights.

We have an annoying shortage of usable south-facing windows in our house, so I use grow lights in our basement. We purchased 4-foot fluorescent shop lights from the local home improvement store and hung them on a metal shelving unit (one light per shelf). The lights are attached to the shelves with short lengths of chain, which enables me to easily raise or lower the lights depending on the size of the plants. Keep the lights low at first, then gradually raise them as the plants grow taller. This prevents seedlings from getting leggy and spindly—ain't nobody wants leggy seedlings. The lights should be on the plants for 16 hours per day, but I can attest to seedlings' ability to survive if you forget to shut the lights off occasionally. Whoops.

Keep the soil moist at all times—especially during the germination phase. Peat or coir pellets dry out quickly, and tiny seedlings don't last very long if they become dry. As the plants mature, they'll need to be repotted into larger containers with potting soil. For repotting, I use either red plastic cups (super classy) or the black plastic packs with four or six cells (the kind you get when you buy potting flowers at the garden store). I reuse my containers year after year and they work like a charm. If you are reusing pots and trays, it's wise to disinfect them to prevent the spread of plant diseases or fungi—many folks do this with diluted bleach, but I prefer white vinegar or hydrogen peroxide instead. Simply spray each container, wipe, and rinse well with water before adding the soil mix and seeds.

## Vegetable Growing Guide

I begin growing in early March when the garden still resembles frozen tundra and the winds whip blinding walls of snow across the pastures. A happy glow comes from the storage room in our basement, and if you peek your head around the corner, you'll find tray upon tray of the tiniest seedlings stretching their way toward the shining grow lights. I felt constant overwhelm the first few years I started my own seeds, as it was hard to keep track of what to plant when. Hopefully this simple guide will eliminate some of the confusion for you during planting time.

Planting in the fall is an option many folks often overlook, although the feasibility will depend on your climate and location. I know many homesteaders in southern states with lovely fall gardens, but my Wyoming fall garden isn't quite as prolific. Flip to page 348 if you need help determining your first and last frost dates.

## BEANS

*Planting Method:* Direct sow seeds any time after your last spring frost date when the soil has reached a temperature of at least 60°F.

*Planting Notes:* Beans do not transplant well, so they will need to be direct sown in the garden. Soak the bean seeds in warm water for a few hours before planting to speed up the germination process. Use your homegrown beans to make Sesame Green Beans (page 135).

## BEETS

*Planting Method:* Direct sow seeds 2 weeks before your last spring frost date. For a fall harvest, plant them 10 to 12 weeks before your first fall frost date.

*Planting Notes:* Each beet seed is actually a capsule with several seeds in one, so plan on thinning the beets as they mature. Beetroot and beet greens are equally appealing and can be used in all sorts of interesting ways. Check out Roasted Beets & Whipped Goat Cheese (page 120) and Beet & Potato Mash (page 113). I grow classic red beets every year, but we also love the golden and white varieties.

## BROCCOLI

*Planting Method:* Start seeds indoors 6 to 8 weeks before your last spring frost date. For an autumn harvest, broccoli seeds can be started indoors 85 to 100 days before your first fall frost date. Transplant the seedlings to your garden when the plants are 3 weeks old.

*Planting Notes:* Set broccoli seedlings outside in the spring when the plants are 5 to 6 inches tall or approximately 2 to 3 weeks before your last spring frost date. Broccoli is susceptible to pests so spray it frequently with homemade pest spray (page 284). Homegrown broccoli is amazing roasted with garlic and olive oil or in Broccoli Cheddar Soup (page 104).

## BRUSSELS SPROUTS

*Planting Method:* Start seeds indoors 6 to 8 weeks before your last spring frost date. You can also direct sow seeds 4 months before your first fall frost date.

*Planting Notes:* Transplant Brussels sprouts in the garden after the danger of spring frosts has passed and your seedlings have their first true leaves. Brussels sprouts are a crowd-pleaser at the table when I roast them with a bit of butter and Parmesan cheese.

## CABBAGE

*Planting Method:* Start seeds indoors 6 to 8 weeks before your last spring frost date. For a fall harvest, start seeds 6 to 12 weeks before your first fall frost date. (The variety of cabbage you choose will determine the exact time frame, so check your seed packet for recommendations.)

*Planting Notes:* Transplant cabbage seedlings when they are 3 to 4 inches tall. You can also direct sow seeds outdoors in the spring when the soil is thawed enough to plant. Cilantro Slaw (page 142) is a fabulous way to serve your homegrown cabbage as a quick summer side.

## CARROTS

*Planting Method:* Direct sow seeds in the garden 3 to 4 weeks before your last spring frost date.

*Planting Notes:* Carrots take forever to germinate—it may be as long as 3 weeks before you see teeny seedlings rising from the soil. They dry out quickly, so keep their rows consistently damp while you wait. In Zone 8 and warmer, you can also plant carrots in the fall or winter. Honey Whipped Carrots (page 130) are a mouth-watering way to serve your harvest.

## CAULIFLOWER

*Planting Method:* Start seeds indoors 4 to 6 weeks before you plan to transplant them. For a fall harvest, start seeds indoors 12 weeks before your first fall frost date; seedlings can be transplanted 6 to 8 weeks before your first fall frost of the year.

*Planting Notes:* Cauliflower can be transplanted 3 to 4 weeks before your last spring frost date, as long as the seedlings are around 5 inches tall. We prefer our cauliflower roasted rather than boiled, with a drizzle of olive oil and a sprinkle of salt.

## GARLIC

*Planting Method:* For the best crop, plant garlic in the fall, about 4 to 6 weeks before your first fall frost date. Break bulbs of seed garlic into cloves and plant each clove pointy-side up.

*Planting Notes:* Garlic can be planted in early spring, but fall garlic tends to produce greater yields. I plant mine in mid-September (this will vary according to your growing zone) and cover the bed with a layer of mulch. I ignore it for the rest of the winter and the green shoots peek through the soil in the spring as the weather warms. Water and weed the garlic bed until the tops begin to brown (usually mid-July for us) and then they are ready to harvest. Garlic is especially delicious in . . . okay, who I am kidding? Garlic is delicious is nearly everything, as evidenced by its inclusion in dozens of recipes in this cookbook.

## CORN

*Planting Method:* Direct sow seeds in the garden 2 weeks after your last spring frost date when the soil has reached a temperature of at least 60°F.

*Planting Notes:* Corn requires a lot of nitrogen as it grows, so amend the soil heavily with compost or other fertilizer for best results. Eat it on the cob or slice it off to make Browned Butter Skillet Corn (page 121).

## GREENS

*Planting Method:* Direct sow seeds as soon as the soil can be worked in the spring.

*Planting Notes:* Greens such as kale, chard, collards, mustard, arugula, and spinach are cool-weather plants that perform best before the summer heat arrives. You can continue to sow rows throughout the summer for later harvests too. Some varieties of greens are especially frost-hardy and withstand very cool temperatures late into the growing season, which makes me especially fond of them here in Wyoming.

## CUCUMBERS

*Planting Method:* Direct sow after your last spring frost date, or start seeds indoors 2 to 4 weeks before your last spring frost date to get a head start on the growing season.

*Planting Notes:* Cucumbers are delicate and very sensitive to frost. Don't transplant them until the soil has reached 65 to 70°F. This is usually at least 2 weeks after the last spring frost date. Pick small, firm cucumbers to make Garlic Dill Icebox Pickles (page 127).

## LETTUCE

*Planting Method:* Direct sow seeds when the soil has reached a temperature of at least 45°F. If you want a jump start on your harvest (especially since many lettuce varieties cannot handle warm temperatures), you can start lettuce seeds indoors as early as 10 weeks before your last spring frost date. Transplant the seedlings as soon as the soil can be worked in the spring.

*Planting Notes:* Lettuce bolts in warm weather, so succession planting can be helpful. Sow a handful of seeds or transplant a few plants each week to extend the harvest as long as possible.

## ONIONS

*Planting Method:* Start onions from seed 8 to 10 weeks before your last spring frost date. Transplant after the danger of frost has passed.

*Planting Notes:* It's entirely possible to grow onions from seed, but I've found onion sets to be a much more low-maintenance option. The sets can be planted early in the spring as soon as the soil can be worked and are hardier than the fragile seedlings. You can find sets at any garden store—they usually come in large bunches for just a couple of dollars.

## PEAS

*Planting Method:* Direct sow seeds 4 to 5 weeks before your last spring frost date when the soil reaches a temperature of at least 45°F.

*Planting Notes:* It's possible to start peas indoors even earlier, but they don't love being transplanted, so be careful with their young roots if you do plan to move them. We love both English peas and sugar snap peas, but they rarely make it into the house, as my dear children have a habit of devouring them as fast as they can ripen.

## PEPPERS

*Planting Method:* Start seeds indoors at least 8 to 10 weeks before your last spring frost date.

*Planting Notes:* Peppers adore heat, so keep the seedlings warm, preferably in a room that stays around 70 to 75°F. Do not plant them outside until your garden temperatures are averaging 65°F during the day and 55°F at night. There are an endless number of pepper varieties, both sweet and hot. My favorites are poblanos, which I add to my Fresh Garden Salsa (page 128) and Chicken Poblano Chowder (page 105).

## POTATOES

*Planting Method:* Direct sow seed potatoes in the garden any time after the soil can be worked in the spring. If your region is prone to very hard frosts later in the spring, wait to plant potatoes until 1 to 2 weeks before your last spring frost date.

*Planting Notes:* Buy seed potatoes from your local garden store or order them online. Avoid using grocery store potatoes, since they may be sprayed with a substance that discourages sprouting. I like to grow varieties that aren't commonly available at the store. (You've got to try purple potatoes at least once!) Cut large seed potatoes into chunks, leaving at least 2 eyes per piece. Plant each piece and mound the dirt higher as sprouts pop through the soil. Potatoes are fairly hardy and can survive a few light frosts in the fall. The possibilities are endless when it comes to potatoes, but Crispy Potato Stacks (page 114), Zesty Oven Fries (page 118), and Scalloped Potatoes (page 117) rank right up there on the list of my favorite spud recipes ever.

## PUMPKINS

*Planting Method:* Direct sow seeds after your last spring frost date when soil temperatures reach at least 70°F. For a slightly earlier crop, start seeds indoors 2 to 4 weeks before your last frost date and transplant once all danger of frost has passed.

*Planting Notes:* If you are planning on making pies, select a pie variety—they have far superior texture and flavor. (My long-standing favorite is the Winter Luxury Pie Pumpkin, an heirloom variety.) Pumpkins prefer rich soil, so add lots of compost to their bed. Ripened pumpkins can be removed from the vine and stored in a cool, dark place for most of the winter. Honey Pumpkin Pie (page 189) will make you extremely thankful you decided to add pumpkins to your garden plans.

## RADISHES

*Planting Method:* Direct sow seeds as soon as the soil is workable in the spring, usually about 2 to 4 weeks before your last spring frost date.

*Planting Notes:* Radishes are a cool-weather vegetable and do best in temperatures of less than 65°F. Plant them as early as you can to avoid them bolting and becoming bitter. You can also plant them in late summer for a fall harvest.

## SQUASH

*Planting Method:* Direct sow seeds 1 to 2 weeks after your last spring frost date. You can start squash seeds indoors 3 to 4 weeks before your last spring frost date. Do not transplant them outdoors until all danger of frost has passed.

*Planting Notes:* Squash are generally divided into two categories. Summer squash (such as zucchini, crookneck, and pattypan) are ready earlier in the season, have thinner skin, and do not store very long. Winter squash (such as acorn, butternut, Hubbard, and spaghetti squash) won't be ready for harvest until late summer or early fall, but have a thick rind that allows them to last in storage most of the winter if conditions are right. Serve summer squash in Summer Squash Gratin (page 133) or make Butternut Pasta Sauce (page 78) with your winter varieties.

## TOMATOES

*Planting Method:* Start seeds indoors 6 to 8 weeks before your last spring frost date unless you live in a very warm climate. Do not transplant tomatoes outdoors until all danger of frost has passed and your soil temperature reaches at least 60°F.

*Planting Notes:* Several weeks before you plan to transplant your tomatoes, harden them off by setting them outside during the day as the weather warms. This helps to minimize transplant shock. Place the seedlings deep into their holes for stronger plants. You'll love having homegrown tomatoes for Warm Cherry Tomato Salad (page 145).

# The Herb Garden

Herbs are an absolute necessity in my kitchen. I would be clueless if I had to cook without them. While I do purchase and use a considerable amount of dried herbs, I grow as many as I possibly can. One of the very best parts about herbs is that it takes exactly zero acres of land to grow them—if you have a sunny windowsill, you've got this covered. Use pots with plenty of drainage (place a tray or saucer underneath to catch overflow) and feed them monthly with fertilizer designed for edible plants and you'll be well on your way to growing fresh flavors for all sorts of dishes. Here's a list of my favorites, which I plant or maintain every year without fail.

### BASIL

An annual you can start from seed or purchase from your local nursery, basil is an herb no homestead should be without. Plant basil next to tomatoes to ward off pests, or put it in a pot in a sunny window. As it grows, pinch off any flowers to keep it producing as long as possible. Use your fresh basil for Warm Cherry Tomato Salad (page 145) and Tomato Basil Galette (page 92).

### DILL

Nothing says "summertime" more than seeing tall stalks of dill poking above the fence in my herb garden. Although it's a biennial like parsley, dill loves to self-seed and will come back year after year once it is established. Dill dries well if you wish to save it for later in the year and is an important addition to Herbed Potato Salad (page 138) and Garlic Dill Icebox Pickles (page 127).

### CHIVES

I have a soft spot for chives, so it makes me happy that they seem to love our harsh climate. They stay green well into the fall, happily come back each spring without any attention from me, and have the prettiest purple flower puffs. I sprinkle fresh-cut chives over any egg dish (try them in Baked Eggs with Cream & Chives, page 28, as well as on baked potatoes or in Beet & Potato Mash, page 113). Mature chive plants can be dug up in the fall and brought inside to overwinter, or they'll happily grow in a sunny window all year long. They don't keep as well as some other herbs, so enjoy them fresh as long as you can.

### LAVENDER

Most people think of lavender as purely a medicinal herb, but its gentle floral flavor makes it a delicious addition to kitchen concoctions too. I like to grow lavender in my front yard flowerbeds—it's gorgeous when it blooms, returns year after year, and will gladly star in the delicately sweet Lavender Honey Custards (page 207).

## MINT

One day in a fit of rebellion, I planted my new mint plants directly in the herb garden, even though all the experts say to only ever plant mint in containers. And sure enough, the two tiny plants have multiplied like rabbits and are currently threatening to take over, just like the experts promised. Once mint is established, it grows like wildfire, so yes, it is indeed advisable to follow the rules and grow it in pots or beds with a clear boundary. (Unless you like to learn things the hard way like me.) You should only have to plant it once, as it comes back each year with a passion. Mint varieties go far beyond basic peppermint, so check your local nurseries to see what interesting variations you can find. (Chocolate Mint is my favorite. Yes, it's a real thing!) Use an abundance of mint to make Homemade Mint Syrup (page 224), and you can also brew peppermint leaves into a tea to soothe tummy troubles.

## OREGANO & MARJORAM

These two gems are related, which explains why I always have to look twice when I'm searching for one or the other in the garden. Both will overwinter in warm climates, but like rosemary, they don't love our hard-core winters, so I do replant them each year. Oregano regularly makes appearances in tomato dishes around our homestead, while marjoram is fabulous in soups and paired with meats.

## PARSLEY

Parsley is a biennial, which means it takes two years to complete its life cycle. I grow both flat-leaf and curly parsley and my motto is, "When in doubt, throw some parsley on top." It dries well and can be saved for use throughout the winter, or keep the plant inside year-round in your windowsill garden.

## ROSEMARY

In warmer climates, rosemary is a perennial so prolific it is sometimes used as a hedge. But alas, here in Wyoming I'm just excited if my tiny rosemary plant doubles in size over the summer. Rosemary doesn't love cold locations, so if you live in a place like I do, you'll have to replant it each year, or at least dig it up and bring it inside over the winter (rosemary likes being a houseplant too). I use rosemary both dried and fresh in soups, stews, stock, and especially for Homemade Bacon (page 37).

## SAGE

I can't get enough of sage. It comes back every year, withstands hard frosts, and pairs beautifully with countless dishes. Interestingly, it isn't as hardy in humid environments, which makes it a perfect fit for our super-dry location. Dried or fresh sage goes into my homemade stocks, as well as into Butternut Pasta Sauce (page 78). It also makes an excellent addition to your indoor herb garden.

## THYME

While I use plenty of dried thyme in my recipes during the colder months, I make a point to add the fresh leaves to every recipe I can in the summer—nothing quite compares to thyme picked right outside the front door. Thyme is another perennial that will happily come back year after year in most locations. It pairs perfectly with soups, roasted chicken, potatoes of all kinds, and countless other dishes.

# eggs, milk & meat

*It's been fascinating to watch the rise of* backyard chickens over the past several years. When we brought home our first flock in 2009, the craze hadn't yet caught on in our area, and I received more than one set of raised eyebrows when I proudly announced we were the new owners of ten Rhode Island Red hens. At that point in history, there weren't assemble-at-home chicken coops for sale at all the local home improvement stores, and while the feed store in town did sell chicks, I had to stalk the sales associates in order to get the exact varieties I wanted before they were gone.

These days, nearly everyone I know has chickens in their backyard. Pinterest is jam-packed with inspiration for designer coops complete with chandeliers and couches, DIY rainbow-colored chicken treats, and instructions for knitting your hens their own sweaters. More and more urban areas are shifting regulations to allow for a handful of hens in urban backyards, so you don't have to live in the country to become a chicken keeper. Backyard poultry is here to stay, y'all.

While I always pause to admire glamorous coops and the creative ways folks entertain their flocks, I personally lean more toward the utilitarian side of things when it comes to poultry. I think of my chickens less as pets and more as working partners in this food-production gig. I don't name my hens (mostly because I can't tell them apart, no matter how hard I try) and knitting sweaters isn't exactly my forte. But I still admire every single blue and brown egg I carry into the house and can't help but smile when the rooster brings his crew up to the front lawn to hunt bugs.

Chickens are the perfect introduction to the animal husbandry side of homesteading. They are simple to get started with, don't take up much space, and provide quick gratification in the form of dozens of eggs. When you break open a grocery store egg next to a homestead egg, the difference is impressive. The vibrant orange yolks of homegrown eggs make their factory-farmed counterparts look pale and anemic. But the richness doesn't stop with the color. Farm-fresh eggs tend to add a deeper flavor to recipes you just can't duplicate with eggs from the store.

# Farm Fresh Egg 101

As much as I love talking all things chicken, it's really all about the eggs for me. Brown, green, blue, white, tan, olive, pink, or chocolate. Depending on the breed of chickens you choose, there's a rainbow waiting to fill your basket. Thanks to the seasonal nature of laying hens, it tends to be either feast or famine when it comes to eggs. I find myself either begging unsuspecting visitors to take them off my hands or rationing them as though they are the only eggs left in the world. For obvious reasons, I much prefer the times of the year when I have more eggs than I can handle, and that's exactly when I'm in the kitchen making Prairie Cream Puffs (page 210), baked eggs (see page 28), and frittatas of all shapes and sizes (see page 27). Excess eggs are also fantastic for bartering with neighbors, and I've traded cartons of freshly laid eggs for veggies or meats grown by homesteading friends more than once.

## Storing Eggs

I keep a chipped enamel bowl full of eggs on my kitchen counter at all times, which I know has alarmed more than one guest when they've walked into my kitchen. Contrary to popular belief, I'm not attempting to flirt with food poisoning.

I like leaving eggs out of the refrigerator for a number of reasons. First, it keeps them easily accessible, which is a definite bonus when you use as many eggs as I do in daily cooking. Second, many baking recipes call for eggs to be at room temperature, and I don't know about you, but I find it nearly impossible to remember to set eggs out of the refrigerator prior to starting any recipe. And finally, farm-fresh eggs simply do not have to be chilled in order to keep them from spoiling.

I just heard the collective gasp. I realize unchilled eggs are a revolutionary concept, but that's really only the case in modern-day America. Great-great-grandma would have left her eggs out without a second thought, and cooks in other parts of the world, most notably Europe, have always left their eggs out of the fridge.

## Washing Eggs

Interestingly enough, the safety of eggs left at room temperature mostly comes down to washing. Because the USDA requires all graded eggs to be washed

and sanitized before they are sold, eggs brought home from the store should immediately be refrigerated. European regulations, on the other hand, require processors to *not* wash their eggs prior to selling them to consumers. Therefore, American eggs would technically be against regulations in Europe, and vice versa. This means as long as you are not washing your homegrown eggs, there should be no problem admiring them on your countertop for a while.

I'm not a fussy person when it comes to homegrown food, so the occasional feather or chicken dropping stuck to an egg doesn't bother me very much. However, I know some folks prefer shiny, uniform eggs, especially if they are selling them or sharing with friends. At first glance, egg washing might seem like a no-brainer, but there are a few things you should know.

Eggshells are porous by nature and naturally covered with a thin film called the *cuticle* or *bloom*. The bloom protects potential baby chicks and slows the process of the liquid part of the egg evaporating through the shell. It's pretty darn amazing when you think about it. Thanks to this bloom, bacteria have a hard time penetrating an eggshell. When you wash an egg, the built-in protection is removed and the porous shell is left exposed and wet. This can create an ideal environment for lurking microbes to enter the egg. If you plan to use eggs immediately after washing, this isn't a huge deal. However, if you plan to store washed eggs, they should be dried thoroughly and kept chilled until use.

I have never used bleach or any sort of chemical wash on my eggs—just water. Only use hot water (at least 90°F) to wash eggs. A cold rinse will cause the contents of the egg to contract and pull bacteria on the shell into the egg. Don't leave eggs soaking in water; just rinse them until they are clean, then dry them thoroughly. Some homesteaders opt out of water altogether and use fine-grit sandpaper to buff off lightly soiled areas. This still damages the bloom on the area where the sandpaper was used, but it keeps the rest of the egg dry, which helps to prevent any contraction inside the egg.

An ounce of prevention is worth a pound of cure. Keep your nesting boxes clean and refresh frequently with clean shavings and you'll save yourself time by not having to deal with dirty eggs.

## How Long Will Eggs Last?

Most experts advise keeping eggs out on the counter for no more than one to two weeks. I usually work through even the oldest eggs in my bowl easily in that time frame, and if I ever do end up with more than I can use, I just pop them in the fridge. I've never had an egg go bad on the counter, even when I've left them out for longer than recommended. However, eggs stored at room temperature will lose moisture at a slightly faster rate. This isn't anything to be alarmed about; it just means the white of the egg will slowly become thicker over time. It happens after long-term storage in the refrigerator too, but takes much longer.

Chilled eggs should last for several months—in fact, I've had cartons get lost in the back of my fridge for over six months and they never went bad. The egg whites were thicker, but otherwise, everything was normal. (If an egg is bad, you'll be able to smell it as soon as you crack it—toss those immediately!) Eggs are amazing, y'all.

## How Many Chickens Do I Need?

The size of your flock will depend on your location and needs. Chickens in the prime of life usually lay an egg a day, with the exact rate varying throughout the year. I usually keep far more chickens than I need (I think I have around forty running around outside at the moment), but I like having eggs to share, and I use plenty in my cooking.

The biggest disappointment of keeping laying hens is when you first realize eggs are a seasonal food. It's easy to overlook this since eggs are so easily available at the grocery store year-round. When daylight hours decrease in the fall, it signals the hens' bodies to slow down egg production or stop it altogether. They usually won't resume laying until spring when the days lengthen once again. So, much to my dismay, there is almost always a portion of the year when I find myself feeding forty chickens, but still buying eggs at the store.

You can trick a chicken into thinking the days are longer with the use of supplemental lighting. A regular 25- or 40-watt bulb left on in the coop is usually sufficient to keep hens laying throughout the winter. Keep the bulb on long enough to bring the total amount of light per day to around 16 hours. (Avoid leaving the light on all night long—this can stress out your birds.)

We have used the lightbulb technique in years past, but these days, I usually just leave the lights off. I feel good about giving my hens a break, and some chicken enthusiasts even claim that forcing hens to lay year-round causes them to wear out faster. (I've yet to see verifiable evidence of this, but it makes sense.)

I've come to terms with eggs being a seasonal food, and I'm at peace if there are times of the year when we don't have scrambled eggs four days a week. We eat as many custards and omelets as we can handle during egg season and then redirect to other dishes during our periodic egg famines.

Even if you *do* use the lightbulb method, you should still plan for a period of reduced egg production once a year when your birds molt. Molting is a natural process of shedding old feathers and growing new ones. It usually takes anywhere from two to five months for a chicken to complete a molting cycle and egg production naturally slows during that time to allow protein to go to feather growth instead. Molting chickens resemble mangy, half-naked ragamuffins, but don't worry—the feathers will return eventually.

## Chicks or Pullets?

It takes chicks five to six months to start laying. This means if you purchase chicks in the spring like most folks, you won't have eggs until late summer or early fall. If you are in a hurry for farm-fresh eggs, it may be worthwhile to check the classified ads for pullets for sale. Pullets (hens less than a year old) cost more than chicks, so it may or may not be worth it to start with them, depending on the urgency of your egg craving. Avoid purchasing birds more than two years old, since a hen's egg production decreases as she ages.

I like to purchase a fresh batch of chicks when my existing flock is two to three years old. This allows me to collect eggs from my mature hens while my chicks are maturing, and ensures I have replacement hens as my previous flock ages.

## Coop Considerations

The good news is, while chickens do require a shelter of some sort, they usually aren't too picky. So if you can't find just the right chandelier to adorn their coop, they'll still love you. That being said, there are a few important things to take into consideration as you prepare to take the chicken plunge.

## Roosts

Birds prefer to be off the ground when they sleep and providing them with a roosting area will also keep them warmer in the winter. Our roosts are 2x4 boards attached to the walls of our coop. I've also seen folks create tiered roosts if they are short on space—I love that idea too. Aim for about 12 inches of roost space per bird, even though they'll probably crowd in tighter than that. Position a board under the roosting areas to catch the accumulating chicken poop. (You can carry the board outside and scrape it off right into the compost pile.)

## Nesting Boxes

Most laying hens prefer a semienclosed space to lay their eggs. Nesting boxes keep eggs off the ground and help to prevent them from getting broken or eaten by other animals. It's also much easier to collect eggs from a box versus hunting all over the yard for them in hidden nests. The sky is the limit when it comes to nesting box construction—you can either build them yourself out of scrap lumber or use cast-off items like crates, bins, or five-gallon buckets (with their bottom screwed to the wall) to create repurposed boxes. Boxes should be sized around 12 x 12 inches, and it's best if you hang them several feet off the ground. I regularly fill our nesting boxes with clean pine shavings or straw, and like to tuck in sprigs of lavender, mint, or dill when the herb garden is in full swing. (Chickens seem to love herbs just as much as we do!)

## Chicken Run or Yard

If given the choice, chickens will always choose roaming over being locked in a small area. Keeping chickens constantly confined in tight quarters can also create unwanted behaviors like pecking or egg eating. You don't need acres and acres for your flock, but you should provide them with a small area to allow them to get fresh air and scratch in the dirt a bit.

We let our chickens range freely and they cover an impressive amount of our barnyard in their quest for the best bugs and seeds. I've learned the hard way how destructive hens are to gardens, so we have a chicken-proof fence around our raised beds. Otherwise, I love to watch them scratch through the cow patties in the corrals and rummage around the compost piles.

If free ranging isn't an option for your flock, you will need some sort of yard to keep them where they should be. If predators aren't a concern, classic chicken wire wrapped around a wooden frame is a simple option. We built our chicken run out of sturdy chain-link kennel panels. It's not as charming as a picket fence, but does a suitable job of keeping out coyotes and determined dogs, and it isn't easily crushed under our massive snowdrifts. If you have problems with predators, you may need to bury a portion of wire under the ground or put netting over the top of your run. So far, we've been able to avoid both of these things by making sure the hens are inside the coop at night with the door shut.

# the chicken bucket

There are lots of things I miss about our homestead when I travel, but there's one thing that feels especially absent when I'm preparing food away from my own kitchen: the chicken bucket.

The humble galvanized pail sits next to my sink. Every bit of scrap food my kitchen churns out ends up in that bucket eventually. Bits of stale bread, carrot tops, celery ends, peels, gristly morsels of meat, spoiled fruit, you name it. Instead of going into the trash, it gets tossed in the pail to be carried outside by the grubby hands of a Prairie Kid, where it's devoured in 15 seconds flat by a horde of hungry birds. The chickens pick out their favorite parts first (tomato bits and strawberry tops are always a hit), then work through the rest. Anything they don't eat is scraped up and added to the compost pile.

The chicken bucket feels so normal to me; I miss it when I'm cooking in a bucketless kitchen. On the occasions where I've found myself cooking meals in a rental house, it's been painful to have no choice but to toss broccoli stems or apple cores in the trash. (I've actually brought home vegetable scraps from friends' houses before.)

There are a few things I don't put into the bucket. Coffee grounds (due to the caffeine), anything with lots of sugar, and anything that is very moldy are the main things to avoid, but most everything else is fair game. (There is some debate as to whether citrus and avocados are safe for chickens, but I've never had an issue with my flock consuming them in small quantities.)

Food waste is an alarming issue, with 35 million tons of food thrown in the trash in America each year. There are a lot of ways we can remedy this massive problem, but I can't help but think a chicken bucket in every kitchen would be a great place to start. If you don't have chickens, find a friend who does and share your scraps with them. Or start a backyard compost bin.

Mobile chicken coops or chicken tractors are another option when it comes to giving your flock room to roam. These contraptions vary in size and complexity, but usually have wheels of some sort so the chicken keeper can shift the location of the flock around the pasture or barnyard for maximum grazing with minimal predator risk. The continual movement also fertilizes the grass—some farmers strategically move a chicken tractor into a pasture where their cattle have just been to break up the cow patties and further nourish the grass. I've always been intrigued by the concept of a mobile coop, but have been hesitant to try it, as Wyoming's legendary winds cause me to have visions of the tractor flying by the window in a flurry of feathers. Perhaps someday we can figure out how to anchor it sufficiently and will feel confident enough to give it a try.

## Ventilation

It's not the most exciting aspect to think about when you're designing your dream coop, but it's crucially important. Chickens need proper ventilation to stay healthy and stuffy coops can create sick birds as ammonia and dust particles accumulate. A buildup of humid air can increase your flock's risk of frostbite as well. Windows, vents, and holes can all assist with airflow, but avoid cold air blowing directly on your birds, since a drafty coop will cause problems of its own.

## Bedding and Flooring

Our chicken coop came with a raised floor, but if I had to start over, I'd definitely opt for a dirt base so I could use the deep-litter method. Deep litter is an in-coop composting approach, where instead of stripping the coop each week, fresh bedding or shavings are added on top of the old and worked in with a manure fork. As the layers grow, microorganisms start to break them down and produce a small amount of heat. This helps to warm the coop in the winter and keeps unpleasant aromas to a minimum. At the end of the season, you're left with a rich layer of decomposed bedding that can be taken to your compost pile. Unfortunately, I can't use deep litter because it will rot wooden floorboards, so instead, I cover our coop floor with a 4- to 5-inch layer of pine shavings (straw is another option) and refresh it every several weeks to keep manure and ammonia odors to a minimum.

## Feeders and Waterers

Feeders don't need to be fancy and can be as basic as rubber pans filled with feed and water. Although I have tried the ever-popular PVC-pipe feeders that are all over Pinterest, I prefer a simple DIY bucket setup. I repurposed a three-gallon plastic bucket that held a shrub from the garden store. We enlarged the drainage holes in the bottom with a hole saw and attached it to a shallow metal pan mounted on top of a frame of 2x4s.

Our waterers are the plain galvanized ones available at any feed store. We suspend them about six inches off the ground with a length of chain attached to the ceiling. This keeps the water cleaner and eliminates the temptation for the ducks to attempt to take baths in the small rim of water (they have a swimming pool outside for that). In the coldest winter months, we switch to a heated dog bowl. It's more work to fill it up daily, but I appreciate not having to constantly break ice.

As far as feed storage goes, invest in a few trash cans with lids to store grain. To discourage mice, keep the lids tightly in place at all times. If you really struggle with rodents, consider only feeding as much food as your flock can consume in one sitting, versus free-choice feeding, which can turn into a 24-hour rodent buffet.

## Electricity

Electricity in your coop isn't an absolute necessity, but I definitely recommend it. Even if you live in a tropical climate where heat lamps aren't needed, you'll eventually end up doing chores in the dark or checking on your birds late at night—flipping on a switch is much handier than fumbling around with a flashlight. Electricity also enables you to provide supplemental lighting to increase egg production or heated water buckets in the winter if you decide to go that route.

THE HEAT LAMP DEBATE—If you homestead in a frigid environment like we do, heat lamps are a frequent topic of conversation and, believe it or not, are pretty controversial in most chicken circles. Heat lamps are notoriously dangerous and have been the cause of countless coop and barn fires, which makes me very hesitant to use them. Chickens are much hardier than we give them credit for. (The exception here would be chicks—young birds do require heat until they are fully feathered, around six weeks of age.)

In the past when I've had heat lamps turned on in the coop, I have personally observed my flock moving as far away from them as possible, even on days when the temperature is well below zero. I've also watched my entire flock go outside of their own accord on the coldest days of the year to roam and forage. This further confirmed my suspicions that keeping their environment at a constant balmy temperature might not be as important as I once thought.

However, just because you might be able to skip the heat lamps doesn't mean you can ignore your birds in the winter altogether. Take special care to make sure they have plenty of feed and unfrozen water and provide roosting areas to keep them off the cold floor and to encourage them to huddle next to one another, which is a position they naturally prefer. While ventilation is crucial, especially in humid areas, drafts can be dangerous. Keep vents and windows up high to avoid having any freezing air blowing in directly on your birds.

If you still can't reconcile the thought of your birds being in an unheated coop, or you are concerned about the combination of humidity and cold causing issues, consider using a heating option with fewer fire risks, such as the plastic heating plates available for dog kennels. If you are determined to use heat lamps, proceed with extreme caution, making sure they are securely bolted to the wall and all wiring is in immaculate condition.

## The Home Dairy

Whenever the topic of home dairying comes up, I can't help but become a bit sentimental. From the very beginning of our journey, dairy animals always felt like the ultimate mark of a successful homestead. I vividly remember lying on the floor with a pile of borrowed goat books as my thoughts raced with the possibilities. At first the notion seemed unattainable. Goats? Raw milk? Us? But like most crazy ideas have the tendency to do, my schemes tumbled around in my brain until I became convinced dairy goats were inevitable.

In the most epic episode of impulse buying ever, we proudly hauled home a pair of pregnant Nubian goats when I was nine months pregnant with Mesa, our first child. The goats and I ended up having our babies just a few days apart. In hindsight, it probably made my postpartum recovery a little wilder than it should have been, but I was in homesteader heaven.

The world of goats felt foreign at first, but quickly became routine. I grew in confidence each kidding season as I helped slippery twins and triplets navigate their way into the world, guided the wobbly babies to find their first taste of milk, and reassured hesitant first-time mamas. Mesa accompanied me on nearly every trip I made into the barn, first as an infant buckled into our barnyard stroller, and then toddling after me in her tiny mud boots as she grew.

And the milk . . . Oh, the milk. After watching so many people turn up their noses at the mention of goat's milk, I was secretly nervous the first time I poured myself a glass of fresh milk from our does. My hesitation vanished upon first gulp. The milk tasted sweet and clean, without one bit of the "goatiness" so many people claimed it would have.

Then one day, for various reasons, it was time to graduate from the goats. With a mixture of pride and wondering what on earth we were getting ourselves into, we hauled home our very first cow. (See below for the pros and cons of goats and cows.) Oakley, a two-year-old Brown Swiss, had never been haltered or milked, and was shortly due to pop out her first calf. Thankfully the easygoing nature of the Brown Swiss made the training process easy, and we've never even needed a stanchion to milk her—she stands patiently at the fence, munches on hay, and waits for me to finish.

A family milk cow contributes to a homestead like no other animal. Her generous supply of milk feeds not only her calf, but also nourishes occasional orphan calves as well. She shares her milk with her humans who, after drinking their fill, can turn it into cheese, butter, yogurt, ice cream, and so much more. Her calves fill the freezer with meat once they mature, or can be sold for a profit, and her manure nourishes the soil and gardens. A good family cow is so much more than mere livestock. She's a partner in every sense of the word and earns her keep extraordinarily well.

Romance aside, home dairying is a sizable commitment, and not one to take on lightly. However, if your schedule and space will allow, consider it. It's one of the most satisfying aspects of homesteading there is, and the rewards for your labor will be sweet and creamy.

## The Great Debate: Cow vs. Goat

Goats were our gateway animals into the world of home dairying, and I'll be forever grateful for them giving me the confidence and knowledge I needed at that time. Even though I just milk cows these days, I'm still very much pro-goat. There are definitely advantages to each type of dairy animal, and it's really up to your preferences and situation to decide which one is exactly right for you.

## THE ADVANTAGES OF KEEPING DAIRY GOATS

**THEY COST LESS**—Dairy goats are much more affordable than a milk cow. Exact costs vary, but expect to pay anywhere from $100 to $400 for a starter goat, depending on the age, breed, and whether it is registered. Like most herd animals, goats do best when kept with a buddy, so plan to get more than one.

**THEY EAT LESS**—The average full-sized goat will consume four to five pounds of hay per day, which is much, much less than a cow eats. Goats are also more prone to eat weeds that cause most cattle to turn up their noses, though they are pickier than many people expect.

**THEY TAKE UP LESS SPACE**—If you don't have acres of pasture or large pens, goats are ideal since they do not require as much space as a cow. If you don't have a lot of pasture space, it's far more cost-effective to feed a goat hay year-round than to feed a cow.

**THEY ARE LESS INTIMIDATING**—Newbies to the world of homesteading often find cows intimidating, especially when you're sitting underneath them to grab a handful of udder. Goats are much easier to handle, haul, and manage if you don't have a lot of experience around large animals. Also, when breeding season arrives, bucks are much easier to handle or borrow than a large and sometimes ornery bull.

**THEY GIVE LESS MILK**—If you have a small family, or don't have the time to deal with the massive quantities of milk a cow can produce, a goat is probably perfect for you. And yes, goat's milk tastes amazing. As long as it has been handled and cooled correctly, it's delicious. And of course, there's chèvre (page 247).

## THE DISADVANTAGES OF KEEPING DAIRY GOATS

**GOATS DON'T BELIEVE IN FENCES**—Goats will climb through barbed wire like it's not even there, and rail fences mean nothing to them. This was a huge factor in us switching over to our milk cow—the idea of re-fencing our entire perimeter fence in wire panels was not appealing. Goats can be fenced in, but expect to use sturdy materials or electric fence.

**THEY GIVE LESS MILK**—Depending on your situation, this can be a good thing or a bad thing. If you plan to use a lot of milk or pursue cheese making as a hobby, you'll probably need to milk several goats at once.

**THE CREAM DOESN'T RISE**—Goat's milk is naturally homogenized, which means the cream does not easily rise to the top. A mechanical cream separator will be required if you hope to make goat butter or whipped cream. As you might have noticed by the recipes in this book, I'm slightly obsessed with cream, so this was always the biggest drawback for me.

## THE ADVANTAGES OF KEEPING A MILK COW

**FENCING IS SIMPLE**—Cows are usually easily contained with basic barbed wire or a wooden fence. Hallelujah.

**SO. MUCH. MILK.**—A milk cow can easily produce four or more gallons of milk per day, which is far more than the average family needs. This gives you lots of options for cheese making or sharing with homesteading friends.

**YOU CAN FEED OTHER ANIMALS**—Excess milk (and there will be excess eventually, I promise) can be fed to pigs to fatten them up, or given in smaller quantities to chickens or dogs as a treat. Some cows give so much milk they can even take on additional calves. Oakley has nursed more than one orphaned calf from the ranches down the road.

**BEAUTIFUL, BEAUTIFUL CREAM**—The first time I opened the refrigerator and found a six-inch cream line in my milk jar, I could hardly contain myself. Cow cream will rise to the top with zero assistance and can be turned into butter, whipped cream, and cream cheese. Oh my.

**CALVES TO FILL THE FREEZER**—You can eat goat meat too, but we've found our dairy steers to make excellent beef after we raise them on grass for about 18 months.

## THE DISADVANTAGES OF KEEPING A MILK COW

**COWS AREN'T CHEAP**—Expect to pay anywhere from $1,000 to $3,000 for a milk cow, with the exact price being determined by the age, breed, and experience of the animal.

**THEY NEED SPECIAL TRANSPORTATION**—You'll need a truck and stock trailer to haul your milk cow (unless you can bribe trailer-owning friends to help you out). In comparison, it is possible to haul a goat in a minivan. Just sayin'.

**COWS NEED SPACE**—One cow usually requires around two to five acres of pasture, depending on the quality and quantity of your grass. We have 60 acres of pasture here on our homestead, but even that isn't enough to feed our animals year around. We supplement with hay from October to April to allow our pastures to rest, which brings me to my next point.

**COWS EAT A LOT**—A full-grown cow may eat as much as 30 to 40 pounds of hay or forage per day. If you have plenty of pasture, this won't be as much of an issue, although you'll likely need to supplement with hay during the colder months.

**SO. MUCH. MILK.**—Initially, this is ridiculously fun. And then you start running out of room in the fridge for anything else. And you can't possibly make enough cheese and yogurt to use it all up. And you start to feel like you're drowning in milk. There are ways to deal with an overabundance of fresh milk, but it takes a bit of forethought.

## My Recommendation

If you are just starting this homesteading adventure, go with goats. They will give you a solid introduction into the world of home dairying, and don't come with as much cost or risk as a cow. However, if you're feeling a bit more adventurous (and really love cream), a cow just might be your perfect solution.

I can attest that both animals have made my personal homesteading story so much more gratifying. The time spent cleaning pens and squirting milk into a bucket feels 100 percent worth it the first time you take a sip of milk from your very own dairy animal.

### WHICH BREED?

Regardless of whether you choose goats or cows, select a breed of animal specifically bred for milking. In the goat world, this would be Nubians, LaManchas, Alpines, Toggenburgs, Nigerian Dwarfs, or Saanens. In the cow world, this would be Brown Swiss, Jerseys, Milking Shorthorns, Ayrshires, Guernseys, or Holsteins.

It's worthwhile to spend time researching the different breeds to decide which traits are most important to you. For example, Holsteins and Saanens give a large volume of milk, but it will have lower butterfat content. This isn't as desirable if you plan to make lots of cheese. Toggenburg goats have stronger-tasting milk, which is prized by some cheese makers, and Guernsey cows are famed for their golden yellow milk that contains more beta-carotene than other breeds'.

## Home Dairy Equipment

Once you've settled on which species of animal you plan to milk, it's time to put together the rest of your home dairy. It's entirely possible to spend thousands of dollars on various pieces of dairy equipment, but you can just as easily collect fresh milk with very minimal upfront cost. Home dairy equipment doesn't have to be fancy to be functional. Fresh milk and saving money—two of my favorite things.

## Milking Machine

If you plan to milk just one or two goats or cows, a milking machine is not a necessity. Not only are they a considerable investment (expect to pay upward of $1,500 for a full setup), they require meticulous cleaning after each use, which takes about the same amount of time as hand-milking a single cow. Therefore, if you just have one or two dairy animals, skip the machine and hone your hand-milking skills instead. Your fingers will be sore the first week or two, but the process becomes easier and more enjoyable the longer you do it.

## Stanchion or Milking Stand

A stanchion is a contraption that holds a dairy animal in place so you can milk in (moderate) peace. We have never used a stanchion for our cows—I prefer to teach them to stand tied while I milk. However, stanchions can be extremely handy if you have a young cow or a wild one, and can play a part in keeping the person doing the milking a little bit safer. When I was milking our goats, we built a milking stand for them, which was simply a small table with a head catch on one side. They would jump up on the platform and stick their head through a hole. I would then lock them into place, and they would stand and eat while I milked.

## Washes and Dips

There are plenty of commercial udder wash options out there, and some folks even use bleach or iodine on their animals. I usually just keep it basic and use a damp hand towel. I wipe down the udder and each teat, and then squirt several streams of milk out on the floor to flush the teat before I begin to milk into the bucket. It's simple and I've never had a single issue doing it this way. However, if you'd like to try something a bit more potent, mix up the essential oil–based spray on page 312.

Once milking is complete, commercial dairies dip each teat in a solution to help remove any mastitis-causing pathogens that may be lurking near the opening of the teat. This isn't something I regularly do for my cows, but if they were struggling with mastitis or other infection, I would absolutely consider it. You can purchase teat dips at your local farm store, but I prefer the soothing DIY option on page 312 instead.

# Homemade Udder Spray

*makes a little over a quart*

1 quart water

¼ cup apple cider vinegar

10 drops melaleuca (tea tree) essential oil

10 drops thyme essential oil

In a quart-sized spray bottle, combine all the ingredients. Spray the udder and teats thoroughly, then wipe off with a clean towel.

# Lavender Teat Dip

*makes one quart*

1 quart water

10 drops grapefruit seed extract

5 drops lavender essential oil

5 drops melaleuca (tea tree) essential oil

In a quart-sized bottle, combine all the ingredients. Pour a small amount of the solution into a cup and dip each teat. (Remember to discard the solution after you are done dipping. Do not pour it back into the main jar.) You can also mix in a spray bottle if you prefer to spray the solution directly on the teat, although it will need to be sprayed very well to ensure all surfaces of the teat are coated.

# when good milk goes bad

Have raw milk that looks slightly, eh, *different* than it did the day you first put it in the fridge? Don't toss it yet! One of my favorite parts of raw milk is the amazing way it never really goes bad—it simply changes forms. As the naturally occurring bacteria in fresh milk begin to break down the milk sugars, you'll notice raw milk will gradually lose its sweetness, though it will still be drinkable for a while. If the process continues long enough, the milk will eventually turn thick and tangy, which is also known as *clabber*. Most of us modern folk are unfamiliar with this process since pasteurized milk doesn't clabber, it just turns smelly and gross.

Because of the acid present in clabber, it was common to combine it with baking soda to act as a leavening agent in baked goods. When baking powder came on the scene, traditional clabber wasn't as necessary and thus it waned in popularity. (But it does make sense why one of the main baking powder manufacturers adopted the name Clabber Girl, doesn't it?)

You can use clabbered raw milk as a substitute for buttermilk in waffles and pancake recipes, or add it to muffins, biscuits, or yeast breads that call for milk. It can even be used to make puddings or smoothies, and some people like to add a dash of cocoa powder and maple syrup to clabbered milk for a tangy chocolate drink. (Remember: Only use soured *raw* milk. If pasteurized milk goes bad, you should just toss it.)

## Milk Bucket

A homesteader's milk bucket will see hard use over the years, so it's worth it to invest in a good one. A 13- to 16-quart stainless-steel bucket with lid will set you back $50 to $150 at most dairy supply stores and is a sufficient size for most milking sessions with your cow. For goats, a 4-quart bucket should be satisfactory, although you might need a smaller size if you have shorter goats.

I only use seamless stainless-steel buckets so they can be properly sanitized and won't leach off-flavors into the milk like plastic has the tendency to do.

There are lidless buckets for sale everywhere, but skip those. Take my word for it—you will want to have a lid to slap on the bucket when you finish milking to keep animals and dust out of your fresh milk.

## Strainer

Eventually something will end up floating in your milk and fishing a goat hair out of your mouth after you take a big sip just isn't fun. Stainless-steel dairy strainers usually run from $20 to $40 and have small disposable discs that filter out hair and dirt. Long ago I discovered the $8 cone-shaped reusable coffee filters with tight wire mesh make the perfect little strainer, so that is all I've ever used. They are easy to sanitize in the dishwasher and can be used over and over again without having to buy any replacement parts. (If you're filtering into a small-mouth jar, set the coffee filter inside a funnel first.)

## Jars

I only store my raw milk in glass—never plastic. Glass is easy to sanitize and doesn't hold on to weird flavors. Quart-sized jars will work for goats, but you'll need to collect many, many gallon-size jars if you are milking a cow.

## Cream Separator

I'm about as low-tech as you can be on this one—I've only ever used a ladle to skim the cream from my milk. A manual (nonelectric) cream separator costs around $650, while fancier models cost even more. Cream separators also require meticulous cleaning after each use, which is another reason I prefer a good old-fashioned ladle. If you are milking goats and really want cream, you will need a separator to collect the cream, as it will not rise to the surface on its own.

# why we went raw

Raw milk is a constant source of controversy, and I'm not sure that will ever change. There are risks associated with consuming raw dairy, but I would argue there are risks connected to many of the foods we consume daily without thought. (Fruits and vegetables alone cause many thousands of cases of food poisoning each year.)

While I personally believe the risks of properly sourced raw milk are very minimal, the decision to consume raw dairy is ultimately a personal one based on your comfort level and the quality of the farms in your area. When on the hunt for a local source of raw milk, look for farms that allow tours of their facilities and are transparent about their herd health, equipment sanitation, and milk handling procedures. Familiarize yourself with what is and is not appropriate so you feel comfortable making the choice if a producer is a match for you.

We made the choice to go raw almost ten years ago and haven't looked back. While private raw milk sales are legal in Wyoming (laws differ from state to state), we don't have an abundance of producers in our area, so we continue to milk our own cows. Here are a few of the reasons we continue to keep home dairy animals despite the frigid morning milkings and constant chores.

## IT'S GOOD FOR YOU

When I first began to research raw milk, the health benefits were what initially caught my attention. Raw milk is a living food that contains higher levels of vitamins and minerals, which are normally lost in the pasteurization process. It also contains beneficial bacteria, amino acids, and enzymes that not only allow it to morph into all manner of tasty things, but are better for your gut.

Some (though not all) folks who are lactose-intolerant report being able to consume raw milk without a problem. Although I've never had an issue with lactose, I've had a tendency since childhood to become congested when I consume considerable amounts of pasteurized diary. Interestingly, I've found I can drink as much raw milk as I like without issue.

## IT TASTES BETTER

Up until the point we got our milk cow, I always avoided drinking large glasses of milk, as it not only would cause me to become congested, but it also always left a sour taste in my mouth. It wasn't until we started milking our cow Oakley that I discovered how much I actually loved the sweet, creamy taste of raw milk.

On a side note, I have heard a handful of people mention they think raw milk has a stronger taste. This isn't something I've noticed in our milk, but if you do find your milk tastes a little too much like a cow or barn, it could be related to the diet of the animal or the age of the milk.

## OH, THE POSSIBILITIES!

When pasteurized milk starts to go bad, it just gets nasty, but raw milk is a different substance entirely. As raw milk ages (or if you leave it out on the counter), it *clabbers*. Clabbered milk is full of probiotics and can be used as a buttermilk substitute in many recipes. It can also be fed to dogs, chickens, and pigs. One of the most magical parts of raw milk is that it doesn't go "bad" in the traditional sense—it just changes forms. For more on this, see page 313.

# How to Milk a Cow and Still Leave Your House

When it comes to keeping dairy animals, the biggest concern for most homesteaders is the commitment level. This particular aspect was the one that scared me the most before we purchased our first dairy goats. However if you are willing to share milk with the baby goats or calves, you have more options than you think. Share-milking, also known as once-a-day milking, has made cow ownership possible for us. I'm a huge fan!

## How to Milk Once a Day

In order to keep a goat or cow at peak production, it must be milked at approximately 12-hour intervals. With share-milking, the baby animal performs one of the milkings for you. Not only does this eliminate bottle-feeding and costly milk replacer, it creates more flexibility in your schedule as you only have to be out in the barn milking once a day, instead of twice.

Obviously, the biggest downfall to this method is that you'll get less milk. But for the average family, the milk collected from one milking each day is sufficient. I usually get more than 2 gallons a day from Oakley when I'm just milking in the mornings. That's plenty for us.

## A Day in the Life of a Share-Milker

Milking in the morning works best for my routine, but you can set up your schedule to accommodate evening milking too. It all depends on your daily schedule and other obligations. Here's a look at my routine.

- Around 8:00 p.m. prior to the day I plan to milk, I separate the calf or baby goats in a pen away from their mama. I always leave them where they can see their mother, so this isn't too traumatic. Put a bit of hay in the pen for them to chew on and make water available as well. Once everyone figures out the routine, the mama usually doesn't seem to mind the separation at all. (I think she secretly appreciates the break.)

- The next morning around 8:00 (I always aim for roughly 12 hours), I head outside with my bucket. Her udder will be full after an evening away from her babies, so I milk her out as much as I can. I usually don't have to worry about there not being enough milk left over for the babies, since most

mothers won't release all of their milk if they know their kids or calf are waiting for them.

- After milking, I release the babies and leave everyone together all day. They'll go out into the pasture, hang out in the corrals, and go about business as usual.

- When 8:00 p.m. rolls around, I repeat the process of separating mother and babies, and the routine starts once again.

- If I will be gone for a day or two, or taking a weekend trip, I simply leave the mama and babies together 24 hours a day. This eliminates the need to find someone else to milk for me during that period.

- To milk in the evening instead, simply reverse this routine. Lock the babies up during the day, milk in the evening, then turn them out together for the night.

The one downfall to this method is that some cows tend to hold back milk when they know their calf is right around the corner. Oakley is famous for this, and it's frustrating. I can milk her until it feels like there isn't a single drop left, but when I turn the calf loose, she'll let down the second flood of milk. This wouldn't be too much of an issue, other than that the richest part of the milk and most of the cream is in the hindmilk (the milk that lets down later in the milking process). Since Oakley holds that back, the calf gets the bulk of my cream.

When we are share-milking I can expect only a one- to two-inch cream line in my jars. I don't love the decrease in butter, but the flexibility it creates in my schedule is worth it. As soon as we wean the calves, the cream line increases to around four to six inches per gallon.

And that is my less-than-conventional approach to keeping a family cow. I use improvised milking equipment to cut costs, and employ share-milking to keep my sanity. We've been doing it this way for over seven years and it continues to work beautifully. I think it's a win-win for everyone involved—including the cow.

# Getting Started with Meat Animals

Every time I post something on the blog about growing our own meat, I'm reminded how polarizing this issue is. I honor the fact that some people feel better with a meatless diet, and if that describes you, feel free to skip this section.

My family and I feel better when we eat meat, so it is something we have intentionally chosen to include in our diet. Our freezers are filled to overflowing with neatly wrapped packages of consciously grown meats raised right here on our homestead. I haven't regularly purchased beef, pork, or chicken at the grocery store in years. I strongly believe that if I'm going to consume meat, I need to be willing to partake in the process of harvesting it. I like knowing our animals were raised in a respectful fashion, and that they were allowed to live the lives they were designed to. Our meat chickens peck grubs and weeds in the sunshine, the beef cattle graze on wide-open grassland, and the hogs spend their days rooting in the mud and enjoying every manner of kitchen scrap imaginable.

Only recently have we as a species become as disconnected as we are from our food sources. Even just 150 years ago, raising your own meat supply was the norm for a massive portion of the population, and I imagine our homesteading ancestors would have looked at a bag of frozen chicken breasts with serious suspicion. In a culture where we do everything possible to erase the fact that the contents of the neatly wrapped Styrofoam packages at the store were ever living, breathing creatures, it feels incredibly radical to butcher an animal you've raised yourself. It's easy to forget that all the meat we eat was alive at some point, regardless of whether you are the one to cut it up and put it in the freezer or someone else does the deed.

We process all our own chickens here on the homestead. We prefer to do them all at once, and usually recruit help to make the assembly-line process more efficient. While we have butchered several of our own hogs and cattle in the past, we recently have been taking them to local butcher shops to be processed instead. Handling beef takes special equipment and the meat is best if it can age for several weeks in a cooler before it's packaged. Our weather rarely cooperates enough to allow us to hang a side of beef for more than a day or two, so at this moment, it's worthwhile for us to haul our steers to town. However, the art of home butchery fascinates me, and it's a skill we plan to bring back to the homestead very soon.

Is it easy to take the life of an animal you know? No, it's not, and I don't expect that feeling to ever go away for me. In fact, I don't want it to go away. Killing should be hard, and if it isn't, we've become too callous. I don't relish

taking a life, and I respect the fact that it makes some people squeamish. However, if we're going to eat meat, we cannot hide from the process. Far too many folks never give their meat a thought, and I believe part of our stewardship as meat eaters involves acknowledging the sacrifice required. Breaking down an animal and watching it transform from flesh to food is a sacred process and causes you to appreciate every bite that much more.

Once I work through my initial emotions on butchering day, I'm filled with the same sense of exhilaration every single time. It's unbelievably empowering to learn the skills of butchering, and each and every time we do it, I can't help but marvel at the process. One of my favorite parts of homesteading is learning and honing new skills, and cutting up meat is no exception. It's amazing to stack meat in your freezer and know you had a part in growing it. And you know the animals were treated fairly, fed well, and lived exactly as they should.

A lot of folks reach out to me before their first harvesting day with concern over how their children will handle it. All kids are different, but ours have never been upset or bothered on butchering day. We don't make a big deal about it, but we don't hide it from them either. They're always outside with us on processing days, but we don't ask them to participate if they are hesitant. Depending on their age, sometimes they want to ask questions and touch, and sometimes they prefer to watch from a distance. We always make a clear differentiation between pets and livestock, so right from the beginning they understand which animals will be living with us permanently and which ones are here just for a short period.

So if you feel a little sad when butchering day rolls around, know that it's nothing to be ashamed about. Acknowledge the emotions, honor the animal, and then take pride in the experience of mastering a forgotten skill in our modern-day world.

If you're ready to opt out of the factory-farmed meats at the grocery store and are intrigued by the thought of home meat production, you have lots of options.

|  | BEEF | PORK | POULTRY |
|---|---|---|---|
| **SPACE REQUIRED** | Beef requires the most space of any homestead meat animal. The exact amount of pasture required depends on your location, the quality of your grass, and the breed of your cow. However, at the very minimum, I recommend at least several acres per animal with supplemental feeding of hay in the winter. Cattle can be kept in smaller pens or corrals, but will need to be fed hay year-round, which will increase the overall cost of raising your own beef. | Plan on at least 150 feet of pen space per pig. Some heritage breeds reportedly grow well on pasture, but will require electric fencing or wire panels to keep them contained (barbed wire won't cut it). I've never had much luck putting my pigs out to pasture though; they mostly just tear it up. | Plan on at least 10 square feet of outdoor space and 4 to 6 square feet of coop space for each bird, although I prefer to give them much more room than that. In the past, we've kept a mixed flock of poultry, but watch the flock dynamics carefully, as the different species have a tendency to pick on each other. Chickens can be extremely destructive, so if you plan to free-range your flock, make sure to fence them out of your gardens (ducks and geese tend to be kinder to plants). |
| **GROWTH PERIOD** | The ideal age to butcher a steer or heifer is between 1½ and 2 years. | The ideal age to butcher a hog is 4 to 6 months, with heritage breeds taking a bit longer to grow out. | Meat birds will be ready for butchering at 8 to 12 weeks of age, depending on the breed. (Heritage breeds take longer to mature.) |
| **BENEFITS** | Cattle don't require fancy fences or shelters. Even if you live in a harsh climate, a simple three-sided shed or windbreak will suffice. | Pigs love kitchen scraps, so you'll never have to worry about food waste or excess milk if you have a milk cow. They also make great Rototillers and will happily dig up your garden in the fall. Pigs do best when they have a friend, so plan on getting at least two. We usually keep one or two for our own freezers and sell the others to family and friends, which offsets some of the cost of raising our own pork. | Thanks their short growth period, you can have a year's worth of chicken in the freezer within just a few short months. Anyone can learn to butcher poultry at home without a lot of expensive equipment, so this can be an ideal option for small-scale homesteaders. |

|  | LAMB | GOAT | RABBIT |
|---|---|---|---|
| **SPACE REQUIRED** | You can keep two to six sheep per acre of land, depending on the condition of your grass and pastures. They are social creatures, so plan on getting at least two. | You can keep two to eight goats per acre of land, depending on the condition of your grass and pastures. Goats are notorious escape artists; electric fencing or wire panels are a necessity for perimeter fences. | Each rabbit will need a hutch roughly 3x2 feet. |
| **GROWTH PERIOD** | The ideal age to butcher a lamb is between 5 and 6 months. | Depending on the amount and type of meat desired, goats can be butchered from 5 months to 2 years of age. | Rabbits are usually harvested between 8 to 12 weeks of age. |
| **BENEFITS** | Sheep are less intimidating (and less dangerous) than a steer. They are generally easy to handle and care for and grow efficiently on grass. | Other than accommodating their escape-artist tendencies, you don't need to invest in fancy facilities or shelter for your goats. They also are willing to eat a wider variety of plants and weeds than cattle or sheep. | Rabbits take the least space of any meat animal on this list and are cheap to feed on grass or hay. Their meat is higher in protein and lower in fat than many other options. While they yield a smaller quantity of meat, they do reproduce easily and have short gestation periods and large litters, so if you get in a rhythm you could feasibly produce a decent amount of meat with rabbits. |

# meat chickens: which breed?

I love incorporating heirloom and heritage varieties of plants and animals whenever possible here on the homestead, but I also have an unapologetically economical side. And so I found myself in a bit of a pickle the first year we raised chickens for the freezer.

Initially, I figured we'd obviously raise a heritage breed of meat birds. Our Brown Swiss milk cow and heirloom vegetables had been slam-dunk choices, so I assumed chickens would be no different. Our local farm store had two varieties of meat birds that first year—Red Rangers (a heritage breed) and Cornish Cross (a more modern hybrid variety), so we got some of each.

I had heard heritage breeds were slightly slower growing, but as the chicks grew, I was shocked at exactly how much slower the Red Rangers were. The Cornish Cross birds were ready to butcher many weeks before the others and yielded a larger amount of meat. Feed for meat birds is expensive, and a flock of birds eats *a lot.* The additional weeks of growing required by the heritage breeds ended up equaling a considerable chunk of cash. In the end, we just couldn't reconcile the added time and expense, so we have raised Cornish Cross birds ever since.

Cornish Cross chickens are a hybrid bird that grows quickly and efficiently. Contrary to popular belief, they are not genetically modified, but can have leg issues if not managed properly. We've had very few issues with our flocks, as long as we do not overfeed them and always butcher them between 8 to 10 weeks of age. Ours have the option of going outside if they wish, but they do tend to be lazier than our laying hens and don't care to roam as much.

Ultimately, the breed you choose should depend on the goals and desires you have for your homesteading experience. If heritage breeds are a top priority for you, look into the Red Ranger or Freedom Ranger breeds. Otherwise, a quicker-growing hybrid will be a more efficient option. There's no right or wrong answer—it's up to you to decide which breed is the best choice for you.

# stocking the larder

The larder, a room or area where food is stored, hearkens back to yesteryear and is a forerunner of the modern pantry. Old-fashioned larders contained root vegetables, ferments, cured meats, preserves, grains, nuts, and seeds. Nowadays, most modern homes have a closet for a pantry, if they're lucky, and it's mostly full of cereal, canned soups, and a few "just add water" instant dinners. It's a far cry from the food storage of our ancestors. Imagine for just a moment if we swapped out the cereal for fresh grains, the red-and-white-labeled soup cans for jars of home-canned stew, and the instant dinners for crates of potatoes and onions. Not only would folks have less of a reason to rush to the store on the heels of a blizzard prediction, but their health would be better for it too.

At any given time we could camp out at our homestead for weeks, even in the dead of winter, without visiting the store. We might run a little low on things like bananas and milk (if the cow weren't in milk at that moment), but we'd still eat like kings. There'd be jars of homegrown tomato sauce over fresh-made pasta, home-canned honey peaches to pair with oatmeal or porridge, and roasted potatoes to go with any cut of meat you could possibly imagine from our deep freezers.

But emergency preparedness is only part of the motivation in keeping a well-stocked larder. The main reason I spend so much time squirreling away food is that I've found a well-stocked pantry to be absolutely crucial to my ability to cook from scratch while living 40 miles from town. I've learned that if I maintain a certain baseline of ingredients, I can cook nearly everything my heart desires. That's especially comforting when the urge for pizza strikes on a Friday night and delivery isn't an option.

We have a small room with concrete walls in our basement that stays consistently cool and dark. It's our *official* larder, but I have food tucked away in multiple areas of the house. The downstairs room stores onion braids, potatoes, winter squash, dry-cured meats, garden seeds, five-gallon buckets of grains, most of my home-canned goods, and a selection of freeze-dried foods for long-term emergency situations. My upstairs pantry cabinets hold baking supplies, bulk herbs and spices, nuts, flour, and anything I find myself using on a more regular basis.

Just like the larders of yesterday, a supply of food in a home still equals security during hard times and ensures you have ample options for making nourishing recipes for your family. And the best part? You don't need a single acre to start building a larder of your own. If you live in a home with limited space, start with a designated cupboard or even a shelf you fill with foundational ingredients for from-scratch cooking, root vegetables, and dried herbs. If you can spare a bit more room, build a food stash in a closet, hutch, or freestanding cabinet. (Pro tip: Use glass jars, baskets, and shelves to organize your food stores. I've found if my larder is attractive—or at least tidy—I'm much more prone to keep it full and functional.) Even with grocery stores in every neighborhood and fast-food joints on every corner, a well-stocked larder is one old-fashioned tradition I'd be happy to carry on.

## A Note on Ingredients

Not all ingredients are created equal. Grocery store eggs are pale and lack the robust flavor of a farm-fresh egg. Cheap butter is white and soft, while high-quality butter is golden yellow and firm. Boxed broth, even organic, tastes like brown water compared to the richness of homemade stock. The ingredients you choose make all the difference in the finished recipes, so choose wisely.

I was so confused by ingredient options when I first jumped into the world of whole foods. It took me years to settle on which substitutes we liked the best in certain recipes, and which ones I should probably just skip. Here is a list of the ingredients I prefer to use when I cook—hopefully this will make the process a little bit easier for you as you sort through all the options.

### Meat

While our short summers and vicious hailstorms make growing vegetables a bit of a gamble, home meat production is one aspect of homesteading we have been able to tackle successfully. If you can't raise your own meat, seek out local ranchers or farmers or look into supporting local 4-H kids by purchasing animals at the county fair.

BEEF—We finish our home-raised beef entirely on grass. Not only do I like to skip paying for grain whenever possible, I prefer grass-fed beef as it contains higher amounts of omega-3 fatty acids and conjugated linoleic acid, a fatty acid

# quick-glance pantry list

Living as far as we do from the store has taught me how to menu plan and cook without relying on daily or even weekly trips to grab this or that, but you won't find the typical boxed dinners or canned soups in my pantries. In addition to the milk and cheese in the fridge, the meat in the freezers, and a handful of frozen homegrown vegetables, I've found I can cook 90 percent of the meals we eat with this list of ingredients. I buy organic whenever possible, and like to purchase in bulk to cut costs. The canned vegetables, salsa, and jellies are usually homemade, although I don't have an issue supplementing with store-bought options when I'm running short on our homegrown supplies. As you stock your own larder, just do the best you can and don't sweat the rest.

- Coconut oil
- Olive oil
- Sesame oil
- Lard (page 251)
- Tallow
- Vinegars (white, apple cider, balsamic, red wine)
- Liquid aminos (soy sauce substitute)
- All-purpose flour
- Hard white wheat berries
- Unsweetened coconut flakes
- Unsweetened cocoa powder
- Organic powdered sugar
- Organic whole cane sugar
- Coarse sea salt
- Fine sea salt
- Cornstarch
- Arrowroot powder

- Vanilla extract (page 261)
- Unflavored gelatin from grass-fed beef
- Raw honey
- Maple syrup
- Blackstrap molasses
- Chocolate chips
- Breadcrumbs (page 262)
- Nuts (walnut, cashews, peanuts, almonds)
- Peanut butter
- Lentils
- Quinoa
- Pasta (spaghetti, rotini, or penne, for quick meals)
- Rolled oats
- White and brown rice
- Popcorn kernels
- Dry beans (pinto, navy, black, kidney, garbanzo)

- Home-canned stock (beef and chicken; page 236)
- Tomato sauce
- Whole and diced tomatoes
- Canned salsa
- Canned peppers
- Unsweetened applesauce
- Dried fruit (raisins, cranberries, apricots, apples)
- Onions (red and yellow)
- Potatoes (usually russets and reds or Yukon Golds)
- Garlic
- Winter squash (seasonally)
- Canned pumpkin
- Various jams and jellies

with substantial health benefits. I've also noticed grass-fed beef has a deeper flavor, although there is a slight learning curve to cooking it. (Choose longer, slower cooking over quicker methods for best results.) If we couldn't raise our own beef, I'd seek out local ranchers and see if they'd be willing to sell us a steer or two. Even if the animals were finished on grain, I'd still much prefer that to grocery store beef. We butcher every 12 to 18 months, which ensures our freezers are jam-packed with white packages of meat all year long. If you don't have room for that much meat all at once, considering going in with friends or family on a half or quarter of an animal. While buying a whole beef or even a portion is a large up-front investment, it's almost always the more frugal option when compared to buying organic beef a few packages at a time from the health food store.

CHICKEN—We try to raise a group of around thirty birds twice a year, which gives us approximately one bird per week for our menu. Although we've tried a couple different varieties, we've found Cornish Cross birds to give us the best meat yield in the shortest amount of time (read more about meat bird breeds on page 326). If you can't raise your own birds, purchase from small producers who allow their flocks to free-range as much as possible.

PORK—Pigs are more of an occasional meat animal for us, mostly because our freezers are already bursting at the seams. We generally raise one or two pigs every other year, which keeps us supplied with roasts and chops to intersperse between the beef and chicken on the menu. Plus, you get lard and bacon, which are good enough reasons to raise pigs all on their own. If you don't plan to keep pigs on your homestead, find a local producer who sells sustainably raised pork and skips synthetic feed additives.

## Fats

One of the very first parts of my diet I changed back at the beginning of my real-food journey was fats. I tossed out the notion that low-fat everything was automatically better, and along with it, I tossed out the hydrogenated fats in my cupboards (good-bye, margarine, shortening, and vegetable oil). I replaced the processed fats with butter, coconut oil, and, yes, lovely lard. It's been gratifying to see more and more people embracing what common sense has said all along—natural fats are healthier than their manufactured, industrial alternatives. Here are the fats and oils I keep on hand in plentiful amounts at all times on the homestead:

BUTTER – I'm not afraid to say it – I LOVE BUTTER. Heck, it might even be one of my favorite ingredients, period. In a perfect world, I'd have ample amounts of homemade butter from the cream skimmed off the top of the milk given to us by our milk cows. But calves and seasons don't always allow that, so when homemade butter is scarce, I opt for organic, grass-fed butter instead. I like to buy it in bulk and store it in the freezer so I'm sure to never run out. (Because running out of butter constitutes an honest-to-goodness emergency at my house.) The recipes in this cookbook were tested with unsalted butter, so if you are using salted, you may need to reduce the amount of salt called for in the recipe.

COCONUT OIL – I love the flexibility of coconut oil, but I don't love everything tasting like coconut. I prefer to use the more neutral expeller-pressed variety to avoid the tropical scent. Coconut oil is a fabulous substitute when a recipe calls for shortening and is also ideal for sautéing and frying. If you don't have access to lard or tallow, coconut oil can be a good alternative in many of the recipes in this book.

LARD & TALLOW – Lard is a beautiful thing, and I'm so glad it's being embraced once again, instead of being demonized as it has been for so long. Tallow is similar to lard, except it comes from cows instead of pigs. If I had to pick between the two, I'd choose lard, because it works for a wider range of recipes. Learn how to make your own lard (page 251), or purchase high-quality lard from one of the sources in the Resources section (page 348). (Avoid the hydrogenated lard available at most grocery stores – it's not the good stuff.) If you don't have access to lard, bacon grease can be substituted in many of the recipes in this book, although bacon grease contains more salt so adjust the salt in the recipes as needed.

OLIVE OIL – I couldn't believe my taste buds the first time I tasted real olive oil. Turns out, the bottles of cheap extra-virgin stuff I'd been buying likely weren't even true olive oil. There is a lot of adulteration in the olive oil industry. For maximum flavor, be sure you're only buying quality oil from a trusted source. Unlike the tasteless grocery store varieties I used to buy, real olive oil can taste fruity, peppery, or even slightly grassy, depending on the type of olives used. Good olive oil will add flavor to your dressings and dishes, so it's absolutely worth it to spend a few extra dollars and invest in the real deal.

## Grains

I hold fast to the mantra of "everything in moderation," so despite their highly controversial nature as of late, we still eat grains. As with anything else, if you include grains in your diet, make sure they are grown organically.

FLOUR—Most of the recipes in this book call for basic all-purpose flour—I've found it produces the most consistent results and the best texture in most of the breads I bake. I mostly use organic, unbleached, unbromated all-purpose flour, although you are welcome to try the recipes in this book with whole wheat flour or other varieties. I've also been venturing into the world of ancient grains, such as einkorn. I'm completely intrigued by their nutty flavors, although it takes a bit of practice to transition to baking with ancient grains, as their gluten content differs from that of the flours we are accustomed to using. When I do use whole wheat flour, I like to grind the wheat berries myself for maximum freshness. I also prefer hard white wheat to the more common hard red—it is a bit milder and not as heavy in texture.

## Sweeteners

It's entirely possible to cook without white sugar—promise! The key is using the right substitute in the right recipe. With a little practice, you'll find that natural sweeteners improve the taste of your finished dishes and provide much better flavor than the white stuff. Here are the sweeteners I use most frequently in my kitchen.

GRANULATED SUGAR—Deciphering all the natural sugar options can be extremely confusing. After trying a number of options over the years, I've found I use dehydrated whole cane sugar, such as Sucanat or Rapadura, the most. It can be substituted in equal measure in most recipes and I use it in breads, cookies, cakes, and lots more. Whole cane sugar is made by crushing sugarcane, then extracting and drying the juice. It's one of the most unrefined sugars and has a higher mineral content than its more refined cousins. It also contains more molasses, which may or may not be welcome in certain recipes. The molasses taste works well with chocolate cakes and cookies, but can be a little overpowering if you are making a lighter vanilla dessert. A slightly less strong-flavored option is coconut sugar, which is still unrefined but without the molasses taste. When a recipe in this cookbook calls for sugar, you can use any of the above options, or even just plain brown sugar if that's all you have.

MAPLE SYRUP—I prefer Grade B maple syrup for its deeper flavor and color, although sometimes it's slightly more difficult to source. If you can't find it, Grade A will work instead. And if you live in an area where you can tap maple trees or make friends with someone who does, even better. As long as you're not buying artificial pancake syrup you'll be set.

HONEY—Raw honey is my preference for drizzling on fresh-baked bread or for using in any recipe that remains uncooked. Since high temperatures negate most of the benefits of raw honey, I don't mind using a less-expensive organic honey in recipes requiring cooking. Local honey is easy to find at most farmers' markets.

## Spices, Herbs & Seasonings

Butter may be my favorite ingredient, but I couldn't live without my collection of herbs and spices. There's an antique spice rack sitting prominently on my counter at all times, and multiple baskets of herbs and containers of spices stashed in the pantry cupboards. Summertime calls for fresh-cut herbs from outside the front door, but during the colder months, dried herbs keep things tasty. Keep a varied collection of seasonings and replenish them often. The herbs and seasonings I keep within easy reach are basil, oregano, rosemary, thyme, parsley, sage, dill, chives, cilantro, bay leaves, marjoram, paprika, onion powder, garlic powder, crushed red pepper flakes, chili powder, tarragon, turmeric, cumin, coriander, cinnamon, allspice, and nutmeg. Whew. It's safe to say I'd be completely useless in the kitchen without my herbs and spices.

SEA SALT—I prefer noniodized sea salt, my favorites being Celtic Sea Salt and Redmond Real Salt. I use fine-ground salt in most of my cooking (it dissolves into the food more easily) and save the coarse or kosher salt for sprinkling on pretzels or for preservation.

BLACK PEPPER—Freshly ground pepper packs more of a flavor punch, so I use it whenever I can. However, I keep pre-ground pepper on hand for recipes requiring larger amounts.

GARLIC—I use fresh garlic as much as possible, but there are times when powdered or granulated garlic is the best choice as it distributes throughout the food more evenly.

VINEGARS—Apple cider vinegar is the most versatile vinegar and I use it the most. I prefer the cloudy, raw kind that still contains the "mother" culture. I also keep balsamic, red wine, and basic white vinegars on hand.

SOY SAUCE—A handful of recipes in this cookbook call for soy sauce, but due to controversial information regarding the health effects of soy, I usually use a soy sauce alternative such as coconut aminos or Bragg liquid aminos.

## Dairy

The notion of producing our own dairy right here on the homestead captured my imagination years ago and remains one of my most-loved parts of our farm life. So much magic can be created from a humble bucket of raw milk that I wish everyone could experience the joy of keeping a milk cow or dairy goat. But alas, I know that's not always possible. If your situation prohibits you from keeping a dairy animal, find a source of organic dairy in your area. We prefer to drink our milk raw (more on that on page 316), but that decision is ultimately up to you.

MILK—I use raw, whole milk almost exclusively, and purchase low-temperature vat-pasteurized, grass-fed, nonhomogenized milk when our cow is dried up or we aren't able to milk for whatever reason. I do avoid ultra-pasteurized (UHT) dairy products—they have been heated to the point of sterilization, which kills off all of the enzymes needed to digest the casein in the milk. If you live in a state where raw milk sales are illegal, look into joining a cow- or goat-sharing program where one can purchase ownership shares in an animal in exchange for fresh milk.

CHEESE CULTURES—At a minimum, keep direct-set thermophilic and mesophilic cultures on hand and stash more specific cultures (buttermilk, chèvre, yogurt) as needed. See Resources (page 348) for where to buy cultures and other cheese-making supplies.

RENNET—Liquid animal or vegetable rennet, or rennet tablets are all suitable options for the recipes in this book. Avoid the grocery store Junket rennet for cheese recipes. It works for some things, but yields inconsistent results for most cheeses, which is incredibly frustrating when you are first starting out. See Resources (page 348) for where to buy rennet.

# water bath canning: quick start guide

Some people love landscapes. Others like photos of cute cats. Me? Well, I love staring at photos of well-stocked pantries. A picture of colorful jars of food lined up in tidy rows will stop my mindless social media scrolling like nothing else.

I suspect it's the desire to savor the bright flavors of homegrown food as long as possible, coupled with the urge to be prepared in an emergency scenario, but homesteading has this strange tendency to turn the most normal folks into food-saving squirrels.

I learned how to can at the beginning of my homesteading journey and the skill has served me very well over the years. I do freeze foods sometimes, but canning is still my preservation method of choice since my freezers are usually bursting with meat. There's a bit of fear surrounding canning (usually passed down from a relative who had a bad experience at one point), but once you understand the basic safety rules, it's very commonsense and quite safe.

The preparation involved in canning different fruits and vegetables varies, but the basic steps for using a water bath canner always stay the same. If you plan to add canning to your repertoire of skills (which I highly recommend), invest in a trusted canning handbook, such as the *Ball Blue Book,* so you can feel confident you're safely preserving all your homegrown produce.

One important note: If you want to preserve low-acid foods like meats, stock, or beans, you *must* use a pressure canner. Water bath canning is only safe for foods naturally high in acid or foods with added acid. (Think applesauce, tomato sauce, pickles, jams, jellies, etc.) Pressure canning isn't hard, but it is a slightly different skill. Master water bath canning first and then you can kick it up a notch by adding a pressure canner to your collection down the road.

## WATER BATH CANNING EQUIPMENT

**CANNING POT WITH LID**—You can use a regular stockpot for canning, but it's worthwhile to invest in a larger pot designed for canning. They hold more jars, which reduces the time you'll spend in a hot kitchen waiting for each batch to finish boiling.

**CANNING JARS**—I use quart-sized jars most frequently, but have plenty of pint and half-pint jars on hand too. I prefer wide-mouth jars so I can fit my hand inside when it's time to scrub them.

**CANNING LIDS AND RINGS**—Rings can be used repeatedly, but lids can only be used once for canning. I keep many boxes of lids in my pantry so I'm always ready for a last-minute canning adventure. (Hey, it happens.)

**JAR LIFTER TONGS**—They're cheap. They work. Get some and save yourself the headache of trying to fish jars out of boiling water with random kitchen utensils. (Been there, done that. It's not fun.)

**LID LIFTER**—It's basically a magnet on a stick, and not absolutely necessary, I suppose. But it is nice to not have scalded fingertips from trying to grab hot canning lids out of a saucepan.

## WATER BATH CANNING WALK-THROUGH

### 1. Clean and (Maybe) Sterilize

Regardless of if your jars are new or old, wash them thoroughly in hot soapy water. Also, save yourself the heartache of lids that won't seal by checking the rims of the jars for chips while you wash. In the past, the National Center for Home Food Preservation recommended sterilizing jars by running them through the dishwasher or by boiling them for 10 minutes before filling. However, they have recently updated their recommendations and you can safely skip this step if you live at elevations less than 1,000 feet and the jars will be processed for at least 10 minutes once they are filled with food. If you live at a higher altitude, simply add 1 minute of boiling time for each additional 1,000 feet of elevation.

## 2. Heat the Water

Start heating your canning pot early in the game—it can take a while to get the water boiling. Fill the pot at least half full with warm water, then place a rack on the bottom and put the lid on top. (You may need to add more water, depending on the quantity and size of the jars you are using—the water must cover the filled jars by several inches.) Turn the burner on high and get the water heating while you prepare the food.

## 3. Prepare the Food

The steps here will vary greatly depending on what you are canning, but usually you'll be cutting, peeling, blanching, or cooking fruits and vegetables before you pack them into the hot, waiting jars. Carefully check your canning recipe for headspace requirements. Headspace is the amount of empty space at the top of the jar between the food and the rim. It matters—over- or underfilled jars can equal a canning disaster.

## 4. Affix the Lids

Wipe the rims of the jars with a clean, damp cloth to remove any food residue, then place the lids on top. I like to gently heat the lids in a saucepan filled with hot water to soften the sealing compound on the edges. Some lid manufacturers have said this is no longer necessary for proper sealing, but old habits die hard, so I still do it. Screw the rings on until they are finger tight only—don't crank them down.

### 5. Bath Time!

Carefully lower the filled jars into the waiting pot. They should be covered by 1 to 2 inches of water—you can add more hot water at this point if you're a bit short. Place the lid on the pot, but do not start your timer until the water returns to a boil. Once the processing time is complete (if you live at a higher elevation, make sure you adjust the time in the recipe as needed—refer back to step 1), turn off the burner and wait for 10 minutes. Use jar tongs to lift the jars straight up—avoid tipping them if at all possible.

### 6. Cool and Label

Set the hot jars on a towel or rack and cool for at least 12 hours. Resist the urge to poke or pry the lids, as tempting as it may be. As the jars cool, you'll be rewarded with the popping of sealing lids—music to a homesteader's ears! Once the lids have sealed, remove the rings (and double-check to be sure each lid has sealed) before storing the jars in your pantry or larder. If a jar hasn't sealed, stick it in the fridge and eat the contents within a few days.

**Safety Note:** As long as you follow the recommended processing times and guidelines for the foods you are canning, there's no reason to be fearful of home-canned food. However, if you ever notice any of the following, do not eat the food and throw it away immediately.

- Lids that are bulging or swollen

- Lids that seem to be loose after the jar has been on the shelf for a while

- Jars that spray out liquid or foam when you open them

- Odd odors coming from the jar

- Mold or discolored food inside the jars

# *five secrets for crunchier pickles*

It's easy to keep icebox pickles (page 127) crunchy, since the cucumbers aren't cooked before going into the jars. However, if you plan to use a water bath canner to preserve your harvest, it can be a bit trickier to steer clear of mushy pickles. (See pages 339–341 for a water bath canning walk-through.) Here are the best tips I've collected over the years for perfectly crunchy cucumbers.

**1. The smaller, the better.** Hands-down, this is the most important factor. If you start with the monster cukes that have been hiding in the garden for two weeks, there's not much you can do to salvage the crunch, no matter how creative you get or how many prayers you say while they're in the canner. Select the smallest, firmest cucumbers possible and save the big ones for eating raw with Buttermilk Ranch Dressing (page 268).

**2. Jar 'em up right away.** As soon as a cucumber is plucked from its pokey vine, the clock starts ticking. The longer they sit on the counter or in the fridge, the softer they will be. Going straight from vine to jar is best, and I usually try to plan room in my schedule for canning on harvest day. However, I've still had good results with cucumbers from the farmers' market, as long as they are firm when I buy them and I can them soon after I get home.

**3. Give 'em a bath.** Soak future pickles in an ice-water bath for several hours before you process them to keep them crisp. A bowl of cold water in the fridge works, as does a bowl of ice cubes and water on the counter.

**4. No blossoms allowed.** The blossom end of a cucumber contains enzymes that may cause increased pickle mushiness. Trim it off just to be safe.

**5. Tea to the rescue.** Many a seasoned canner swears by the addition of tannins to their pickles. Tannins are naturally occurring compounds found in oak leaves, grape leaves, and black tea. Although this trick is frequently recommended, I've never had stellar results with it. If you have oak leaves or grape leaves handy, it can't hurt to toss one in each jar just for fun, though I can't guarantee the results. If you don't have access to leaves, add ½ teaspoon loose black tea to each jar instead.

To live is the rarest
thing in the world.
Most people exist,
that is all.
—OSCAR WILDE

# a final word

Wilde may seem like a lofty quote with which to end a book about homemade biscuits, roast beef dinners, and brown gravy, but I can't think of a better sentiment to encapsulate the reasons behind our choosing this crazy homestead life. At first glance, homesteading might seem simply defined by chickens or a few homegrown vegetables in the backyard. However, as those who have chosen this lifestyle can attest, it's so much more. On a deeper level, homesteading truly symbolizes an awakening.

For most of us, gone are the days when we must devote the majority of our hours to simple survival. Technology has made everyday life easier than ever, and we can order food, wash our clothes, and heat our homes with the press of a button. People don't *need* to grow their vegetables, make their own bread, or spend extra time sourcing locally raised meats. Yet we are. And our ranks are growing each and every day.

The homesteading journey often begins as a mission to improve our diets and personal food supply. However, when a richer, more meaningful existence is discovered hiding among the cartons of farm-fresh eggs, between the rows of crisp, homegrown lettuce, and in the pots and pans of nourishing, homemade meals, this hybrid modern and heritage lifestyle quickly becomes more meaningful.

What starts as a basic fascination with better food ends with more confident, self-sufficient individuals who are able to finally master the art of slowing down long enough to taste the simple joys of this life. Modern homesteading proves to us that with a bit of determination, you truly can create the life you want, no matter where you live.

May this simple cookbook be the catalyst to your learning how to not just exist in this world, but to truly live.

Happy homesteading, my friends.

—Jill

# acknowledgments

When the concept of this cookbook first entered my consciousness, I had no idea what amazing relationships and collaborations would develop in the process. The creation of a book like this is never a solo venture, and you wouldn't be holding this volume in your hands today if not for the many amazing folks who poured so much time and effort into this project. It's hard to fully express all the gratitude I feel right now, but I'll do my best.

To my husband, Christian: Thank you for pushing me to dream bigger and for believing in me, even when I want to bring home flocks of chickens and herds of milk cows. Being married to you has made me a better person.

To Mom and Dad: Thank you for supporting our dreams, even from 1,100 miles away, and for teaching me how to be disciplined and consistent in all my pursuits. (I guess I forgive you for making me take those darn creative writing classes.)

To my sister, Jenna: You're always there to listen to my ramblings and talk me through my insecurities. Thank you. You keep me sane.

To Lindsay Linton Buk of Linton Productions: Girl, you captured my vision better than I could have ever imagined. Your photography upleveled this book beyond my wildest dreams, and I cannot imagine doing this project without you. Wyoming women, unite!

To Greta Eagan, food, wardrobe, prop, makeup, hair, and pickle stylist extraordinaire: You brought an incredible new dimension to my homestead style. Thank you for making everything look so stunning. And for bringing some serious powdered sugar action to the table.

To my agent, John Maas: Thank you for taking a chance on a first-time author and for your continual patience and expertise in guiding me through this new adventure. You have made this entire process extremely enjoyable.

To my editor, Kara Rota, and the entire team at Flatiron: Thank you for believing in this project and making it infinitely better with your suggestions, edits, and ideas. Also, thank you for breaking me of my ellipsis addiction.

To Dr. Eric Zielinski: Thank you for making introductions and giving me the nudge I needed to pursue a "real" book. This cookbook would not exist if it weren't for you.

To Candy Moulton: Thank you for bringing depth and definition to my understanding of homesteading history and for freely sharing your extensive knowledge with me.

To the best kitchen crew EVER, who stuck with me during a marathon two-week photo shoot: Summer, thank you for washing the dishes and scrubbing down the kitchen a billion times. Laura, thank you for bringing the muscle and being the official on-set animal whisperer. And Julie, thank you for keeping the kids content for days and days on end.

To the readers of *The Prairie Homestead* blog: Thank you for continuing to read, comment, share, and encourage me over the last nine years of blogging. Your stories keep me going—this book was created for you!

And to my Creator: Thank you for placing these dreams and passions in my heart, and for taking me on this unorthodox, yet never boring, path.

# resources

All these suppliers carry high-quality ingredients and tools to give your homestead kitchen efforts a boost.

**Baker Creek Heirloom Seed Company**
An excellent selection of affordable, heirloom seeds with fabulous stories
www.rareseeds.com

**Blendtec**
Professional-grade kitchen blenders
www.blendtec.com

**Bragg Live Foods**
Organic, unfiltered apple cider vinegar, as well as my preferred soy sauce substitute, liquid aminos
www.bragg.com

**Cultures for Health**
Dairy cultures, fermented food cultures, and cheese-making supplies
www.culturesforhealth.com

**Fatworks**
A good source of pasture-raised lard and tallow if you can't make it yourself
www.fatworks.com

**Jovial Foods**
Quality olive oil, einkorn flour, and wheat berries
www.jovialfoods.com

**King Arthur Flour**
A variety of high-quality whole wheat and unbleached, unbromated all-purpose flours
www.kingarthurflour.com

**Kettle & Fire**
I'll always recommend making your own stock, but if you can't, this is a great option.
www.kettleandfire.com

**Lodge Cast Iron**
Pre-seasoned cast-iron cookware
www.lodgemfg.com

**NutriMill**
Electric grain mills and wheat grinders
www.nutrimill.com

**Redmond Real Salt**
Unrefined sea salt with the natural minerals and no additives
www.realsalt.com

**Thrive Market**
An online natural food supplier that carries a wide variety of foods and brands if you don't have a health food store in your area
www.thrivemarket.com

**Tropical Traditions**
Extra-virgin and expeller-pressed coconut oil
www.tropicaltraditions.com

**US Wellness Meats**
Grass-fed and pasture-raised beef, poultry, pork, and lamb. A great option if you can't find a reputable local producer.
www.grasslandbeef.com

# Additional Tools for Your Homestead Journey

Visit theprairiehomestead.com/cookbookbonus for exclusive bonus content I created just for my cookbook community, including:

- A tour of exactly how we set up our chicken coop

- Printable shopping guides and pantry checklists

- Step-by-step directions and photographs for setting up your own DIY indoor seed-starting system

- For hands-on video tutorials and heritage kitchen techniques, check out my Heritage Cooking Crash Course at heritagecookingclass.com.

- The Homestead Skills Bucket List

## FROST DATES
Determine your last spring frost date and ideal planting times by using the map at www.ncdc.noaa.gov/file/day-last-spring-freeze-map.jpg. It's much more accurate than relying on common zone charts and can prevent a lot of heartache caused by frozen seedlings planted too soon. If you are not in the United States, a quick online search for the last frost dates in your country should provide all the information you need.

# index